WHIPS' NIGHTMARE

Christopher Gill.

Whips' Nightmare

Diary of a Maastricht Rebel

by

CHRISTOPHER GILL

To Jean Hughes

With Best Wishes

Christopher Gill

St George's Day 2004

The Memoir Club

First published in 2003 by
The Memoir Club
Whitworth Hall
Spennymoor
County Durham

British Library Cataloguing in
Publication Data.
A catalogue record for this book
is available from the
British Library.

ISBN: 1 84104 086 X

Typeset by George Wishart & Associates, Whitley Bay.
Printed by Cromwell Press Ltd

Dedication

To my family and other members
of the kitchen cabinet.

I would like to thank my wife Patricia and secretary Vicki Stevens without whose invaluable help production of this book would not have been possible.

Contents

Illustrations

Foreword

VERY OCCASIONALLY British politics have been convulsed by issues that transcend party loyalties. Mercifully they are few, but today's divisions over Europe match the upheavals over the Corn Laws in the 1840s and the turmoil created by the Irish Home Rule a generation later. Christopher Gill writes about Europe and his membership of the Commons for two Parliaments from 1987 to 1997; he leaves his third Parliament, from 1997-2001, hopefully for another book.

I know Christopher as a conscientious Shropshire MP and a good and dependable neighbour. This book demonstrates that he was a wholehearted defender of British national institutions. He arrived at Westminster relatively late, aged fifty, and without ambition to climb the political ladder or seeking patronage. He was beyond the discipline and embrace of the Whips.

It is this quality that makes him a fascinating chronicler of the agonies that beset the Conservative Government whilst it struggled with the Maastricht Treaty.

I have my own prejudices on this matter. It seems to me that after the Thatcher Government passed the Single European Act – a much greater centralising measure than was then anticipated – Conservatives wanted a long period of calm. The general mood was to accept membership of the European Union, and to see how open trade in goods and services evolved. This was not to be. The President of the European Commission, Jacques Delors, argued that Europe was like a bicycle: you kept pedalling or else you fell off. The drive to expand the role of the European Union led to the Maastricht Treaty with a commitment to a single currency and monetary union.

I do not believe that John Major had his heart in Maastricht, in either its timing or its ambitions. Had he lost the 1992 General Election I believe the Conservatives would have generally opposed the Maastricht proposals. Of course, Major *won* the Election and was able to adjust the Maastricht provisions for Britain in respect of the Social Chapter and the Single Currency. He regarded this as a negotiating coup: 'Game, Set and Match,' he proclaimed. It was a victory that did not ring true to Gill and his fellow sceptics.

There followed a drawn-out Parliamentary battle, aided by the Danish referendum and the Government's narrow majority. It became clear that the sceptics had many sympathisers including members of the Cabinet. The sceptic cause also became a lightning conductor for Conservatives who were generally dissatisfied with Major's leadership. Christopher Gill writes with admirable candour about the various factions within the sceptic camp. His own passion and unwillingness to compromise is evident. He must have been a Whips' nightmare.

The great upheavals over the Corn Laws and Irish Home Rule had their political giants, Disraeli and Joseph Chamberlain. The Euro-rebels of the 1990s had no towering personalities – although the 1970s produced Powell and Roy Jenkins – but they produced Parliamentarians who stuck to their beliefs. They lost the votes but their gestures were not wholly in vain. Now in Opposition the Conservative Party has generally moved in a sceptical direction. I believe it would have done so had the Tories been defeated in 1992 and then had the freedom that Opposition can provide. The Corn Laws and Protection and Irish Home Rule issues had a political life of decades; my bet is that Europe will follow suit. The debate continues.

The Right Honourable Lord Biffen of Tanat DL

Author's Note

WHILST I HAVE HAD to rely upon memory and enquiry for the introductory chapters to these memoirs the account of the 10 years from my first election to Parliament in 1987 to the General Election held on 1 May 1997 is based upon the daily diaries which I kept throughout that period.

Having regard to the political developments which took place in that decade I have felt it important to provide the reader with as accurate an account of what actually happened, albeit from my own perspective as a backbencher, as is possible. Without recourse to the diaries in which I recorded events as they occurred I have no doubt that the accuracy which I have sought to achieve would have eluded me because of the tricks that time inevitably plays upon memory.

As I compiled these memoirs often was the occasion when my recollection was at odds with the dates and details recorded in my diaries. Deliberately I have resisted the temptation not to let truth stand in the way of a good story.

Prologue

MY EARLIEST RECOLLECTION of politics is as a young boy pushing leaflets
through letterboxes in Upper Zoar Street. Zoar Street lay to the west of
the Cotymundy Patch, an area of derelict land so called because when the
slums that had previously stood there were being demolished between the
wars it is said that a strange unrecognisable creature ran out. Throughout
Wolverhampton this legendary creature was known as the Cotymundy.

That I found myself electioneering in this rather less than salubrious area was
because I had been roped in to help by the local councillors. At that time my
father and other businessmen in the town such as James Beattie (grandson of
the founder of the eponymous department store), Arthur Baker (master
butcher), Peter Farmer (bookseller), Harold Fullwood (Chairman, Staffordshire
Tyre Company), Reg Guy (Director of Billinghams, Ford motor main agents),
Dudley Haselock (Director of D & G Haselock, wholesalers to the hairdressing
trade), Percy Morrell (joint owner of the Levedale Dairy), Walter Nelson
(principal of Nelson & Co., Chartered Accountants) and Bert Windridge
(Director of Windridge Prams Ltd, famous locally for their slogan: 'Why worry,
wheel a Windridge') served on the Wolverhampton County Borough Council
and were an integral part of the well-oiled election machine spearheaded by the
local Member of Parliament, the late J. Enoch Powell. When in 1959 I became,
as a branch secretary, a small cog in that impressive machine it was to discover
that in every ward there was a strong branch structure and that at election time
there would be a team of workers in every polling district within that ward, each
with its own dedicated committee room keeping tabs on whether or not our
pledges had voted. In due course it was to be that proficient organisation which
ensured my success in wresting for myself a place on Council from the sitting
Labour councillor but in the intervening period there was my education to be
completed and National Service too.

At Birchfield Preparatory School for boys on the outskirts of Wolverhampton the Headmaster, N.R. Brown – the boys never knew what the N.R.
stood for and it is doubtful whether the parents did either – advised my
parents that I should go on to Sedburgh School in Westmorland (now
Cumbria). Not unreasonably Father concluded that getting my younger
brother and I to and from school in Shrewsbury would be an altogether more
practical proposition and so it was that in the autumn of 1950 I was sent, as a
rather diffident new boy, to the Schools.

Barely five years after the end of World War II and with the Korean War just started it is hardly surprising that an important feature of the school curriculum was the Combined Cadet Force. After one term in the Initial Training Corps – as far as I recall rather like glorified Boy Scouting – boys joined the Army section of the CCF, the highlight of which was the annual field day when virtually the whole school was transported into the surrounding countryside to practise its martial skills. Thus it was that early one summer day in 1951 I fell in to march to Shrewsbury station to board the specially chartered train that was to take 'the Corps' to Cressage Halt in the Severn valley just to the north of Ironbridge.

To cross the River Severn just below the Schools it was necessary to 'break step' so that the structure of the Kingsland Bridge was spared the potentially damaging effects of 500 pairs of boots crashing down in unison. What followed was to prove a relatively small but significant turning point in my early life. After crawling around all day on my belly in the water meadows of the River Severn, never knowing what was going on nor really what I was supposed to be doing, I there and then resolved to join the Naval Section!

There may have been other factors in that decision but at the time I think that they were probably less compelling than the impression created by the day's events and the quite dreadful packed lunch that accompanied it. I do recall the great N.R. Brown advising parents that the only boys who knew what they wanted to do in life were those who wanted either to farm or to go to sea. By the time that I entered Parliament in 1987 I was able to count myself lucky enough to have done both but there was another rather more prosaic factor. As the 'doul' – 'fag' in other schools but, as befits a Classics school, actually Greek for slave – to the Ridgemount head of house I was tasked to polish J.R. Tusting's uniform boots till they shone and to ensure that his white webbing and every other part of his naval uniform were maintained in immaculate condition.

Diligent application to this task had its own reward when subsequently R.G. Wood, the officer in charge of the Naval section, stood in front of the assembled company having carried out his weekly inspection and said that the 'smartest cadet on parade was Gill'.

Russell Wood or 'Rusty' as he was popularly known, was a charismatic young New Zealander whose university studies had been interrupted by war service in the Royal New Zealand Naval Volunteer Reserve. In 1946 he resumed his studies at Oxford where he took the History Honours degree before joining the staff at Shrewsbury School in 1949. Apart from myself the other aspiring politician to whom Rusty taught history was Michael Heseltine. Given the demonstrably different views that Michael Heseltine and I were to hold on the vexed question of Britain's membership of the European Union, Rusty in later life would occasionally venture the opinion that he had had more success with the younger of his two pupils than with his better known contemporary.

By 1952 I was seized by the importance of ensuring as far as I possibly could that I would do my compulsory National Service in the Royal Navy. Accordingly I was given time out from school to travel to Salthouse Dock, Liverpool to join the Mersey Division of the Royal Naval Volunteer Reserve as an O/D (Ordinary Deckhand) – one step below Ordinary Seaman! That was a decision that I never came to regret any more than I had cause to regret my decision not to seek a place at university. For three years from the beginning of 1955 until the end of 1957, courtesy of HMG, I attended the university of Life and it was during this time that I came to know what it was that I was going to do with the rest of my life.

Leaving aside the circumstances which resulted in me watching the landing at Suez in the autumn of 1956 from the relative safety of an armchair in the wardroom of HMS *Harrier* (then the Naval Aircraft Direction School at St. Anne's Head in Pembrokeshire) rather than from the deck of my former ship, HMS *Modeste*, in the Red Sea, 1957 found me aboard the flagship of the Mediterranean Fleet, HMS *Birmingham*.

One Sunday lunchtime in Grand Harbour, Malta, at our invitation the Commander-in-Chief Mediterranean, Vice Admiral Sir Ralph Edwardes, came on board to have drinks in the Gunroom with the ship's Midshipmen. All was going well until the C-in-C wheeled on me and said, 'And what are you going to do when you leave the service?' Without a moment's hesitation I blurted out that I 'intended to go into business to make enough money to make myself financially independent before going into national politics.' Afterwards I could scarcely believe what I had said and told this story to not a single soul until I had secured my election as the Conservative Member of Parliament for Ludlow thirty years later.

In answering the Admiral I had also, again quite involuntarily, said that if I could find three hundred kindred spirits we could put the 'Great back in Britain' and thereby hangs this tale.

I took up my bed…and walked

T HE 10 APRIL 1987 found me lying in a hospital bed recovering from a fairly routine operation earlier in the week. Visiting me that evening my wife brought the news that our sitting Member of Parliament, Eric Cockeram, would not be seeking re-election. Subsequently it became clear that he had been given little choice in the matter because the Ludlow Constituency Conservative Association Chairman, Captain Michael Lumsden, had made it clear to him that, he being under suspicion of having fraudulently applied for privatisation shares in BT, the Association would not have him.

Being due to be discharged from hospital the following morning I spent the rest of the day going over and over again the reasons why I should, or should not, throw my hat in the ring to succeed the beleaguered Eric Cockeram, one time PPS to former Chancellor of the Exchequer, Anthony Barber.

On the back of the proverbial used envelope I listed all the pros and on the reverse all the cons. I concluded that this was the golden opportunity that I had been hoping for although it has to be said that I had recognised another window of opportunity way back in 1974 when my then MP, Enoch Powell, had suddenly announced that he would not stand as a Conservative candidate at the forthcoming General Election.

The first that we Party workers in the constituency knew of Enoch's shock decision was when we saw the story break on the 9 O'clock News on Thursday 7 February 1974. At 0630 the following morning I got the Chair-man of the Wolverhampton South West Conservative Association, George Wilkes, out of bed to ask him to put me on the top of the list of candidates to succeed our illustrious Member, a request I was subsequently obliged to withdraw for business and family reasons. At that time the family business depended entirely upon my own day to day involvement and on the domestic front the situation was somewhat complicated by the fact that I had only recently bought a farm in Shropshire and, because of the state of the property market, was unable to sell my house in Wolverhampton. In these trying circumstances I hit upon the then novel idea of part exchanging my detached house for a semi-detached house which in due course I part exchanged for a terrace house before finally exiting the Wolverhampton residential property market altogether.

In the event the Wolverhampton SW Association chose Nicholas Budgen as

Son-in-law Russell, wife Patricia, self, son Charles, elder daughter Helen, taken prior to my adoption meeting as the Conservative Parliamentary candidate for the Ludlow Constituency.

Enoch's successor and whatever his faults as perceived by his constituents Nick went on to prove himself an outstanding Parliamentarian and a worthy successor to that exceptional man of courage, foresight and integrity who left such an indelible mark upon the nation's political history.

On Saturday 11 April I took up my bed and, figuratively speaking, walked. First to my mother and father living close by and then to all the other members of my immediate family. The question was, should I do this thing? With the exception only of my elder daughter the rest of the family said that if this was what I really wanted to do then go for it. Helen's comment was that she would have thought that I'd got enough to do already, a comment which I was to recall when in the second half of the year my learning curve seemed to be practically vertical. As far as the family business was concerned we cut a deal. In exchange for an undertaking not to sell out, son Charles and Managing Director Alan Paget gave me their blessing and I was on my way.

In spite of feeling well below par because of where I had spent the past seven days I now went into overdrive to contact all those people that I knew in the Ludlow constituency in the hope that I could start a band wagon rolling in support of my candidature to be the Prospective Parliamentary Candidate. This was to pay a massive and entirely helpful dividend in that when it came to the final selection meeting at the Overton Grange Hotel, Ludlow on 14 May, 200 of the 300 Association members present were people that I knew. Against this local coalition the runner-up, Peter Butler, who went on to become the Member of Parliament for Milton Keynes North East in 1992 and ironically PPS to another Chancellor, later confided that he realised that he never stood a chance. The other runner-up, Joan Hall, previously Member for Keighley, I never saw again but when, some years later, I learnt that she was a confidante of Margaret Thatcher I realised why the Iron Lady's initial welcome to me as a new colleague had been somewhat less than fulsome.

In the month between leaving hospital and actually becoming the PPC there were various hurdles to be overcome, not least the initial selection interviews. Although I was not to hear it for a long time after the event, and the subsequent happenings which I shall relate make it sound most improbable, Captain Lumsden was apparently heard to exclaim, 'Well, beat that!' after I had attended for the final short-listing interview. Nor could I have anticipated that the banner headline on the front page of the *Shropshire Star* which I picked up on the way to Overton Grange would have read 'MP Makes Comeback Bid'. This I found rather unnerving given that Eric Cockeram's hash had, I thought, been settled weeks ago.

With the virtual certainty of an early General Election in prospect there was no time to lose and the Chairman (Lumpy as he came to be known), the Agent, Sheila Poole, and I met to make our plans for the campaign. During the daytime the object of the exercise would be to see and be seen in as many parts of the country's 11th largest constituency as possible – the Ludlow division comprised 48 per cent of the land mass of Shropshire, itself England's biggest inland county – and in the evenings to address up to four but never fewer than two public meetings in village halls. At those meetings a member of the Association would be invited to take the Chair to introduce the candidate, in this case myself, to conduct the meeting and generally to keep order. On the occasions when Lumpy himself presided at those meetings the most difficult and awkward question would invariably come, not from the floor, but from the chair! This always struck me as being a rather bizarre way of helping a novice candidate. Coupled with the fact that the plan of campaign seemed destined to oblige the candidate to appear in both the east of the constituency and the west on the same day, the distance in between being potentially seventy miles, I determined to take a much bigger hand in planning any future campaign.

One of the biggest bonuses of the campaign, apart from increasing the majority, was meeting the person who subsequently became my secretary.

While canvassing together in Diddlebury, a typical South Shropshire village in the beautiful Corvedale, Vicki Stevens said that should I need a secretary she would be only too pleased to help. At the time I told her that I wasn't entirely convinced that I would but that I would certainly bear her in mind. Within days of my being elected I realised that dealing with the mass of correspondence and other literature that is the bane of the modern politician's life was not something that I could cope with single-handedly. I dialled the telephone number she had given me and we have worked together ever since.

The subject of secretaries cropped up again when, in my first few weeks at Westminster, I sought the advice of some of my new colleagues. Some said that it was vital to have someone in the House, others that the best solution was a good woman in the constituency and one, Nick Budgen, bless him, that there was no need to have one at all. I decided to compromise and having allowed myself to be interviewed by Mary Cranston who had previously worked for Sir Patrick Wall, the former Member for Beverley, consequentially found myself with two secretaries – Mary in the House and Vicki in the Constituency. Never was a Member as lucky as I. To find one good secretary was a blessing but to find two who were both competent, loyal and entirely trustworthy was something else.

CHAPTER TWO

...the culmination of a fairy-tale

ON 11 JUNE 1987 Margaret Thatcher swept to her third election victory but because, by tradition, votes were not counted in the Ludlow division until the following day it was not until the afternoon of the 12th that I knew for certain that I was part of that phenomenon.

Even though I had increased the Conservative majority (and would do so again in 1992) this was no time to rest on my laurels. My arrival in Westminster a few days later was the culmination of a fairy-tale. Barely four weeks had elapsed since my selection as the PPC and here I was, the Honourable Member for Ludlow. The significance of having achieved a life-long ambition at the first attempt and of having gained the nomination without ever having been on the Party list of approved candidates escaped me until I was able to compare notes with my newfound colleagues. I suspect that the Party never forgave me for beating the system and subsequently the rules were changed so as to make it virtually impossible for there to be any repetition. In these rather unusual circumstances Conservative Central Office did their best to shut the stable door after the horse had bolted by insisting that I should attend for interview. Since I had already secured the nomination what purpose was served by this futile exercise I shall never know. Obliged to take a day off campaigning I duly reported to Smith Square and was, in due course, ushered into the presence of the Party Chairman. By this stage in the Election campaign Norman Tebbitt was clearly experiencing a degree of understandable frustration because although himself the duly appointed Chairman he was having to contend with a back seat driver in the shape of the Leader's protégé, David Young. I have no recollection of his other questions – they were commendably few – but I do recall him asking me what I did for a living. When I replied that I was a butcher he swiftly retorted that 'we could do with one of those round here' and the interview was at an end.

When the newly elected Parliament first met I fondly imagined that the Party would find use for a mature person with a record of running a successful business. As a butcher and farmer I somewhat deferentially volunteered my services to the then Agriculture Minister, John McGregor. It took me a little time to appreciate that this is not the way it works and instead of being put on the Agriculture Select Committee found myself in no time at all on the Standing Committee of the latest Social Security Bill – a subject area of which my knowledge was virtually nil. My second mistake was to

9

Being congratulated by LCCA Chairman Michael Lumsden on being selected, 12 June 1987.

believe that I was joining a team. Far from it, as evidenced by the lengths that the said Agriculture Minister and his minions went to in trying to ensure that I was no part of his official visit that autumn to the South Shropshire Hills – in my constituency.

One of the strangest features of being elected to Parliament for the first time is that one is given absolutely no guidance as to what facilities are provided and least of all any indication of when they will be made available.

CHAPTER THREE

...being right in politics is not the way to win and influence friends

COMPARED WITH what was to follow the next three years were a breeze although it wasn't long before I was in the Whips' very bad books because of my opposition to the Party's flagship policy – the ill fated Community Charge.

In 1981, in an unprecedented move, the ordinary members of the Wolverhampton Chamber of Commerce had demanded an Extraordinary General Meeting to voice their concerns about the rapidly increasing General Rate imposed by the Labour controlled local authority. Leading the charge was Andrew Rutherford whose steel fabrication business, like so many others, was struggling to cope with rising overheads, major components of which were totally beyond our immediate control. The upshot of this meeting was the formation of a Rates Action Committee of which I was to become Chairman. Given that I was known to be somewhat of a political animal and probably, at that time, the only member of the Chamber to have served on the local Council, perhaps it was inevitable that I should find myself cast in this new role.

Under my chairmanship the Rates Action Committee met regularly and achieved the very satisfactory distinction of pressurising the Councillors into pegging the rate. As a committee we then turned our attention to the proposals which were starting to emerge from the Conservative Opposition. After much deliberation and having considered all the alternatives we recommended to Patrick Jenkin, then Shadow Environment Secretary, that the least preferred option was any form of Poll Tax. Perversely the Party concluded otherwise and committed itself in the 1987 Queen's Speech to introducing the Community Charge.

In the meantime, whilst being interviewed for the candidacy for the Ludlow seat, I had been asked if there was any aspect of Conservative Party policy with which I disagreed. Without a moment's hesitation I said that there was just one thing and that was the government's proposals regarding the Rates.

David Lightbown, the Whips' Office equivalent of the terminator, was singularly unimpressed with my refusal to vote the ticket on this highly contentious policy. Likewise I was singularly unimpressed by the way he went about it and warned my own Whip that Lightbown and I were on a collision course. Anthony Durant responded by saying that it was all very well me being opposed to the Community Charge but what would I put in its place?

Drawing upon my previous experience as a Councillor on a County Borough (i.e. all-purpose) Council I had no difficulty in quickly coming up with a different strategy. The solution to this problem was to make the cost of Social Services and, in particular, Education a charge against the national taxpayer with the costs of all other local authority services remaining a charge against the ratepayer. At a stroke the subsidies from Whitehall to Town Halls could have been ended, local government finance would have been made less opaque and the health of local government itself restored by the more transparent accountability which would ensue. This was a theme that I was to return to time and again over the next fourteen years but with all major parties, for whatever reason, in thrall to central control it is an idea whose time has not yet come. Perhaps I should not have been surprised that there was no response or reaction to my letter to Tony Durant and maybe that helped me to stick to my last. However good in theory, the 'Poll Tax', as it came to be known, was never going to work in practice – as subsequent events proved – and I abstained throughout, starting with the Divisions on the legislation to impose the charge in Scotland in advance of its being introduced in England and Wales.

When, several years later, Lightbown's wife Ann told me that it was people like me who were ruining her husband's health – he was grossly overweight and subsequently died of a heart attack – I was reminded of the not so subtle technique he used to bully new Members into submission. In the first few weeks and months of a new Parliament new Members are put under inordinate pressure by the Whips and those who succumb are forever regarded as lobby fodder. Once a Member has caved in on a principle that Member is compromised and therefore potentially vulnerable. The Whips know that someone who has surrendered on one principle can be pressured into giving way on another principle and for those who want to cut a deal there is always the inducement of patronage to help them make the 'right' decision. Another technique much favoured by the Whips is to bounce their charges into making a premature commitment to support, or maybe oppose, a measure before the individual in question has had time or opportunity to study its implications. When the Member subsequently realises that he has made a mistake and wishes to change his mind the Whips are on hand to point out that honour demands that he stick to his original undertaking. Backtracking usually results in the Member being described by the Whips as a complete shit but then again the Whips' vocabulary does on those occasions tend to be rather basic, if not entirely predictable.

Given its Third Reading in April 1988, more than two years were to elapse before the Community Charge was cited as the principal reason for Margaret

Thatcher's failure to defeat the challenge to her leadership, the other one being, of course, the European dimension.

The passage of the Local Government Finance Bill, to give it its full title, was an object lesson in more senses of the word than one. Firstly, it illustrated the sheer impossibility of persuading governments to compromise, let alone change their minds. Secondly, it would in due course demonstrate that governments are reactive rather than proactive: when the Poll Tax legislation became unworkable it had to be scrapped but no amount of pointing out the pitfalls in advance was going to stop the Government going full steam ahead at the time. Thirdly, the whole sorry saga underscored the importance of Parliament retaining the ultimate power to repeal or amend legislation which in operation proves to be either deficient or unworkable. Finally, it highlighted the common sense of letting contentious legislation run the gamut of a Select Committee procedure before being given its Second Reading in the chamber of the House of Commons. Creating the opportunity for members of the public and other interested bodies to input at the outset of the legislative process might offend the *amour propre* of Government Ministers and departmental officials but the quality of the resultant legislation would be significantly improved.

What this experience also showed was that being right in politics is most definitely not the way to win and influence friends. If you're proved right then the rest of your colleagues are proved wrong and they don't like it one least little bit. Political careers are not ruined by going with the flow: on the contrary. The fact that the policy pursued may be ruinous to individual lives, whole industries or even the entire country is not the consideration that the average politician makes when he delivers his vote. The predominating consideration is whether or not this represents a good career move – sad but true and, in the age of the professional politician, likely to get worse rather than better. For understandable reasons politicians who have no experience beyond politics are driven to succeed in a way that those with a successful career in other fields are not. Climbing the greasy pole of politics becomes an end in itself. Parliament is littered with those who either fell or were pushed off the greasy pole who now have neither principles nor position to console them. Politics is a cruel mistress and as Enoch Powell once said, 'All political careers end in failure.'

CHAPTER FOUR

...the sound of the dawn chorus

ALMOST BEFORE I knew where I was and certainly before I had got my bearings all hell broke loose in Shropshire. The Health Authorities – at that time a massive Regional HA in Birmingham and a District HA in Shrewsbury – decided to close the county's cottage hospitals, six of which were in my constituency. Endless public meetings, dozens of deputations and countless letters ensued but, as my colleague in Shropshire North was to observe, the fact that I was to be seen publicly standing up for the interests of my constituents would stand me in good stead.

Shortly after being selected to fight the Ludlow seat I received a phone call from John Biffen who suggested that we might meet for a chat. Flattered that such a senior, respected and recently defenestrated Cabinet Minister should wish to take time out to talk to the likes of me I was only too pleased to make my way to the Mytton & Mermaid on the banks of the River Severn at Atcham to meet the great man. Our meeting took place not long after the PM's Press Secretary, Bernard Ingham, had famously told journalists that John Biffen was a 'semi-detached' member of the Cabinet and as we parted I found it impossible to resist asking for his own explanation as to how he had run foul of the Iron Lady. 'Oh,' he said, 'I think by pointing out to her on just one too many occasions that her slip was showing.'

The other neighbouring Parliamentarian who was kind enough to telephone offering his congratulations upon my selection was Peter Temple-Morris. By and by the Member for Leominster was to approach me to ask if I would be interested in becoming Secretary of the Conservative backbench European Affairs Committee. My initial response to Peter's invitation was to tell him that I was not desperately keen to take on the suggested position but that if he would allow me to sleep on it I would let him know the following day. The next morning I woke up thinking to myself that it was just possible that Europe might one day become a topical issue – if not in this Parliament, then perhaps in the next – and that I would let my name go forward. The irony of this arrangement was not finally played out until Peter crossed the floor of the House barely six months after the 1997 election because he considered the Conservative Party too hostile towards the European Union. That was some three years after I myself had had the party Whip withdrawn for defying a 3-line Whip by abstaining on a motion to send more money to Brussels.

Fighting to 'Save the Cottage Hospitals'.

Apart from my first run-in with the Whips' office over the Community Charge and the 'little local difficulty' concerning the proposed closure of the cottage hospitals my first three years in Parliament were relatively uneventful.

There were no repercussions resulting from my principled opposition to the Poll Tax other than an entry in the Whips' bad books. On the hospital front an enormous amount of time and effort had resulted in only one of my six cottage hospitals being closed and I settled down to being one of Margaret Thatcher's loyal foot-soldiers, confident in the knowledge that if on occasions she got her knickers in a twist she was more than capable of sorting the problem out without any great political fall-out.

Quite apart from being an admirer of her dynamic leadership I was also, as a businessman, enthusiastic about the obvious benefits that her policies were bringing to the national economy. Having had a hand in setting her on the road to fame and fortune I also had a personal vested interest in her success.

In 1969, as the Chairman of the Wolverhampton Local Education Authority, I had been invited, together with the Conservative chairmen of other LEAs, to attend a meeting at the Carlton Club to discuss the Party's Education policy.

The meeting was addressed by Sir Edward Boyle, the then shadow Education Secretary. Absent from his address was any reference to Grammar Schools and so when it came to questions I stood up and asked him if, when the Conservatives were returned to power, he would reverse the policy of Grammar School closures.

Edward Boyle declined to answer the question and I stood up again and repeated it.

Again he refused to answer and I was obliged to say to him yet again, 'Will the next Conservative Government reverse the process of Grammar School closures, Yes or No?'

Again he refused to answer.

Before the day was out Edward Boyle had been sacked and replaced by a junior member of the Shadow Cabinet called Margaret Thatcher.

What had happened, according to my mole in Conservative Central Office, was that the whole proceedings of the meeting at the Carlton Club had been recorded – quite a novelty in those days – and, when played back in CCO later in the day, so angered the Leader, Ted Heath, that Edward Boyle was sent packing without further ado. The fact that more Grammar Schools continued to close under Margaret Thatcher's regime does not form part of this narrative. Suffice it to say that, with the benefit of hindsight, it is now all too apparent that more, much more, should have been done on the Education front during the eighteen years of Conservative administration which followed Margaret Thatcher's election as Prime Minister in 1979.

But the emphasis was very much upon completing the programme of privatising the public utilities begun in the last Parliament – a process that was eventually completed by John Major's administration when it returned the railways to the private sector on the eve of the 1997 General Election.

Education and the Health Service, by far and away the biggest public sector undertakings of them all, lived to fight another day. Given that there will ultimately be so very little else for national parliaments to get their teeth into once the terms of the European treaties are fully implemented, perhaps there was some method in this strategy that was not recognisable at the time. In the meantime the nation continues to pay a high price for a second-class Education Service and a National Health Service that is no longer – if it ever was – 'the envy of the world'.

To de-nationalise or, to use the modern idiom, to privatise whole industries struck me as being massively complicated compared with the act of bringing them into public ownership in the first place.

The Bills to privatise Water and Electricity were complex and dense. The consequence of this was that the House was obliged to sit until all hours as

Self with pedigree South Devon cattle.

the battle to complete the necessary Parliamentary stages was fought out. Often in the Summer sitting I would find myself walking home in the early hours of the morning listening to the sound of the dawn chorus. Initially my wife, Patricia, would ask me what had gone on since she last saw me when I left to go to the House at 0930 the previous day. At 2 or 3 or 4 o'clock the following morning the last thing I wanted to do was to rehearse the events of the past twenty-four hours. My priority was to snatch a brief few hours sleep before it all started happening again.

Being transplanted from the open spaces of rural Shropshire to the confines of a small flat in Westminster was not easy for either of us but for Patricia, with the whole day on her own, the change of lifestyle was traumatic.

The sale of our pedigree herd of South Devon cattle in the Summer recess following the 1987 election in June represented another heartfelt break with the past. Our whole world was rapidly changing but given the choice there is little doubt where Patricia would have preferred to be.

When I told our son, Charles, that his mother would no longer be at home to wash his socks it wasn't long before he made alternative arrangements. On 5 December he announced his engagement to Lisa, married her the following September and in due course presented us with two of our four delightful grandchildren. Our elder daughter, Helen, having married and our younger daughter, Sarah, having started college in London in 1986 at least we had only ourselves to please. Compared with other colleagues with young families and commitments to match we were in a much better situation and I also soon began to realise how lucky I had been in another respect.

My life's plan had envisaged making myself financially independent by the age of 40 but as I approached the rubicon the national economy was going from bad to worse. Scrawled in the mud on the back of a lorry I read, 'Vote for Ted, 3 days at work 4 in bed.' It said it all. The high hopes of Ted Heath's General Election victory in 1970 had evaporated and his brief administration was limping towards an ignominious capitulation. Just as I was ready to fire up the emergency electricity generator that I had bought second-hand from the Lea & Perrins sauce factory in Worcester in order to keep the Gill factory running, Ted caved in to the miners and the rest, as they say, is history. Undaunted and seemingly untainted by having lost the argument about who governs, Parliament or the Trades Unions, Sir Edward, as he now is, was to haunt the political scene (and his recognisably more successful successor) for a further twenty-seven years. Only with the passage of time is the irony of Ted Heath's battle as to who governs this country seen in its proper perspective. It was he, as Prime Minister of Great Britain and Northern Ireland, who had negotiated Britain's accession to the European Economic Community (later to become the European Community and latterly the European Union) and who, by dint of his signature on the Treaty of Rome, had set in motion the very process by which the UK would progressively surrender the sovereignty of the Westminster Parliament and the inalienable right to call itself a self governing nation.

So much for 'who governs', the watchword of the 1974 election.

Nonetheless I have this much to thank Ted for. Had it not been for his disastrous administration which plunged the economy and the whole of industry into such unprecedented turmoil I might have been in a better position to realise my original ambition. Had that been the case doubtless I should then have been even more frustrated as a younger man than I was as a more mature person entering Parliament for the first time at age 50. As one gets older one mellows, recognises that Rome wasn't built in a day and learns to accept that there is more to life than personal ambition. On the other hand if Ted had not acted as he did in another direction, the opportunity that presented itself in Wolverhampton South West would simply not have arisen. Had he not propelled the UK into the benighted EEC, with effect from 1 January 1973, then it follows that Enoch Powell would not have kicked over the traces in February 1974.

…not the last time I would experience a major conflict of interest

ARRIVING IN THE Palace of Westminster before the official State Opening I tried to ascertain which office I had been allocated. In the absence of any positive response to that question and acting upon the rumours circulating amongst the new Members I tried putting my mail in the office of my predecessor only to discover that it rapidly found its way back to the House of Commons Post Office from where I had collected it in the first place. What the Serjeant at Arms' Office were able to do as an interim measure was to issue me with a key to a locker of which there are literally hundreds dotted about the corridors. Finding the locker corresponding to the numbered key that I had been issued with proved to be another interesting experience because the lockers are not sequentially sited. Nevertheless for the first three weeks of the Summer sitting that was my office until allocated a space in the East Cloisters – effectively a passageway approximately 10 feet wide where I and thirteen other Members sat at desks placed back to back down its length.

In contrast to the lack of any written guidance the old hands were invariably helpful but with the exception of Nick Budgen and Anthony Steen (South Hams) I didn't know any old hands. Nick Budgen I had met as a result of our mutual interest in pedigree South Devon cattle and Anthony Steen when he visited Wolverhampton in his capacity as Director of the Young Volunteers organisation at the time I was Chairman of the Local Education Committee. Had Enoch Powell survived that election he would have been another Member that I would have known but sadly the electorate of South Down had decreed otherwise. To me this was a huge disappointment and I dropped Enoch a line to say so. With typical Powellite economy he replied that 'some are surprisingly found and others surprisingly lost'. It was a sad end to a long and distinguished Parliamentary career.

Before venturing into the Members' Dining Room on my second evening in Parliament I had learned that protocol decreed that one sat wherever there was a space at an occupied table and only sat at an unoccupied table if there wasn't. Entering the Dining Room by the central doorway I spotted several vacant chairs at a table in the middle of the room and proceeded to sit myself down upon one of them whereupon Alan Beith, Member for Berwick-upon-Tweed, leant over and politely explained that this was the Liberal Democrat table. He went on to say that if I didn't mind sitting at their table they certainly wouldn't mind either, a sentiment which I reciprocated. What nobody had told me was that seating in the Members' Dining Room is strictly segregated – and for good reason too. Looking up I could see David Evans, Member for Hatfield, and others of my intake gesticulating madly from the far end of the room whereupon I excused myself from the Liberal table and beat a hasty retreat in the direction of the Conservative tables! The beauty of these arrangements is that one is randomly thrown together with colleagues that one might not otherwise encounter and because one is supposedly amongst 'friends' the conversation can be, and often is, uninhibited and frank to the point of indiscretion.

As an exemption to the general convention it was sometimes the case that one found oneself dining in enemy territory. On an occasion when the Conservative end of the dining room was full to capacity Sir Iain Lloyd and I seated ourselves at the Labour end where he proceeded to give me what proved to be very sound advice. 'Remember,' he said, 'that you can have more influence as a backbencher without ambition than ever you will if it is known that you are hungry for office.' Never once did I regret following that sage advice but in any case I had no burning ambition to be the junior Minister in charge of drains, only a strong determination to be my own man. Perhaps not the best way to advance a career in politics but not a bad recipe for ensuring a decent night's sleep when one's head eventually hits the pillow.

The debating Chamber in the House of Commons is very much smaller than is popularly imagined. On occasions such as State Opening, Budget Day and moments of high drama it is physically impossible for all 659 Members to sit and many find themselves standing at the Bar of the House, behind the Speaker's Chair or ensconced in the Galleries. That was hardly the situation when I made my Maiden Speech on 23 October 1987. Attendance on a Friday, other than in exceptional circumstances, is never great and a debate on 'Health' attracted what is commonly known as a 'thin House'. Nevertheless I did my stuff, possibly to the surprise of one of the Government Whips, David Lightbown, who, enquiring as to my intention on the previous day, had intimated that half the maiden speakers don't go through with it when the time comes.

It is axiomatic that in making a maiden speech new Members pay tribute to their predecessor, irrespective of party affiliations, but in so doing I was determined also to mention Sir Jasper More who had represented Ludlow from 1960 to 1979. His widow subsequently told me that he had very much approved of what I had said but sadly, five days later he died at 8 p.m. on my 51st birthday. Lady More, who became a staunch and loyal ally, used to tell the tale of one of their experiences whilst canvassing in Church Stretton. On answering the doorbell the lady of the house directed Jasper and Clare to the top of the garden where she said they would find her husband tending his donkey.

'And what do you call the donkey?' says Clare.

'We calls 'im Jaaspurr.'

'That's an unusual name for a donkey,' says Jasper.

'Yes,' he says, 'we calls 'im Jaaspurr after your grandfairther – 'is name was Jaaspurr'!

Looking back after an interval of nearly fifteen years I have no cause to regret what I first told the House in October 1987. As predicted the Common Agriculture Policy has proved to be the ruination of British farming (and fisheries too), the proliferation of quasi autonomous Government organisations, Quangos, has continued apace and the problems created by the state's virtual monopoly in the provision of Health care have simply continued to compound and grow. At a more mundane level I advised the House that the way to a healthy life was through eating a balanced diet of which an essential component is meat and two veg. Speaking as a butcher representing one of Britain's premier livestock areas this was not, I considered, out of place.

One of the things that the Conservative Party has always done well is to give former colleagues a good send-off. On 20 November Sir John Stradling Thomas (Monmouth) representing the Speaker of the House of Commons, Stephen Dorrell (Loughborough) representing the Prime Minister and other luminaries such as former Foreign Secretary Lord Pym, journeyed to Ludlow to join the huge gathering in St. Laurence's Church for the Thanksgiving Service for the life of Sir Jasper More. When earlier in the month I had gone to see Speaker Weatherill to tell him about the arrangements for Jasper's memorial service he was kindness itself. Taking pity upon a very recent, rather unsure and somewhat overawed new Member, the person who now held the highest elected office in the land modestly described how at school he had regarded himself as the 'Senior Inferior'. He extended an open invitation to 'Whisky and Sympathy' after the 10 o'clock votes whenever I felt the need, an Adjournment debate if required and advice on how to succeed in Parliament simply for the asking. I don't pretend that Bernard Weatherill treated other backbenchers any differently but at a time when my 'learning curve' seemed almost vertical, my confidence less than boundless and the fear of failure quite real, his hand of genuine friendship was a real boost to flagging morale and an absolute tonic at a critical juncture.

My baptism of fire eventually ended on 25 April 1988 when the Local Government Finance Bill implementing the Community Charge received its Third Reading. I am not proud of the fact that I consistently abstained on all votes to introduce this ill starred method of financing local government, believing as I do that one should be either positively for or positively against whatever is proposed. However this was not the first nor sadly would it be the last time that I would experience a major conflict of interest between adherence to a principle on the one hand and loyalty to the Party under whose colours I had been elected on the other. The other consideration which on occasions makes the decision even more difficult is that constituents may also have a strongly held view of what's best. This was certainly the case regarding the Poll Tax where farm workers, for example, living in tied cottages, were strongly opposed to the principle of having to pay exactly the same amount as their very much better off employers.

Two days later I was the guest of Michael Heseltine at Wilton's for lunch. Having resigned from Cabinet in January 1986 over the Westland affair Michael was widely regarded as having exploited party differences regarding the Community Charge to advance his own prospects of one day becoming Leader. That he harboured such an ambition was something that I had instinctively known ever since we had been at Shrewsbury School together more than thirty years previously. To this day I retain a picture in my mind's eye of the teenage Heseltine striding across the Site, a mane of blond hair streaming out behind him, en route to the School debating society. To have pursued this burning ambition so assiduously from such an early age is no criticism of the man but in politics, as I knew from my own experience of being chosen to fight the Ludlow seat, being the right man in the right place at the right time is everything. In Michael's case it also has to be said that it was he himself who was to observe that 'he who wields the knife never wears the crown'.

For the time being the battles over the 'Poll Tax' which had included Michael Heseltine's insurrection in the shape of the Mates' amendment* were all water under the bridge.

But not for long. Two years later the same cocktail would be served up again with catastrophic consequences for one of the finest leaders the Conservative Party had ever had.

In the interim my time was fully occupied trying to ensure that the six cottage hospitals in my constituency remained open, arguing for lower taxes, sticking up for the agriculture industry and generally trying to honour the commitment I had given at interview to be a good constituency MP.

On 16 February I had asked the Prime Minister about Monetary Compensatory Amounts and Pigs. Throughout my Parliamentary career I made it my practice to ask my own questions and to ask only the questions for which I wanted an answer. Asking planted questions or questions just for the sake of gumming up the works wasn't my style. The Whips might have thought this rather untoward but my principle was to be able to stand behind whatever I said or did. Refusing to speak in the House about subjects that I knew nothing of was an irritation to the Whips but whereas they would change and go on to other jobs I would continue to plough my own, sometimes lonely, furrow.

---

*The Mates' amendment had been initiated by Michael Mates, Member for East Hampshire, and sought to substitute a system of 'banding' for the flat rate charge written into the Bill.

Rather surprisingly the Prime Minister's Parliamentary Private Secretary, Archie Hamilton, raised no objections to my proposed question about pigs but the reaction of other colleagues was interesting. John Biffen (Shropshire North) thought it too long but in any case why not ask about teachers as there were going to be a number of Shropshire teachers in the Public Gallery that afternoon but 'there again,' he said, 'there are probably more pigs in Shropshire than teachers so you go ahead.' Richard Ryder, a junior Whip representing Mid Norfolk, a county with a large pig population, was most encouraging and Edwina Currie (Derbyshire South) whose hour of fame as far as Agriculture was concerned was yet to come, said to hype it up by flattering the PM – that, she confessed, was how she had got on!

In terms of knowing how to get on I was already the beneficiary of Julian Critchley's advice. Over dinner one night he said that in return for a stick of black pudding he would tell me how to succeed in politics. The very next morning he was to be heard on the airwaves telling the world at large how he had met this new Member of Parliament who made black puddings and how he, Critchley, had got the better of the deal by offering to advise him in exchange for a common or garden stick of black pudding. Whilst never exactly bosom pals Critchley and I were, at that stage, on good terms and he was kind enough to opine that it was 'a great achievement to have been selected by one's own people', Ludlow being the constituency in which I had lived since 1972 and whose boundary is a mere six miles from my birthplace in Wolverhampton. Critchley would be forever telling me that it was his ambition to live in Ludlow but this never materialised until suddenly, immediately following his re-election at Aldershot in 1992, he removed himself to 44 Mill Street, scarcely ever to be seen in Westminster again.

To welcome him to the Ludlow constituency I offered to stand him lunch at the nationally acclaimed Poppies restaurant at Brimfield. Arriving a few minutes late because of a rather protracted constituency 'surgery' I found Critchley tucking into lobster and the best bottle of Chablis the establishment could provide. I paid the bill and the rest, as they say, is history.

Thereafter he proceeded to bite the hand that had fed him by waging a virulent campaign against the Party that had sustained him, the Prime Minister who had caused him to be knighted and his own Member of Parliament, i.e. myself, whom he publicly announced he wouldn't vote for. Carelessly overlooking the fact that we had both attended the same school he accused me of being poorly educated and like so many of his ilk could never bring himself to accept that someone from a commercial background might conceivably have as much to contribute as those who had never had a real job outside politics. With friends like that who needs enemies but, as all thinking people knew, the real bone of contention was Europe. Since his days at the Sorbonne Critchley had been an ardent Europhile and was an enthusiastic supporter of European Union. I was not, as will become apparent as this story unfolds. After a false start in July 1988 when I was, to my lasting shame, the only Shropshire MP to vote in favour of the Second Reading of the European Communities (Finance) Bill. I subsequently declined to support it at either Report stage or Third Reading. Six years later my refusal to vote in favour of yet another European Communities (Finance) Bill resulted in my having the Party whip withdrawn, but more of that anon.

After a year in the House I felt totally exhausted even though the real battles were yet to come. Perhaps I should have heeded the advice of Enoch Powell who, on performing the opening ceremony of a new factory for the family business in 1971, had light-heartedly advised against going into politics and to stick to making black puddings instead. I know what he meant and can appreciate the huge frustration that Enoch must have experienced when he unavailingly sought to warn against the twin perils of mass immigration and the abandonment of national sovereignty.

CHAPTER SIX

1989

…my learning curve still practically vertical

B Y THE TIME the New Year came round my learning curve was still practically vertical but in terms of getting to grips with my new career I was over the worst. In February I became a Freeman of the City of London, three months in advance of my esteemed Leader, Margaret Thatcher. In March, having heard Prof. Martin Holmes describe the CAP as 'the greatest single engine of poverty', I joined the Friends of the Bruges Group which had been formed to support the principles enunciated by the PM in her famous 1988 Bruges speech and in April I was accorded the distinction by the Adam Smith Institute of being amongst the top five Parliamentary Free Marketeers.

Back in the constituency I was floating the idea that the Bank of England should be privatised and on 26 October 1989 tabled a question to the PM asking whether 'it is her policy to restore the independent status of the Bank of England' only to withdraw it on the advice of friends less than ten minutes before the then Chancellor, Nigel Lawson, announced his resignation. The significance of this was that Lawson, speaking in the House five days later, went on to advocate an independent Bank but regrettably a further eight years were to elapse before the incoming New Labour Government took the momentous step of making the setting of interest rates the sole prerogative of the Old Lady of Threadneedle Street, a decision which now appears to have paid off handsomely.

Conservative MPs who were opposed to Bank of England independence were, in many cases, fearful that this would play into the hands of the European Union, a resurgent resistance to which was by now just starting to manifest itself. John Redwood's Early Day Motion tabled on 16 May stating that

this House congratulates the Prime Minister on the strong leadership that she is giving to the United Kingdom and to Europe by making it clear that the best way to build a successful European Community is through the willing and active co-operation between independent sovereign states; fully endorses her view that it is right to keep the running of the economy of the United Kingdom and the running of taxation of the United Kingdom in this Parliament; and also endorses her statement that the Delors Report aims of a federal Europe, a common currency and a common economic policy, including fiscal policy are completely unacceptable

Newly elected Freeman of the City of London, flanked by l-r son Charles, daughter-in-law Lisa, wife Patricia, Mother, younger daughter Sarah and Father.

and my letter to *The Times* supported by Messrs. Cran, Janman, Porter and Redwood were but the opening salvoes in a battle for the heart and soul of the Conservative Party that was to run and run. These were the outward and visible signs of a discontent that was to reach epic proportions at the time of the passage of the Treaty on European Union in the 1992/3 session. Meanwhile it seems probable that, prompted by her Bruges speech, the forces of darkness were already plotting clandestinely to overthrow the Iron Lady – an objective that they would achieve in the autumn of 1990 after the failure of 'stalking horse' Sir Anthony Meyer (Clwyd North West) to attract sufficient votes to trigger a full-scale leadership contest in 1989. On this occasion Margaret Thatcher attracted a massive 314 votes but what was about to befall the Parliamentary party was the very antithesis of what the Opposition Chief Whip, Derek Foster (Bishop Auckland), described as 'the impressive way in which the Tory Party sticks together and closes ranks in a crisis'. When he made this observation to me in a conversation on the Terrace of the House of Commons on the last day of June 1989, I concluded, given the recent history of the Labour Party, how envious he must be. Little did I realise at the time that the traitors within the Conservative Party were already at work and that the knives were well and truly out for Maggie. Removing her from the seat of power now became the Europhiles' top priority, determined as they were to ensure that the project (of European integration) should not be prejudiced by any latter-day Boadicea standing in its way.

Addressing the full 1922 Committee at the end of the summer sitting, the Prime Minister tried to meet the threat by saying that 'we belong to Europe…and will continue to fight for what we believe in.' Clearly this was said to keep both wings of the Party happy and before announcing that she too would be taking a holiday this year stressed that our 'future success depends upon sticking together' – a message that would sadly fall upon an increasing number of deaf ears.

A few days later there was a Ministerial reshuffle and when the PM announced, as she invariably did at Question Time, that her engagements included an audience with the Queen one of the Labour backbench wags, Tony Banks (West Ham), called out, 'Is she being reshuffled too!'

Whilst Prime Ministers obviously have the final say in who shall be Ministers the election of officers to backbench committees is exclusively the province of backbenchers themselves. In 1988 the election of officers to the backbench committee on European Affairs had passed almost unnoticed but by the time it came round again in December 1989 things had clearly moved on. In the first place a huge number of colleagues turned up to cast their vote in the Committee Room appointed for the purpose and more significantly, when the result of the ballot was announced, it was clear that the Europhiles had been routed. Out went Ian Taylor (Esher) as Chairman to be replaced by Bill Cash (Stafford) and, as Vice Chairmen, in came Euro realists Tony Favell (Stockport) and Roger Knapman (Stroud).

Prior to the ballot Government Whip Tristan Garel-Jones (often referred to as the Member for Madrid because of his Spanish wife but actually representing Watford), who was to play a significant if not ignominious part in the European wrangles ahead, had warned Bill that should he get the Chairmanship of the European Affairs Committee his prospects of advancement would be non-existent. The battle lines were clearly being drawn. A fight to the death between those of us who believed in the preservation of the Nation state and colleagues who put European integration as a higher ideal than National sovereignty was now seemingly inevitable.

CHAPTER SEVEN

1990

'Tory MPs bemused by the confusion they have created.'

IN THE New Year Honours List there is a Knighthood for Christopher
Prout. Christopher has been Shropshire's MEP since the first direct
election to the European Parliament and is destined to be the Leader of the
Conservative group in Strasbourg for the five year period 1987-92. A
Federalist at heart, Christopher's advancement through the political ranks was
remarkable in that it was directly inverse to the pattern of electoral success.
Fewer Conservative MEPs were returned to Strasbourg in the previous year's
European Parliament election than in 1984 and fewer still would be elected in
1994, the year in which Christopher lost his own seat and was rewarded with
a place in the House of Lords. Admiral Byng, had you but lived in our times!

Ever the optimist I went on 23 January to meet the Minister of State at the
Department of Trade and Industry. Douglas Hogg (Grantham) had previously
warned me that I wouldn't change his mind on the subject of Government
grants in aid to industry but I was still determined to try. My case was, and
remains, that grants and subsidies distort the economic patterns that would
otherwise prevail and that Government largesse (with taxpayers' money)
should, by and large, be used only on projects which individual taxpayers have
an equal opportunity to access e.g. infrastructure projects. I instanced how, in
my own county of Shropshire, what had made all the difference in terms of
success or failure for the new town at Telford was not the inducements to
individual companies to locate there but the advent (somewhat belatedly) of
the M54 connecting Telford to the national motorway system.

All of this was not going down at all well with Douglas who became more
and more agitated and started to beat the arms of his chair with the palms of
both hands. The dust from his armchair was rising in clouds but when he
proceeded to tell me that he knew nothing about business the advantage was
suddenly mine. 'Why then do you not take any notice of someone who does?'
I was then able to tell Douglas how several years previously at the St. John's
Hotel in Solihull, in front of an audience of 200 businessmen, I had heard his
father, Quintin, say the very same thing.*

In my diary I recorded a most unsatisfactory meeting with a bumptious,

---

*In fairness it has to be said that Lord Hailsham, Quintin Hogg as he was then, was deputising at very short
notice for a Cabinet colleague with relevant departmental responsibilities.

28

arrogant pipsqueak. What he might have thought of me I may never know other than that he told me at the time that I was a 'fundamentalist'. For many years after that event we were as oil to water. He was a man of Government, I was not. He was a federalist, I was not. He was a QC, I but a humble butcher and farmer.

In September 1997 I found myself chosen to sit next to Douglas at dinner. The occasion was the meeting of the remnants of the Parliamentary party in Eastbourne after the massive electoral cull that had occurred on 1 May. The Press rather unkindly described this gathering as a 'bonding session' but entering into the spirit of the occasion I determined that by the end of our dinner together Douglas and I would be on good terms...and so we were. Out of a deep mistrust there grew to be a mutual respect to the extent that he subsequently confided in me that he had voted for me in the 1997 elections to the Executive of the 1922 Committee and for my part I remain the greatest admirer of his forensic skills as a backbench debater and effective Parliamentarian.

One evening in 1999 we fell in step walking home after the House had adjourned and he asked me whether I considered that the time had come when we should make a little trouble for the Government on account of their apparent determination to ban foxhunting.

The following Monday evening we kept the Government out of their beds for rather longer than they had bargained for as a result of pressing to divisions business that they thought would go through on the nod. Acting as a Teller for the 'No' Lobby I struck up a brief conversation with my opposite number, a Government Whip, Bob Ainsworth (Coventry N.E.) who wanted to know 'what's this all about?' 'In a word,' I said, 'hunting,' to which he replied, 'Oh, I'm all for the class warfare!' Now we know.

It is now apparent that the back-lash against the Community Charge (Poll Tax) is real and growing. By the time we come to the autumn and the wreckers' next opportunity to mount a challenge to the leadership the PM will, as a consequence, have seriously depleted her store of political credit and be very much more vulnerable than when challenged by the 'stalking donkey' last November.

Putting things into perspective, Nick Budgen tells Bill Newton-Dunn MEP (Lincolnshire) that MEPs have an entirely futile existence. Those of us who recognise that the European Parliament would be more accurately described as an Assembly, a mere talking shop, are bound to agree with his judgement but later in the year, as the terms of the Treaty on European Union begin to emerge, how many Westminster Parliamentarians will stop to think that a vote for this unprecedented ceding of sovereignty will put them in the same category? It is doubtful whether the rough ride that Newton-Dunn had at the hands of the European Affairs Committee that March made the slightest difference and it was no surprise when, shortly after the European Parliament elections in 1999, he defected to the ultra-federalist Liberal Democrats.

By now the pace of European integration is accelerating and having been browbeaten by both Chancellor Nigel Lawson (Blaby) and Foreign Secretary Douglas Hurd (Witney) at the EU Heads of Government meeting in Madrid in 1989 Margaret Thatcher reluctantly agrees to join the ill-fated Exchange Rate Mechanism. The announcement that we have joined comes on 5 October. On the 16th Tony Favell resigns as Parliamentary Private Secretary to John Major (Chancellor of the Exchequer October 1989-November 1990 and briefly, in the period July-October 1989, Foreign Secretary) and the next day is reported as saying that he wants to be free to speak out about the European Union into which, in his own words, we are 'sleepwalking'. Several months will elapse before Tony confides that he wishes he hadn't prevailed over John Major to prevent him making a strongly federalist speech whilst Chancellor.

A month later on 13 November Geoffrey Howe (Deputy PM July 1989-November 1990) delivers his infamous and vitriolic attack on the Prime Minister – the speech that wags say took Elspeth (his wife) five minutes to write and Geoffrey five years to deliver – and the Party is plunged headlong into a Leadership contest.

Two days later the battle lines are drawn – a straight fight between the incumbent, Margaret Thatcher, and the upstart, Heseltine. The ballot on 20 November results in 204 votes for Thatcher, 152 for Hezza and 16 abstentions, a convincing enough victory in itself but sadly not quite good enough to satisfy the arcane rules of the 1922 Committee.

The Labour Party are cock-a-hoop and can scarcely believe their luck. Eric Martlew (Lab. Carlisle) observes that the Tories don't know what to do – 'they haven't got as much experience in these matters as Labour'! – and tomorrow's *Daily Telegraph* will carry the headline 'Tory MPs bemused by the confusion they have created.'

Whilst there might be confusion in some colleagues' minds there is none in mine. I tell them that I'm not going to see the greatest peacetime PM bounced out of Number 10 by Andreotti, Geoffrey Howe, Michael Heseltine or anybody else. Even if I am entirely alone I shall continue to cast my vote for Thatcher. Sadly this prospect expires at one minute past 9 o'clock on the morning of 22 November when the Iron Lady announces that she will not contest the next round. It is the end of an era.

Confusion reigns supreme. The wreckers have done their worst and now we must choose from the best of a bad bunch – Heseltine, Hurd or Major.

My constituency Association Chairman is content with my decision to back

Major but (being an old Etonian) prefers Hurd. The Treasurer agrees that Major is the man. Amongst the Conservative Councillors there is some support for Major but their preference for Heseltine is definitely not shared by the 'punters' who come in off the street to tell me, at my regular Saturday morning surgery, not to vote for him. Never before nor since have I experienced such unsolicited antipathy towards one specific individual politician.

Back at the House I twist Graham Bright's arm – he is Member for Luton S. and John Major's new PPS – to let me have ten minutes with his boss so that I may seek his personal assurance that he will not go soft on Trades Unions, nor Europe, and that he will be prepared to look at radical reform of the method of financing local government expenditure. I venture to suggest that the problems in this area will not go away until local authorities are put into the position of having themselves to raise £1 for every 100p they spend. I also venture the opinion that he will do very well in the ballot tomorrow which indeed he does. Voting is 185 for Major, 131 for Heseltine and 56 for Hurd.

Hurd and Hezza concede and John Major is our new Leader and Prime Minister. It will be a while before I and others realise how comprehensively we have been duped by this closet integrationist but even before the set-piece battles regarding the forthcoming Treaty on European Union commence the storm clouds are gathering. At this stage Britain's membership of the Exchange Rate Mechanism is of less than eight weeks duration. In two years time the economic ramifications of this misguided decision will be plain for all to see and the political consequences will by then have left an indelible blot on the Conservative Party's escutcheon.

In the meantime I hold out the hand of friendship by inviting the new PM to visit the Ludlow constituency (29 November) where Norma his wife was born, and a fortnight later (13 December) fire a shot across his bows before he goes off to the European Council meeting in Rome.*

---

*Mr Gill: When my right hon. Friend goes to Rome this weekend, will he bear it in mind that, in the final analysis, the British Government must go whichever way gives British agriculture and industry the best prospects of creating wealth for the people who live in these islands? Will he tell our European partners that wealth creation through free trade remains our top priority? (*Hansard* col. 1107)

CHAPTER EIGHT

1991

By now everyone is talking about Europe...

SOME SIX MONTHS later, having battled with my conscience and concluded that there really is little point in being a Member of Parliament unless one expresses one's point of view frankly and honestly, on 6 June I find myself asking the PM yet another leading question.* When I give Downing Street advance notice of what I am going to say they are none too happy and ring back suggesting some anodyne alternative question about Agriculture.

This has a rather hollow ring to it because I have lost no opportunity in trying to interest the Party hierarchy in helping the farming industry by scrapping the iniquitous Common Agriculture Policy and nobody wants to hear of it. Mentioning such a heresy at a luncheon convened by the PM at No. 10 specifically to discuss Agriculture ensures that I am never invited again. The consideration as far as the top brass are concerned is not that the CAP will ultimately destroy the livelihood of British farmers but rather the fear that leaving the CAP will wreck the European project. Why a Conservative Government should wish to uphold a Collectivist system is a question that still needs an answer but Major's second administration, as we shall soon see, will go through fire and brimstone to ratify a treaty that enshrines in law all that the Conservative Party has historically been opposed to – destroying in the process its own reputation, the fundamentals of Parliamentary democracy and any hope of being re-elected in the foreseeable future.

As a regular participant in Agriculture debates there was nothing unusual about my catching the Deputy Speaker's eye in a late night sitting of the House to consider a Money Resolution relating to an Order about Suckler Cows. I was well into my stride when Harold Walker (Lab. Doncaster) suddenly called, 'Order, Order, What's beef got to do with suckler cows: the Honourable Gentleman must stick to the point.' Respectfully I pointed out that the very best quality beef comes from suckler herds whereupon the Deputy Speaker kindly allowed me to continue. Upon resuming my seat after

---

*Mr Gill: My right hon. Friend is aware of the tremendous support among Conservative Members for his views on economic and monetary union. Is my right hon. Friend aware that those same views, clearly articulated by my right hon. Friend the Chancellor last week and my right hon. Friend the Foreign Secretary on the 'Today' programme this week, command the support of the majority of British voters, as evidenced by a recent opinion poll showing that 63 per cent oppose the single currency? (*Hansard* col. 403)

I had finished speaking one of my younger colleagues leant over and said, 'Chris, what's a suckler cow?' How well I answered that question can be judged from the fact that a little while later my young friend was on his feet in that same debate telling the world all about suckler cows and not so long after that was made a Minister of Agriculture!

As 1991 wears on the European issue comes more and more to predominate. The reaction of colleagues to my question on 6 June is mixed – some are cool towards me, others congratulatory. Michael Spicer (Worcestershire West) who will play such a key role in the revolt over the Maastricht Treaty tells James Cran (Beverley) and I what a good job we're doing and his good friend Nicholas Ridley is interested to hear that I've been 'handbagged' for my pains. This he attempts to counteract two days later by publishing an article in the *Evening Standard* – he says he hopes 'that'll get the Stasi off your back.'

On the same day that Nicholas Ridley's article appears in print Bill Cash (Stafford) gets wind of an operation to pack the evening meeting of our European Affairs committee. In the event an unprecedented number of colleagues attend what is clearly a well orchestrated attempt to destabilise our Chairman (Cash) and to put us so-called Eurosceptics in our place – news which soon finds its way on to the *Today* programme and into tomorrow's newspapers.

Peter Temple-Morris denies that the Lollards (a group of Conservative Members on the left of the Party) are behind the plot and suggests that maybe it had its origins in the Whip's Office – a suggestion which Government Whip Tim Boswell (Daventry) is quick to deny. George Gardiner (Reigate), Chairman of the '92 Committee representing Members on the right of the Party, observes that the time of the meeting on the official Whip was given as 1730 whereas it should have stated 1700 thus giving an unfair and possibly intended advantage to the plotters. Be that as it may, by the time the annual election of officers to the committee comes round again in November it is obvious that the hand of Government is at work. Messrs. Cash, Cran, Favell, Knapman and I are unceremoniously voted out in a massive turnout of colleagues estimated to be somewhere in the order of 200, in other words practically every Conservative backbencher except the payroll (i.e. those Members with a job or position dependent upon Government patronage). Robert Hughes (Harrow W. and former PPS to Edward Heath) tells the Press that the voting was 4 to 1 in their favour but more reliable estimates suggest that the result was 60/40. Either way the gloves were off. This was confirmed when William Powell (Corby) let slip that orders had gone out from Downing Street to get rid of Cash. Once that instruction had been issued we never stood a chance but as John Biffen was to observe this was 'Government behaving as one would expect Wrekin District Council to behave'. In this

Rt. Hon. John Biffen MP, LCCA Chairman Jackie Williams and self.

respect Government were making a big mistake quite apart from the fact that it had always been understood that backbench committees were the exclusive prerogative of backbenchers and absolutely no business of Government.

Even though the Major administration hasn't yet celebrated its first anniversary it is digging in on the European issue seemingly oblivious to all signs of dissent. When a politician of Nicholas Ridley's stature and experience points out that the man on the proverbial Clapham omnibus can read in the newspapers that the Home Secretary is against the dismantling of national frontiers; that the Foreign Secretary is against the EC being the means of our Security; that the Defence Secretary is against the EC being the vehicle of our Defence; that the Employment Secretary is against the Social Chapter; that the Chancellor has reservations about the Single Currency and that the Agriculture Minister wants drastic reform of the CAP, he's entitled to ask what on earth we're doing wasting our time at Intergovernmental Conferences. The logic is faultless but the juggernaut of European integration brooks no opposition whether built on logic or not.

The PM is fully committed to the ERM – a necessary prelude to joining the Single Currency – but after barely nine months gestation, unwelcome signs are appearing. Addressing my colleagues in the '92 Committee in July I tell them that I am diffident about raising the subject because the die is already cast but do they realise that our Government is riding a tiger (the ERM) and that it will be a close run thing as to whether we are able to fight and win a General Election before the chickens come home to roost? Discussion on this topic indicates that many of my colleagues haven't the remotest understanding of the danger in which we are now standing and will simply continue to go with the flow. Judged by the reaction to my debut at the '22 Committee a couple of months earlier perhaps I shouldn't have been surprised. On that occasion I had warned colleagues about the dangers of irrevocably fixed exchange rates and a single currency but to little avail. Nick Budgen subsequently told me that in his opinion a few words in the privacy of the '22 Committee would gain more publicity than a speech in the Chamber but any thoughts that I might have had of stimulating a discussion or a debate amongst colleagues were sadly disappointed. The prevailing mood appears to be one of keeping any dissenting views to oneself and hoping for the best. All of my instincts point in the opposite direction – if there's a problem looming then it's best to thrash it out before it's too late. In the fullness of time events will clearly demonstrate which of these approaches makes the most sense.

The summer sitting ends with the Leader, John Major, addressing the '22 Committee in the time honoured fashion. He repeats his pledge not to agree a treaty at Maastricht unless it is in Britain's interest. Knowing his man, Tony Favell fears that Major will sign on the dotted line and then bring the treaty to Parliament for ratification which is, in due course, precisely what happens.

Earlier in the day, acting on a tip-off from Charles Irving (Cheltenham) my wife and I repair to the House of Commons terrace where we are introduced to the PM's guest, President Gorbachev of Russia. As Chairman of the Catering Committee Charles is a useful man to know because nothing much happens in the Palace of Westminster without the knowledge of the Catering Department. The other recognised sources of inside information are the House of Commons policemen – particularly the one on duty behind the Speaker's chair – Government Ministers' chauffeurs and the splendid platoon of doorkeepers (traditionally retired members of Her Majesty's armed services).

Before being returned as the Member for Cheltenham Charles had been the Prospective Parliamentary Candidate for South East Wolverhampton. Knowing of my association with the town he once regaled me with the story of his attendance for interview at the offices of the SE Wolverhampton Conservative Association offices in Wellington Road, Bilston. Needing to use the facilities he was directed to the top of the stairs where he would find what he was looking for. Hanging his jacket on the back of the WC door and dropping his trousers his next sensation, as he put it himself, was of dropping through the floor and ceiling below 'clutching the porcelain to me as I went'.

Hardly a safe seat but Charles made a sufficient impression to win the nomination and went on to become an immensely popular PPC.

The Bilston constituency is obviously a very different kettle of fish to Ludlow where at the end of a particularly sticky dinner Christopher Prout is reputed to have turned to his hostess and enquired as to whether things were still quite as feudal in Shropshire as they used to be. 'Not at all,' came the reply, 'that's why you're here!'

I had originally encountered Christopher Prout when he was my MEP and found him an attentive listener when I, as a livestock producer and abattoir owner, had tried to explain how the European Beef Regime was ruining one of Britain's most successful industries. Notwithstanding the effect that European policies were having upon his country and, more to the point, upon his constituents, Christopher never wavered in his support for European integration. With the passage of time our relationship became somewhat strained because whereas Christopher, in respect of the European Community, could see no wrong I could increasingly find no good.

Our first clash came at a constituency Euro function in October when he exhorted the assembled company to get behind John Major when he returned from Maastricht '…regardless of the deal'. As a businessman I was certainly not in the habit of doing deals regardless of the terms and now as a politician I was certainly not in the business of riding roughshod over the views of the people I represented, particularly when the deal would result in the diminution of Parliamentary democracy and the political freedom which had underscored our personal liberties for centuries past. Indeed, the very following week I was pleased to have the opportunity to speak alongside Tony Favell, in support of the Freedom Association's 'Referendum First' campaign launched at a fringe meeting at the Conservative Party conference in Blackpool. Whilst an audience of barely forty people scarcely constitutes a 'full house', those present were to hear the Chairman, Norris McWhirter, tell them 'they will one day be proud to have been in at the beginning of something of great national importance.' Notwithstanding the fact that it would, within the next twelve months, become quite clear that John Major would never under any circumstances concede a referendum on the Treaty on European Union, a decade later we have a Labour Government committed to holding a referendum before entering into the final stage of Economic and Monetary Union and the Conservative Party pledged to oppose the Single Currency as a matter of principle.

On returning to the House that autumn my first (fortuitous) encounter is with the Chief Whip, Richard Ryder. I lose no time explaining that I shall be supporting the Government in the lobbies this evening (on Defence cuts to which as a former Naval Officer I am bitterly opposed) but only so as to keep my powder dry for the forthcoming European Community debate. I tell him

The Freedom Association

invites you to the launch of

Referendum First Campaign

35 Westminster Bridge Road, London SE1 7JB
Tel: 071 928 9995 Fax: 071 928 9524

Tony Favell, MP (RFC, Parliamentary Advisor)

Chris Gill, MP

Norris McWhirter, CBE (RFC, Chairman)

John Murray (RFC, co-founder)

Philip Vander Elst (Editor, Freedom Today)

The Referendum First Campaign aims to unite all who wish to have a referendum before any further moves towards European economic and political union are approved by Parliament.

Sign the Parliamentary Petition and get involved

Time: 1pm - 2.15pm.
Date: Wednesday 9 October.
Venue: The Grand Theatre,
25 Church Street.

Cash Bar and Refreshments

that wild horses won't get me to vote for more federalism and for good measure mention that I'm now a referendum man – 'an Irish solution' he says as he retreats into the sanctuary of the Speaker's Secretary's office. I don't relish the prospect of 'an Irish solution' any more than he does but the fact of the matter is that a referendum is now seen as the only way forward by those of us who are totally opposed to European Union. With all the political parties represented in Westminster being in favour of European integration and the people of the UK never having been consulted it is difficult to see any other way out of the present impasse.

At the State Opening of Parliament I tell my good friend Michael Shersby (Uxbridge) that my interpretation of the draft Treaty proposals put forward by the Dutch Government which currently holds the Presidency is at variance with what is being reported in the Press. From the time that I joined Parliament four years ago Michael has been unfailingly helpful and once again I am happy to take his advice to obtain a second opinion from the House of Commons Library.

The very next day the Library responds with an interpretation of the draft Treaty which is far from comforting.* When I show it to colleagues at a '92 Committee dinner a few days later Michael Portillo (Enfield Southgate) urges me to circulate it to all Conservative MPs including Government Ministers and the Prime Minister himself. Interestingly Michael says that he 'cannot identify the force which is compelling us in the direction of ever greater European integration.' To this day that remains, particularly as far as the Conservative Party is concerned, the $64,000 question.

Over the course of the next forty-eight hours I ensure that all my Conservative colleagues are sent a copy of the Library letter which is by now causing quite a stir. When Gerald Howarth (Cannock & Burntwood) who is serving as her PPS shows Margaret Thatcher a copy of the letter she hits the roof. Overall I am left in no doubt that I have touched a raw nerve and maybe struck a significant blow in the battle against Federalism and the Single Currency.

It will be another twelve months before the Bill to ratify the Maastricht Treaty reaches the Commons but for the past six months, even before the first draft was available, interest has been mounting. In years to come ill-informed commentators will try to ascribe the robust and principled opposition to the treaty as a personal attack, or a vendetta even, against the Prime Minister, John Major. Nothing could be further from the truth although one suspects that Major will go to the grave believing that it was. Perhaps if he had taken the trouble to understand the true nature of the objections he would have seen matters in a different light but the fact is that from beginning to end there was

---

*Appendix A.

little or no attempt at real dialogue. All the warning signs were there but Government wasn't listening. With an overall majority of 88 Government didn't have to listen but when, following the General Election in April 1992, the majority was cut to 21 it still didn't listen.

Out of a very comfortable majority, 9 abstentions and 6 votes against a Government motion outlining the negotiating objectives for the forthcoming IGC at Maastricht was small beer. Government Whips might have thought that the abstainers, Cash, Cran, Favell, Gill, Gorman, Jessel, Teddy Taylor, Tebbitt and Ann Winterton, would come back into line once they had made their protest. They might also have calculated that Messrs. Biffen, Body, Browne, Fairburn, Richard Shepherd and Nick Winterton would be a small enough group of long-term dissidents to be manageable. How wrong they were but with the man management skills for which the Conservative Whips' Office was once famed now but a distant memory it may have been too much to hope that the coming confrontation could have been avoided.

At 1000 on Tuesday 26th, Downing Street rings to know what my question to the PM that afternoon will be. I take the opportunity of requesting a meeting with the PM which is usually a sure fire way of sending PPS Graham Bright into spasm. At 1545, to my great surprise, the Chief Whip asks if I would like to see the PM and within the hour I find myself, together with other Euro realists Chris Butler, Den Dover, Ivan Lawrence and Michael Lord, face to face with John Major. His line is that some agreement at Maastricht is necessary if the UK is to avoid a run on the pound and sustained economic difficulties. The fact that our membership of the ERM will lead to horrendous economic difficulties before any of us are very much older does not seem to occur to him. When it is suggested that the Treaty might be put to a referendum his hackles rise and he emphasises that he is sticking to his stated position because he doesn't want a recurrence of the accusations made earlier in the year that he is 'dithering'. He appears to be totally insensitive to any suggestion that a sell-out or fudging of the issue will have an adverse effect upon electoral prospects. We come away from the meeting wiser but generally unconvinced.

That evening James Cran joins me at home for dinner for the inaugural meeting of the Maastricht group at which we agree a list of ten names to be approached to form an initial caucus. Later that same evening Michael Spicer observes that a lot is riding on the success of the Gill/Cran axis, more perhaps than even we at the time appreciated.

The following day the Chief Whip stops me in the Central Lobby to ask about last evening's meeting with the PM. With rather more frankness than tact I tell him that John Major is clearly not a conviction politician and, that being the case, his popularity will inevitably decline; that I believe that were he to exercise a Veto at Maastricht the British public would give him three rousing cheers and, in the absence of any other popular appeal, a chance of winning the next General Election; that he shouldn't underestimate the strength of backbench feeling on the European question (which he says he doesn't) and that just as I have been proved right regarding the Community Charge I will be proved right on this issue too. I point out that I have no axe to grind and stress my credentials as an independent voice – precious little good it does me, but at least the management can't say they weren't warned.

By now everybody is talking about Europe and Downing Street is in overdrive trying to soften up those most likely to prove recalcitrant. Aitken, Cran, Gorman and Gardiner are one group seen by the PM on 3 December. Other groups include Cash, Conway, Janman, Jessel, Marlow, McNair Wilson, Townend, Twinn and Ann Winterton. Michael Shersby is scheduled to meet the Foreign Secretary (Douglas Hurd) for the same treatment tomorrow.

On 5 December Ann Winterton, Teresa Gorman, Toby Jessel and Hugo Summerson attend the first meeting of the Maastricht group which elects James Cran and myself as its joint Secretaries. We all go away pledged to canvass the views of other colleagues some of whom, surprisingly in the case of Tim Janman and Michael Lord, appear rather 'wobbly'.

As luck would have it, on the very eve of the Maastricht IGC, I am drawn high up in the ballot of Members to ask a question at Question Time. I pose the question as to whether the Foreign Secretary would not agree that '*if he and the Prime Minister were tonight to reject Monetary and Political Union the British people would give three rousing cheers?*'

That same day (10 December) James tells me that he has been offered a job as a PPS but, to his lasting credit, he has told them that he couldn't possibly consider it until the Maastricht business is finished.

Patronage is a very powerful tool in the hands of the Government Whips whose task it is to see that the Government always gets its business. It isn't their only weapon and they're not averse to using a little blackmail or taking advantage of a Member down on his luck if it achieves the desired effect. Working on the principle that every man has his price they achieve some most remarkable conversions. Many are those broken on the wheel of politics who start out with high ideals but wind up with their principles broken and their ambition unfulfilled.

Amongst the many accusations that would be levelled against we so-called rebels was the one that we were aided and abetted by Margaret Thatcher and that we danced to her tune. Given that it was Margaret's Government that had forced the Single European Act through Parliament on a guillotined motion hers was not, at least as far as I was concerned, the best example to follow but it was nevertheless a rare privilege to be invited to dine with the great lady at her home in Belgravia together with nine other right inclined colleagues not all of whom, it has to be said, were so passionately opposed to federalism (a polite word for European integration) as myself. Margaret was positively fizzing with anger at the likely outcome of today's events in Maastricht and, looking rather pointedly in my direction, announced that if she could find a safe seat she would stand again in spite of her previously announced intention to leave the Commons at the end of this Parliament. What was more revealing was the contempt she reserved for those who had deceived her – 'the ones who let her down but whom she never suspected'. Harking back to Maastricht she was to exclaim, 'How do you think I feel when I hear all this? What an awful Christmas it's going to be for us all.' There was no shortage of conversation that evening but it would be fanciful to pretend that it added up to anything remotely like a plan of action; indeed from that point of view I wondered what purpose it had served.

One of Margaret's Cabinet Ministers who could never be accused of knowingly sharing her instincts was John Gummer who served as Agriculture Minister from 1989 to 1993. At a meeting with him on 11 December he blankly refused to even consider scrapping the CAP not least, I suspect, because he feared that leaving the CAP would go against the grain of European integration to which he is so committed. Because of my ongoing interest in Agriculture we would cross swords again and in due course we would be at daggers drawn about another of Britain's basic industries, fishing.

In the House the PM's statement on the agreement reached at Maastricht is generally well received on our benches but the fact remains that notwithstanding the opt-outs negotiated on the Single Currency and the Social Chapter it is a deeply integrationist and, to many of us, totally unacceptable treaty. Downing Street now moves to put its own gloss on it and I feel obliged to speak to Graham Bright at No. 10 and subsequently Norman Fowler (Sutton Coldfield) who has joined the chorus, to say to them that they should kill the 'Eurosceptics marginalised' story because two can play at that game and our line will have to be 'how we prevented the Government from selling out'. The contents of the celebrated 'Library letter' are still being recalled and John Taylor (Solihull) tells me that it has been the subject of a Whips' Office meeting.

John Biffen has agreed to become President of our Maastricht group and his experience and advice will be invaluable as his opposition to the European project goes back to the days of the Treaty of Accession in 1972. He has written a paper for us and is quite convinced that if we go into opposition, as seems likely, the Party will come over to our point of view.

Amongst all the excitement occasioned by the Maastricht Treaty the Government pushes through the new Council Tax legislation on a guillotined Third Reading but nothing can stop the mounting interest in a Government motion tabled for the last day of the Autumn sitting to 'congratulate the Prime

Minister on achieving all the negotiating objectives set out in the motion that was supported by the House on 21st November; and warmly endorses the agreement secured by the Government at Maastricht.'

Deputy Speaker Paul Dean (Woodspring), indicates that I have no chance of being called in the debate. In contrast to four years ago this subject is now top of the political agenda and all the great and the good are vying to speak. On such occasions the custom and practice is to give priority to Privy Councillors and those who might be considered to have a specialist interest by dint of the office they hold, as chairman of a relevant committee for example.

When it comes to the vote it is apparent that the number of disaffected Conservatives has grown since the original Division on 21 November. Those abstaining now total 15 (Butler, Cash, Cran, John Carlisle, Farr, Gill, Gorman, Gerald Howarth, Janman, Jessel, Ridley, Spicer, Thatcher and two Wintertons) and the number of those voting against (Biffen, Browne, Budgen, Favell, Richard Shepherd and Tebbitt) is swelled by the addition of Bill Walker (Tayside) who has resigned as Vice Chairman of the Party in Scotland in protest.

Michael Heseltine is exultant. He tells Gerald Howarth that he has worked for this outcome for four years and in a side swipe at myself invites the journalist he has been briefing to 'have a word with one of the minnows'. When I point out that I will be proved right he retorts, 'And so were the people who led us into war in 1914 and 1939,' thereby placing himself firmly in the camp of the appeasers.

As 1991 draws to a close emotions are running high. Margaret Thatcher is heard to say that if ever Heseltine becomes leader she will leave the Party. The new Leader, after barely twelve months in office, has opened up a schism in the Party which he will never heal and we all know that within the next six months we shall have to go to the country.

CHAPTER NINE

1992

Henceforth we will refer to ourselves as the Fresh Start Group

WITH A General Election looming colleagues are in no mood to rock any boats although a spontaneous rebellion over the Consolidated Fund (No.2) Bill in February finds 16 Conservatives in the 'No' Lobby.

By mid-February Michael Spicer is anxious that the Eurosceptics should meet again and wants me to act as their Chief Whip. A month later, Nick Budgen, in what his friends describe as an uncharacteristic act of generosity, offers to buy me a cup of coffee in the Members' Smoking Room. He flatters me by describing me as a good House of Commons man, someone who knows the people and someone who would, more to the point, be able to identify likely support for a stand against ERM in the event of a Conservative Government being returned with a much reduced majority. It later transpires that he has asked Michael Spicer if he may join our group and Michael has referred him to me. For reasons which escape me Budgie is a Kenneth Clarke (Rushcliffe) fan as, surprisingly, is Norman Tebbitt (Chingford). Nick Ridley on the other hand says that the Right of the Party must start to think about getting their own man in place because 'win or lose the Election, Major won't last the year'. His preferred choice is Michael Howard (Folkestone & Hythe). Another Cabinet Minister avers that Major is instinctively with the centre-Right but subsequent events will demonstrate that Peter Lilley's assessment is somewhat wide of the mark.

Anticipating that the General Election will be on 9 April Messrs Cash, Cran, Spicer and I meet on 10 March and agree that we should be prepared to meet again on 10 April. The following day our prediction is fulfilled and the Dissolution of my first Parliament ensues. As they leave for their constituencies the predominant mood amongst colleagues is one of resignation, the general feeling being that this is an election which we will be lucky to win.

That was my opinion too until one day, canvassing on the Clee Hill at dusk as the rain turned to snow, I knocked on the door of a council house. When the occupant saw my blue rosette she said, 'We're Labour,' but as I was about to turn on my heels she said that there was something else that I ought to know. She insisted on telling me that her family were Welsh, at which point I concluded that there really was no point in continuing this conversation until she then said, 'But we wouldn't vote for that Pillock.' This was the day after

Re-elected with a record majority, 10 April 1992.

Canvassing in Broad Street, Ludlow, with wife Patricia flanked by Cynthia and Rosemary Scott.

the aforesaid Kinnock had made his triumphalist speech at Sheffield and it was then that I knew that we were in with a chance. Sadly I couldn't find anyone to take my bet that we would be returned with an overall majority of 20 which, come the day, was actually 21. But for this chance encounter I would never have believed that we were going to win as it was by now clearly established in most people's minds that we were destined for opposition. Indeed many would argue that this was the election the Conservatives needed to lose in order to reconsider strategy, re-assess their tactics and not least so as to pass the poisoned chalice of European Union to Labour.

In the event the Conservative majority in the Ludlow constituency increased from 11,699 to 14,152 which, rightly or wrongly, I took to be a vindication of my having stood up for my constituents' interests in the matter of Agriculture, Cottage Hospitals, the ill-fated Poll Tax and a host of other complaints against an increasingly arrogant Government which, to cap it all, was keen to hand over our country's very sovereignty to the unelected and unaccountable in Brussels.

The General Election over, our very first task is to elect a new Speaker and I am happy to follow the lead of my Shropshire colleague John Biffen who has proposed Betty Boothroyd (Lab. Sandwell). Dining in Pimlico that evening I chance upon the Crawley Food Mountain and take the opportunity of congratulating him upon his appointment as Parliamentary Under Secretary at the Ministry of Agriculture, Fisheries and Food. He responds by saying that he is responsible for all the things that I'm interested in like Meat, Animals, Abattoirs etc. and hopes that I am 'not going to bring down the Government'. At this point other diners in the restaurant are seen to gag on their food and I bid the Honourable Nicholas Soames a hasty good night.

Swearing-in at the beginning of a new Parliament is a prerequisite of receiving the Parliamentary salary and, in the case of new members, swearing-in for the first time can be significant because seniority amongst those of the same intake is determined by the order in which they first signed the register. My own urgency to sign the register on this occasion was much more prosaic and I am grateful to the bulky form of Geoffrey Dickens (Littleborough & Saddleworth) who kindly interposes himself between the mass of humanity and the presiding Clerks thus creating a lee in which I am able to place my right hand on the Testament, take the Oath of Allegiance to Her Majesty and reach Heathrow in time for my flight to a spot of rest and recuperation in sunnier climes.

The State Opening of Parliament is on 6 May and the following day I am on my feet at the first meeting of the '22 Committee to express the opinion that it is a great shame that the Maastricht Treaty is being taken through the House as Government business rather than on a free vote and that the people of the United Kingdom haven't been sufficiently involved in the debate.* This goes down like the proverbial lead balloon but the Chairman, Cranley Onslow (Woking), undertakes to pass on my views to the Chief Whip.

Four days later all hell breaks loose, when the Press report that in her speech to the European Parliament tomorrow the Queen intends to say that sovereignty is insignificant compared with the many other important issues affecting the Parliament.

As luck would have it I am the first Conservative on the Order Paper for Prime Minister's questions (Thursday 12 May) and the Lobby correspondents are pressing to know what I am going to say. After congratulating the PM on leading the Conservative Party to an unprecedented fourth consecutive General Election victory I then proceed to ask him whether '*he would not agree that his strongly anti-federalist stance was instrumental in securing that general election victory? In view of today's press reports, will he reassure the House that British sovereignty is not insignificant?*'

That evening I have arranged to dine at the Carlton Club with fifteen colleagues of similar persuasion. To enter the Club premises in St. James

*Appendix B.

Street we all have to run the gauntlet of the press and media who have got wind of our meeting and are camped outside. At least one of our number, anxious to avoid unwelcome publicity, decides that discretion is the better part of valour and returns to the House without ever alighting from his cab.

Over our tomato and tarragon soup and *demi-poussin bonne femme* we discuss tactics and determine to do our level best to prevent the Bill implementing the Treaty on European Union from reaching the statute book.

The only person present who fails to contribute to the debate is the member for Spelthorne, David Wilshire, thus giving rise to speculation, fairly or otherwise, that he is a Whips' Office 'nark'.

During the course of the evening Nick Budgen nips out of the club to do a TV interview but subsequently discovers that my PMQ earlier in the day has stolen the limelight.

We conclude by all signing a letter which Richard Body (Holland with Boston) will send to newspapers in Denmark encouraging the Danish people to vote 'No' in their forthcoming referendum. Whether or not this action had the least effect upon the eventual outcome we shall never know but what is certain is that when, on 2 June, the Danes rejected the Treaty on European Union our own Prime Minister was presented with a heaven sent opportunity to kick the whole issue into touch. Before Parliament reassembles after the Summer recess Major will have been given yet another reason to dump the Treaty but, stubbornly, he will plough on regardless of the catastrophic damage he will inflict upon his Party in the process.

For the following evening Michael Spicer has arranged a drinks party at his home in advance of a '92 dinner at the St. Stephen's Club. As a 'networker' Michael's skills are unsurpassed. On this occasion he has invited several members of the new intake including Margaret Thatcher's successor at Finchley, one Hartley Booth, who will subsequently be obliged to resign from his position as a PPS after revelations of some indiscretion involving a secretary. Hartley impresses me with his rhetoric on the subject which is fast becoming the major topic of conversation but, as with so many of my colleagues, it is quite apparent that when push comes to shove he will be unwilling to prejudice his future promotion prospects by defying the Government Whips.

Members attending the '92 Dinner vote to support John Butterfill (Bournemouth West) in the election for chairmanship of the backbench European Affairs Committee but Peter Hordern (Horsham) declares that he too will be a candidate having announced that he 'absolutely agrees with the PM's line on Europe'. As far as James Cran and I are concerned it is, given the disgraceful way in which the Government mounted its operation to cut out Eurosceptics last November, a matter of supreme indifference. Figuratively speaking the dogs have barked and the caravan has moved on.

The following day elder statesman John Biffen gives a splendid talk to colleagues assembled in Committee Room 13 as a result of which I am optimistic that a few of the new members may be encouraged to vote the right way when the European Communities (Amendment) Bill comes up for its Second Reading next week.

Addressing the Annual Dinner of the Ludlow Constituency Conservative Association (LCCA) that Friday evening Lord Deedes, in a rather cryptic speech, throws out some veiled hints about not rocking the boat and about the Member of Parliament being allowed always to have time to play golf. Is this, I ask myself, an alternative to 'spending more time with his family' rather than making a nuisance of himself in Westminster!

A week after having Question 5 at Prime Minister's Question time (PMQs) I am lucky enough to be drawn to have Q3. Whilst my question does not attract the same level of press interest as a week ago it elicits the response that '*all the matters to which my Hon. Friend has referred are extremely important and I give him the assurance that we shall fight to preserve British interests up to, during and after the ratification of the Maastricht Treaty.*' Whilst at the time this appears to be an entirely satisfactory reply, in due course it will come to be seen that there is a world of difference between what the so called Eurosceptics define as being in British interests and the Prime Minister's own interpretation of that same term. Irrespective of the fact that John Major's game of cat and mouse with the dissidents within his own ranks will ultimately destroy Conservative Party morale and any prospect of future electoral success, it is a game that he plays with consummate skill and with far more guile than his reputation for honesty would imply.

Attending the House on Wednesday 20 May for the commencement at 3.40 p.m. of the Second Reading of the Maastricht Treaty it is 3.09 a.m. Thursday before I am called to speak, prefacing my contribution to the debate by saying that '*I have not a scintilla of doubt about my voting intentions tomorrow night. I shall be right to vote against the Bill and will do so for many reasons.*'

True to my word, in company with 21 Conservative colleagues, 59 Labour members and 11 Ulster Unionists, I vote against the Second Reading and seldom have I felt more confident that my vote was recorded in the right place. Interestingly, Bill Walker, who has resigned as a Party Vice-Chairman in Scotland on account of this issue, the soon to be knighted Roger Moate (Faversham) who has been a constant opponent of European integration for as long as he's been in the house (22 years) and Roger Knapman who has been with us every inch of the way so far, will abstain. Not that it makes much difference because the voting is 336 in favour of the Bill and 92 against. What is also interesting about this particular division is that it fairly accurately indicates the level of support that we shall get from our Conservative colleagues throughout the protracted passage of this highly controversial and groundbreaking Bill. Consistently the 'rebel' vote will be somewhere in the region of 25 – not always the same 25 but rarely either more or less.

Lest the reader should think that a revolt of 25 within its own ranks will be sufficient to defeat a Government with a majority of only 21 it needs to be pointed out that, in spite of the games they will play, the Opposition's motive at every stage of the Bill's progress is simply to defeat the Government and precipitate another General Election. On the other hand they are not in the business of defeating the Bill that furthers European integration of which they are strongly in favour. Paradoxically the rebel position is precisely the opposite. We wish to kill the Bill but we most certainly don't wish to bring down the Conservative Government.

Accusations will be made that we are acting as we are to spite Mr Major and to undermine his administration. We shall be further accused of co-operating with the Labour opposition but even if this were true it would be totally unprofitable because it is obvious from the outset that the Labour Whips will either impose a 3-line Whip or 'slip' some of their members not in any way to assist the Conservative rebels but simply to cause the maximum embarrassment and difficulty for the Government. At no time are we under any illusion that the Opposition are going to assist us in achieving our objective. We are in the business of defeating the Treaty, they are in the business of defeating the Government. The dilemma from our point of view is that if the Labour Party achieves their objective then we will inevitably lose ours. Our only hope is that by argument and attrition we will finally persuade our own side to recognise the folly of their ways and abandon the whole collectivist project. Given the number of 'fellow-travellers' on the Conservative benches this is possibly a forlorn hope but for many of us there are no circumstances in which we are going to vote 1000 years of our nation's history into oblivion.

After this historic vote John Butcher (Coventry SW) suggests a drink on the Terrace. John is a slightly enigmatic character and whilst on this occasion I am left wondering what it was that he really wanted to talk about, subsequent events will prove him to be a doughty champion of our cause and a source of much sound advice in difficult times. Regrettably, this inconclusive conversation scuppers my plans for a fast getaway at the beginning of the Whitsuntide recess. Time and again Governments bring their most controversial motions to the House on the eve of a recess hoping thereby to defuse potentially explosive situations by facilitating the escape of members to their constituencies or foreign parts immediately the difficult division is over.

This does not always work out quite how the Whips intend and whilst resting and recuperating in sunny Salcombe I entertain and am entertained by the local Member, Anthony Steen, who surprises me by saying that he will

help with the amendments which are crucial if we are to defeat the Maastricht
Treaty Bill. Unlike other international treaties, all of which are negotiated and
agreed by Ministers acting under the Royal Prerogative, the European treaties,
because they inevitably necessitate consequential changes to domestic
legislation, must be brought to Parliament for ratification. If we can in any
way amend the Maastricht Treaty in the Westminster Parliament it ceases to be
the treaty that the Prime Minister and the Foreign Secretary have agreed with
their counterparts in each of the other European Community member states.
In that eventuality the Treaty cannot be ratified. Given that the Bill
implementing the Treaty has obtained its Second Reading with a massive
majority in favour, the only remaining possibility of preventing it reaching the
Statute Book is to wreck it by amendment. At this point my constituent, the
honourable Member for Stafford, Bill Cash, comes into his own and will in
due course produce scores of amendments which will ensure that the Bill's
passage through Parliament is long and protracted. The Government have the
option of accelerating the Bill's progress through the Commons by means of a
timetable (guillotine) motion but given the febrile atmosphere and their
slender majority this is something that they dare hardly even think about, the
prospect being that this would convert a principled objection to a specific
piece of legislation into a full scale mutiny.

Back in the House after a welcome break it is business as usual. At a
meeting of our Euro group Budgie (Nick Budgen) needles Michael Spicer by
saying that whilst upsetting the Government we cannot expect to be thought
respectable and neither should we be at all apologetic for what we're about.
When I ask Biffo (John Biffen) if he will take part in the Committee stage of
the Maastricht Bill scheduled to start tomorrow he says that he will attend and
contribute 'as the spirit moves' but, he says, we can rely on Budgie to
'contribute at length and with erudition'. This being a Bill of major
constitutional importance the Committee stage will be conducted by a
committee of the whole House, rather than in a Standing Committee upstairs,
which means that all Members will be able to speak to any of the selected
amendments. As the Whips for the rebels it will be down to James Cran and I
to ensure that on the one hand we have an adequate number of speakers to
cover all the debates and on the other hand that our people are sensible in
terms of not antagonising our colleagues with silly filibusters. We will also
have the job of ensuring that they are all on hand when divisions are called
and that they cast their votes in the correct lobby. With a little bit of luck and a
lot of planning and attention to detail we will be able to wrest control of the
Parliamentary timetable and cause the Government maximum inconvenience
as they attempt to give away our country's freedom and independence. The
prospect of abandoning our historic liberties and democratic institutions is
deeply depressing and being paired for the evening, I decide to try and lift the

gloom by taking my wife out to dinner where, at Simply Nico, we find ourselves once again dining in the company of the Crawley Food Mountain. Home in time for the 'News at Ten', we are delighted to hear that the Danes have rejected Maastricht so that a day (2 June) which had started in depression ends in elation. Michael Spicer calls me half an hour before midnight and I suggest that in the light of the latest development we should insist upon seeing the Chief Whip but, rather surprisingly, he says that he thinks we should just let matters take their course.

The following morning Michael and I speak again and I am puzzled by the fact that not only is he reluctant to seek a meeting with the Chief Whip but neither is he wanting to meet the new Chairman of the '22 Committee, Marcus Fox (Shipley). Whether this reluctance to take the issue head-on stems from timidity or a deeper understanding of the tactical situation I cannot tell. Nevertheless, together with other colleagues, we meet in his office at 1430 and set about drafting an Early Day Motion in the light of the fact that the Government have decided to pull today's business.

Whilst drafting EDM 174* we learn that far from abandoning the Treaty the Government have simply decided to postpone its further consideration and the wording of our EDM has to be amended accordingly.

By 2030 we have obtained 72 signatures which significantly include 26 of the new intake. Derek Conway, my constituency neighbour at Shrewsbury & Atcham, signs but later withdraws which is disappointing, not least because in the '83/'87 Parliament Derek had been one of only 11 brave souls to defy a 3-line Whip to vote against the Single European Act – the irony being the fact that on that occasion the business was being steered through the House by another Shropshire MP, then Leader of the House, John Biffen, who had the job of introducing the guillotine motion which speeded its passage.

In terms of the Executive getting its own way the existence of the 'guillotine' is extremely useful but when on 4 June Teddy Taylor (Southend E) tells the '22 Committee that Gerald Kaufman (Lab. Manchester, Gorton) has committed the Labour Party to voting against any 'guillotining' of the Maastricht Bill it becomes even clearer that the Government are not going to be able to take any short cuts. This is confirmed by my 'pair' Jeff Rooker (Lab. Birmingham Perry Barr), who tells me that Labour believe they can prevent the Government introducing a 'time table motion' and thereby delay them from getting their business.

My purple patch continues and I am drawn at Q4 for PMQs. I take the opportunity, as usual, of keeping up the pressure on the perennial subject –

---

*EDM 174 states: 'That this House urges Her Majesty's Government to use the decision to postpone the passage of the European Communities (Amendment) Bill as an opportunity to make a fresh start with the future development of the EEC and in particular to concentrate its efforts on the chosen agenda of the British presidency which is to extend the borders of the EEC and to create a fully competitive common market.'

Europe. The question goes well and once again I get a mention on the TV News at 9 o'clock which in itself is not altogether surprising given the propensity of the BBC not to miss any opportunity to use material which they think might embarrass the Conservative Government.

I had prefaced my question to the PM by drawing his attention to EDM 174 which possibly accounts for the fact that later in the day the Vote Office are obliged to run off additional copies. In the meantime, however, the Whips have been busy trying to persuade colleagues to withdraw their names and there is more than a strong suspicion that they have intercepted the additional names which James Cran collected yesterday. One of the new Members believes that he saw the envelope addressed to me and containing the extra signatories being removed by one of the Whips from the letterboard where James had put it ready for my collection.

Our bandwagon is starting to roll and we are encouraged by indications, however delphic, that big names like Ken Baker (Mole Valley) and David Howell (Guildford) may be coming over to our side. Peter Fry (Wellingborough) says that he can't support the Government again over Maastricht and Vivian Bendall (Ilford N) says that he has told the Chief Whip where to get off, but not just on the issue of Maastricht!

On 9 June my name is on the Order Paper to ask another question but sadly there is a letter from 10 Downing Street advising me that the PM will be visiting South America this week and therefore unable to attend PMQs which will be answered in his stead by the Leader of the House, Tony Newton (Braintree). In the PM's absence his other alter ego, PPS Graham Bright, is busy in the Lobbies but goes very much on the defensive when I try to tell him which side his boss's bread is buttered. He says they 'know who is opposed as a matter of principle or belief and who is opposed for other reasons.'

Meanwhile that old warhorse Teddy Taylor, who's been fighting the European battle ever since resigning as Under Secretary of State for Scotland in protest way back in 1974, is saying that we should forget Maastricht for the time being and concentrate all our attention on the ERM. In the sense that the ERM is potentially more dangerous to the Government than the Treaty he is probably right but the question is whether we can afford to open up a second front and if we do will it not make it look as though we're just serial troublemakers?

Hardly a day passes now without a meeting of our group which exceptionally is still without a name. On 10 June we actually decide against having a formal name but in favour of a dinner later in the month. The following day Michael Spicer telephones me to stop me going ahead with the arrangements for the dinner and once again I find myself wondering why he is so reluctant to act more decisively. The following day when Michael Lord (Suffolk

Central) stands up in a debate about Agriculture to say that the Common Agricultural Policy (CAP) should be scrapped, Agriculture Minister John Gummer (Suffolk Coastal) pointedly walks out of the Chamber. There are no surprises there because Gummer is well known for his collectivist views and the only question is how these are thought to be compatible with being a Conservative. The surprise is when Michael Lord subsequently sows a seed of doubt in my mind about the motives of our colleague Michael Spicer. This is a conversation that I shall recall more than once as the year progresses especially when James Cran suggests that maybe someone is pulling Michael's strings. There is certainly no lack of evidence that the 'management' are worried, as evidenced by the fact that the usually forthright and independent Member for Welwyn Hatfield, David Evans, has been persuaded to withdraw his name from our EDM.

The BBC are also following our activities with interest and on 15 June they tell the world that the Eurosceptics are meeting to launch an attack on the ERM. On the 9 O'clock News that evening they report that new Members went to No. 10 for lunch and were told by the PM that they were making difficulties for him and given a dressing down. This is not substantiated by the new Members I speak to such as John Horam (Orpington), John Whittingdale (Colchester S & Maldon) and others who say that the PM did not address them collectively at all and that the subject of Maastricht as a specific issue was not even raised. One is left wondering whether the Press Office are putting the poison down to provoke Conservative Constituency Associations into bringing pressure to bear upon wayward Members or whether it is simply the BBC trying to hype things up to discomfit the Government.

As far as launching a concerted attack on the ERM is concerned it transpires that Teddy Taylor is behind this idea and I feel bound to tell him that trying to open up a second front could prove counter-productive to the central aim of defeating the Maastricht Treaty. On the other hand I am also thinking that the time has come when we must start to reach out beyond Parliament itself and I talk to Tony Favell (Stockport) about organising a fringe meeting at the forthcoming Party Conference in Brighton where, in due course, we shall have some fun and games. In the meantime it transpires that Michael Spicer is opposed to taking a high profile at conference and once again James Cran and I are left wondering about the sincerity of his commitment.

According to the *Daily Telegraph* (16 June) at yesterday's lunch for new Members the PM described Eurosceptics as naïve, a description which is somewhat resented by Michael Shersby (Uxbridge) and other senior and respected backbenchers who are generally distinguished by their loyalty to the Party – loyalty which is now being put severely to the test by Ministers such as our Minister for Europe. Notwithstanding the result of the Danish referendum Tristan Garel-Jones (Watford) tells me that the Treaty will be brought back to the House and he being so cocksure about it I am constrained to ask him if he has done his arithmetic.

As a result of this brief exchange it is clear that the Government are not in any way deterred by mounting evidence of resistance to the Treaty nor apparently are they likely to be swayed by force of argument. In the circumstances it is clear that we shall have to adopt guerrilla tactics to thwart them although John Biffen suggests that it might be thought altogether more *communautaire* to adopt the tactics of the Maquis!

From our point of view the object of the exercise remains that of defeating the Maastricht Treaty although my friend John Farbon from Herefordshire, who will play such a crucial role in the moment of high political drama which unfolds in 1995, is already starting to chivvy us into referring to the Treaty as the Treaty on European Union rather than Maastricht – which, as he quite rightly points out, doesn't convey its awesome significance.

By the rising of the House on 18 June our group of anti Maastricht dissidents at last has a name. Henceforth, at the suggestion of Roger Knapman, we will refer to ourselves as the Fresh Start Group, believing as we do that the best thing that Government could now do is to draw a line under the past and start afresh to negotiate a Treaty which instead of imposing European Union (Economic, Monetary & Political) reflects more accurately the principles which the vast majority of the electorate thought that they were voting for in the Referendum in 1975.

Back in the constituency there is tremendous interest in what I am up to on the European front and, at this stage at least, Conservative Association members appear to be entirely supportive. As the going gets tough later in the year this happy state of affairs will be put to the test as Party members become divided between those who support the principle that their Member of Parliament is fighting for and those who feel that, regardless of the issue, the thing that matters most is loyalty to the Party and its Leader. As the situation develops it will become apparent that those who support the 'rebel' cause are, generally speaking, the activists who are actually in contact with the voters and in the other camp the 'armchair Conservatives' who feed on their own recycled prejudices.

As June draws to a close I am becoming increasingly depressed by endless meetings and discussions and resolve to allocate less time to talk and more to action. In this spirit I get stuck into Douglas Hurd (Foreign Secretary) when on 24 June he attends the backbench European Affairs Committee (EAC). I remind him of the succession of Parliamentary Questions (PQs) that I have asked these past two years about 'subsidiarity' and suggest that it is a terrible indictment of Government when he himself is, after all this time, saying that the word is 'clumsy and ambiguous'. Isn't it even less satisfactory that only a month ago he was prepared to ask the House to ratify the Maastricht Treaty whilst the definition of subsidiarity remains unclear? He has created the impression that he sees nothing intrinsically wrong with richer countries transferring massive funds to the poorer countries of the EEC which many of us regard as pure socialism. I go on to express my personal opinion that Maastricht is a socialist treaty and ask him 'if he is aware of the potential for this treaty to split the Party if Government insist on bringing it back to the House?' Furthermore 'would he recognise that responsibility for splitting the Party will be his and the Government's – not mine as a backbencher without the power, the influence nor the wish to split the Party?'

Committee Chairman Peter Hordern (Horsham) must by now be regretting calling upon me to ask the first question but it sets the tone for the meeting at which the Foreign Secretary is given a right royal roasting. Afterwards Michael Neubert (Romford) says that he has never witnessed such a seminal backbench committee meeting in the whole of his eighteen years in Parliament. Michael Lord and John Wilkinson (Ruislip-Northwood) provide the star turns but Douglas Hurd is unable to answer any of us satisfactorily. James Cran in the meantime has had a stormy meeting with Deputy Chief Whip David Heathcoat-Amory, which is brought to a conclusion by James walking out 'rather than be treated like a sixteen-year-old'. He subsequently tells his own area Whip that his priority is to defeat the Maastricht Treaty and if, in order to organise to do that, it proves necessary to miss votes on 3-line Whips then that is what he will do. Almost simultaneously another Government Whip, James Arbuthnot (Wanstead and Woodford) has had an encounter with Michael Carttiss (Great Yarmouth).

Carttiss:	'If I was a Whip I shouldn't have any problem getting colleagues to vote.'
Arbuthnot:	'How would you do that?'
Carttiss:	'Ah, that's what you've got to learn!'

John Major's answer to Teresa Gorman (Billericay) on 25 June illustrates his reluctance to give any quarter to those of us who are opposed to his wretched treaty:

Gorman:	'May I recommend the attitude of one of his predecessors, my right hon. Friend the Member for Old Bexley and Sidcup (Sir Edward Heath), who allowed a free vote of the House in similar circumstances?'
Prime Minister:	'The House has now debated and voted on the Maastricht agreement on three occasions. As I indicated a moment ago...we contested the General Election on that proposition...The Maastricht Treaty was negotiated in good faith by all member states. I have no

intention of breaking the word of the British Government that was given on that occasion; nor do I have any intention of compromising.'

He returns to the House the following Monday to report on the outcome of the weekend meeting of heads of Government in Lisbon and loses no time in demonstrating his determination to press on regardless. The next evening colleagues are incited to virtual mutiny when Norman Lamont (Kingston-upon-Thames) addresses a dinner of the '92 Group. He speaks about his support for the Exchange Rate Mechanism (ERM) – as Chancellor he cannot do otherwise but even those of us who are convinced that it will all end in tears cannot at this stage know that in precisely eleven weeks time Norman will meet his nemesis and that both his own reputation and that of the Conservative Party for financial prudence and probity will be utterly destroyed in the process.

My question to Foreign Office Ministers on 1 July* gets a dusty answer but there is support from an unexpected quarter, Patrick Cormack (Staffordshire South). *'Will my right hon. Friend think again about the answer that he gave to my hon. Friend the Member for Ludlow (Mr Gill)? Does he accept that many of us who are not Euro-sceptics believe that there is a great deal to be said for thoroughly informing the people of this country about the benefits of Maastricht?'*

The most encouraging aspect of this day's Question Time is the physical appearance of Minister of State Tristan Garel-Jones. He looks like a broken man – all his natural bounce, self-confidence and general cockiness appear to have deserted him but it is too much to hope that he will give up the unequal struggle and quit.

Hardly a day now passes without reference to the Maastricht Treaty. On Sunday 5 July my constituent Bill Cash comes over for a brief (two hour) chat at home at the beginning of yet another week of planning, cajoling, canvassing and generally doing what we can to win and influence friends. On the Terrace of the House of Commons the midnight oil is burnt discussing tactics for the Party Conference with Messrs. Cash, Cran, Butcher, Marlow and Spicer but the best idea comes from Danish referendum 'No' campaigner Knud Pedersen who says that getting an actual copy of the Treaty to the people seems to have been a decisive factor in their successful campaign.

Working on this positive suggestion I get busy trying to find benefactors to put up the money to enable me to purchase bulk copies of the Treaty from HMSO with a view to making them available at a knock-down price to delegates at the Party Conference in October.

---

*'My right hon. Friend will be aware of the precedent in the last Parliament whereby certain aspects of Government policy were brought to the attention of every household. If the Treaty on European Union is in the best interests of the British people, why is my right hon. Friend so keen to stifle wider public debate by refusing the public a referendum and denying them the essential information on which to reach their own conclusions?'

In the event the only thing wrong with this idea is that the Party, notwithstanding that it is the party of Government and that it is Government policy to ram the Maastricht Treaty through Parliament by fair means or foul, would prefer that its members were kept in ignorance of the Treaty's contents. Such is the Government's paranoia that no less a figure than Party Vice-Chairman Tim Smith (Beaconsfield), is despatched to the foyer of the Brighton Conference Centre where I am busily selling copies of the Treaty on European Union (cover price £13.30) for £1 to order me to stop doing so.

'On what grounds do you order me to stop making the truth available to our members?' I ask.

'On the basis that the money you have obtained from your sponsors is money that would otherwise have come to the Party,' he replies.

The fact that my backers are putting up the money because they share my repugnance at what the Government is doing and the way in which it is being done seems to elude him but then, as subsequent events were to prove, Tim Smith's ideas of the proper use of money and mine were somewhat different.

It beggars belief that the Party should go to such lengths, or indeed any lengths, to prevent its members from reading the truth about these matters. What I am providing is not propaganda. On the contrary, it is the official document printed and published by HMSO upon the express instruction of Government. It is no more or less than what the public are entitled to see but if ever it was in doubt it is now glaringly obvious that the gloves are off and that this is going to be a fight to the finish.

In this operation the real star is John Butcher. Recognising Michael Spicer's reluctance to publicly associate himself with our exercise he literally rolls up his sleeves and takes charge of the operation, giving our small band of helpers their instructions and not being shy about telling the press and media what we are up to.

In one respect the operation is somewhat over the top because all that people really need to see is the preamble to the Treaty which tells them all they need to know.*

On the other hand the likelihood is that unless they receive the whole document and can thereby satisfy themselves that it is the genuine article they will simply discard it amongst the mass of other leaflets and pamphlets which proliferate at political conferences.

Up until this time the grassroots have been kept in the dark and whilst the relatively small amount of opposition to the Treaty stimulated by our Conference activities will be insufficient to cause Government to shelve their plans the cat is nonetheless well and truly out of the bag.

---

*Appendix C.

Before we reach Conference, however, all hell breaks loose when on 16 September Britain's membership of the ERM proves unsustainable. Throughout the day the Chancellor, Norman Lamont, with a series of interest rate hikes, tries to sidestep the inevitable but by mid-afternoon, Minimum Lending Rate having reached 15 per cent, the game is up. With the benefit of hindsight it is all too plain to see that this was the moment when three things should have happened. Lamont should have fallen on his sword, Major should have recognised another opportunity to dump the Treaty and the Government should have apologised for getting it all so horribly wrong – by this time unemployment figures have practically doubled from 1.67 million in October 1990 to 2.85 million, countless thousands have seen their homes repossessed and a huge number of businesses have been forced to close. None of these things happened – as far as the Major administration was concerned it was business as usual.

What occurred then was that the economy, unlike the reputation of the Conservative Party, slowly began to recover. A pattern would emerge remarkably similar to the one which followed Britain's exit from the Gold Standard in 1931. Within three months of abandoning the ERM interest rates would halve from 12 per cent to 6 per cent just as within nine months of leaving the Gold Standard interest rates were slashed from 6 per cent to 2 per cent. With lower, more realistic interest rates economic activity was rekindled and unemployment which, incidentally, had more than doubled between 1925 and 1931 from 1.25 million to 2.9 million, started to come down. The fact that fixed exchange rates prejudice economic activity was now plain for all to see but, nothing daunted, Major was clearly not going to allow a little local difficulty to soften his determination to make the UK a fully paid-up subscriber to the European Union. His third opportunity to abandon the project will come after the vote in the House of Commons on 4 November but before that happens Parliament is recalled on 24 September to debate the ERM debacle.

On the eve of Parliament the Fresh Start Group dine together in the Rodin Restaurant at 4 Millbank where we had last met just before the beginning of the Summer recess. The evening is disastrous. The upshot of it is that James Cran, infuriated by the irresponsibility of some of our colleagues' pronouncements, says that he's through with them. Michael Spicer says that he'll quit too so I have my work cut out trying to keep the show on the road. Privately I explain that whilst they may not like the attitude of some of our colleagues the reality is that they are all we've got and that in any case, regardless of their own intentions, I am determined to stick with it.

The Rodin dinner having proved such a disaster I am relieved when my second initiative, the convening of a business meeting, goes very much better. After last night's temporary aberration James Cran is back on side and before

Lunching with Nick Winterton and His Excellency the Ambassador at the Danish Embassy.

the 10 o'clock vote we collect 70 signatures for EDM 549,* which is the product of the meeting held in Committee Room 12 earlier in the day.

After a Summer recess punctuated by the drama of events surrounding 16 September, Black Wednesday as it became to be known, and a highly charged Party Conference at which I had the pleasure of telling Danish Television how they had so nearly saved our bacon by voting 'No' to Maastricht, it is time to return to Westminster.

In the Members' Lobby at the House of Commons there are two L-shaped upholstered benches, one in each of the corners immediately adjacent to the entrances to the Whips' Offices. From now on James and I will spend as much time as we possibly can occupying the bench outside the Government Whips' Office. By this ploy we will put ourselves in the best position to see and be seen by all of our colleagues, intimidate the Whips by appearing to be just as well organised as they and give encouragement to the waverers by demonstrating that we are not mere will-o'-the-wisp characters who are here today and gone tomorrow.

With or without our efforts a strong groundswell of spontaneous opposition to Maastricht is sparked off when on 22 October Nick Budgen tables a notice of Motion.

This comes hard on the heels of another unpopular measure, this time initiated by Michael Heseltine, Secretary of State for Trade & Industry, who wants to shut thirty-one coal mines. The strength of public opinion against this proposition is almost unprecedented. From the Ludlow constituency,

---

*EDM 549 states: That this House welcomes the Government's decision to leave the ERM; and urges a fresh start to economic policy, in particular the abandonment of fixed exchange rates and a commitment to sound finance, stable money and the right climate for steady growth.'

where the last colliery has long since closed, I receive 302 protest letters and a petition from one village alone containing 313 names. Hezza, according to a letter I receive from his PPS Richard Ottaway (Croydon South), would like to speak to me, not about pit closures but about a motion which the Government intend bringing to the House on 4 November. This is the first intimation of the Maastricht Paving debate and prompts me to write to all those colleagues who have indicated their opposition to the Maastricht Treaty Bill inviting them to attend a meeting on the eve of the debate.

Come the day and 34 colleagues, plus Willie Ross (Londonderry East) acting as observer for the Ulster Unionists, meet in Committee Room 19 where all points of view are expressed and discussed, the overwhelming body of opinion being that we should go through the 'No' Lobby in both of tomorrow's likely divisions. Robert Jones (Hertfordshire West) is practically alone in not speaking at the meeting but subsequently assures James and I that he will definitely be voting with us. In the event we are not entirely surprised when he votes the other way.

With 34 pledges at the meeting which include some who intend to abstain, plus others not able to attend, we have enough to win.

Sharing a table in the Cafeteria with Ann Winterton (Congleton) later that evening she makes no secret of the fact that she is excited at the prospect of being in on what could be the beginning of a sea change in Westminster politics – the day when the backbenches actually assert control over the Executive.

The Executive, for their part, know that they are up against it but even after their coup earlier this evening they must know that as things stand the risk of their losing the vote is still very real.

The coup that the Whips have pulled off centres around George Gardiner (Reigate) who has managed to elude me all day. I finally run him to ground in the Members' Lobby at 1645 but rather than answer my questions about the voting intentions of he and his four henchmen he says that he will meet to discuss the matter with James and I at 1800. What we then learn is that in the meantime he and Rhodes Boyson (Brent North), Bob Dunn (Dartford), James Pawsey (Rugby & Kenilworth) and John Townend (Bridlington) have been to see the PM. Not only have they already sold the pass but then, contrary to the assurances they give James and I, they go to the Press to publicly announce their intention to support the Government in tomorrow's votes. The irony of this incident will become apparent at a later stage when both George and John become staunch Maastricht refuseniks.

After days of feverish activity trying to ensure that we maximise our potential support, the day of the Paving debate arrives. James and I, who have spent much of the previous weekend together contacting supporters and potential supporters, meet early on Wednesday 4 November to verify numbers and by the time we leave home to go to the House we have a potential majority of 10 in our pocket. En route to the House I stop off at St. Matthews Hall in Great Peter Street to address the British Housewives League on the subject of 'A Future for Parliament'. The irony of speaking on this subject on the eve of the day made famous by Guy Fawkes, who is reputed to have imported his gunpowder from the town of Maastricht, is uncanny. Equally ironic is the fact that when I go to be interviewed by the BBC they tell me that it is proving impossible to get Ministers to go on air to put the Government case.

At the House the Government machine moves into overdrive as they realise that they are going to lose. In the event they win by a margin of three but only after Vivian Bendall (Ilford North), Michael Carttiss (Great Yarmouth) and Peter Fry (Wellingborough) change their colours, Warren Hawksley (Halesowen & Stourbridge) and Walter Sweeney (Vale of Glamorgan) having been persuaded to abstain. Gerry Vaughan (Reading East), under pressure from Michael Heseltine not to rebel, also abstains and I am witness to Harry Greenway (Ealing North) being physically manhandled into the Government lobby. In the meantime Nick Budgen's Constituency Association Chairman, Roseanne Williams, has apparently been asked if, in order to persuade Nick to toe the line, it would help to threaten him with having the Party Whip withdrawn. Similarly it is alleged that a Central Office agent has been despatched to the Vale of Glamorgan to see what leverage can be exerted there where, with a majority of only 19, Walter Sweeney is seen to be extremely vulnerable. In the case of Michael Clark (Rochford) the threat to cancel his place on a foreign visit is somewhat less draconian and in my own case the promise by Nicholas Soames, Parliamentary Secretary at MAFF, to 'close every abattoir you own' unless I vote the ticket is, given the state of the abattoir industry, hardly the threat he imagines.

In point of fact the crucial vote is on a Labour amendment which would have the effect of postponing the Committee stage of the European Communities (Amendment) Bill until after the forthcoming Edinburgh summit, a matter of a mere five weeks, but essentially it is, as far as the Government is concerned, a vote of confidence in their European policy. A defeat at this juncture would stymie ratification of the Maastricht Treaty which is already stalled by the negative outcome of the referendum in Denmark.

The Whips have done their stuff. The Government has got its business and in normal circumstances that would be that. But these are not normal circumstances and, as James Cran observes, from now onwards it will be 'trench warfare'.

The following day there is criticism of our action at the regular weekly meeting of the '22 Committee with well known Europhile Peter Emery (Honiton) chewing on about 'disgraceful behaviour', 'a party within a party', 'even appointing their own Whips' etc. Former RAF fighter pilot John Wilkinson (Ruislip-Northwood) gallantly retaliates by instancing the 'deplorable tactics of the Government Whips' but such is the mood of the meeting that he might just as well have saved his breath.

For my own part a note from 33 South Eaton Place saying: 'That was splendid work yesterday. You will not live to regret it. Yours ever, Enoch,' provides some solace as does a note from constituency neighbour Derek Conway (Shrewsbury & Atcham) exhorting me to 'recover in the knowledge that those of us too cowardly to be with you this week deeply respect your courage.'

The immensity of what we so called 'rebels' have achieved this week only begins to sink in when on Friday I am sitting on the train home to Shropshire reading the daily newspapers. Whilst we haven't won the crucial vote we have certainly had the effect of kicking the Treaty into the long grass and the more I think about it the more the significance of our operation dawns upon me. In bringing their Motion to the House the Government clearly intended to rub out the 'sceptics'. What they failed to appreciate is the effectiveness of our organisation and the strength of our support. By coincidence James Cran is the guest speaker at the Bridgnorth Supper Club this evening and reports that there is a good level of support for us there too, as indeed there is at Cleobury Mortimer when I attend Sunday's Remembrance Day service.

Anticipating that it won't be long before the battle moves on to the home front I decide that now is the time to take steps to ensure that as far as possible I have officers in the Ludlow Constituency Conservative Association (LCCA) who will support me. My immediate aim is to line up a sympathetic Vice-Chairman to follow Michael Wood when his three year term in that office expires in March 1994. A telephone call to Pam Twitchell results in an invitation to dine at Whitton Court where Michael and I tell Pam how important it is that she lets her name go forward for Vice-Chairman at the next AGM. She promises to consider the proposition and in due course a successful lobbying exercise results in her being elected by a very substantial majority to the obvious chagrin of Alan Screen, the other contestant.

In a few days time the Chancellor, Norman Lamont, will make his Autumn Statement. At a backbench committee we are warned by Paymaster General John Cope (Northavon), that it is going to be tough. In the event the reverse is true. Instead of cuts there will be an increase in borrowings forecast at £37 billions in 1992/3 and £44 billions in 1993/4. It is little surprise that at this rate the National Debt will double by the time the Conservative administration hands over its 'golden legacy' to Labour on 1 May 1997.

On the same day as the Autumn Statement (12 November) the PM addresses a '92 Committee dinner and assures the assembled company that there will be no recriminations against the Maastricht rebels. We shall see!

Perhaps at this stage he doesn't envisage any further opposition to the project but if that is his view he couldn't be more mistaken. The Fresh Start Group is up and running and we are actively planning how to oppose the Committee stage of the Treaty at every turn. Bill Cash has put together a team of researchers and when the time comes will table scores of amendments in the knowledge that even the slightest alteration to the approved text will render the ratification process null and void. If we succeed in amending the Treaty during the course of its Parliamentary passage then it ceases to be the Treaty that the Heads of State have agreed. In that circumstance it is simply a question of 'back to the drawing board' and start again.

By this time we are starting to make our presence felt again in anticipation of the Committee Stage of the Bill due to commence on 1 December. Government Whip Tim Kirkhope (Leeds North East) jokingly says that the benches outside the Whips' Office, where James and I are often to be seen sitting with intent to waylay colleagues and intimidate Whips, are going to be removed.

For the next eight months whenever the Maastricht Bill is being debated in the House a game of cat and mouse will be played out between the Government, on the one hand, who will want to suspend the 10 o'clock Rule and the rebels, on the other hand, who will not. Under Standing Orders the 10 o'clock Rule which prevents debate proceeding beyond 10 p.m. may be suspended if the House agrees either on the nod or by a majority of votes cast in a Division. Generally speaking Governments prefer to suspend this Standing Order so as to obtain more debating time at night rather than lose whole days which they may wish to devote to other business. Those opposed to the business of the day have an altogether different objective. If they can prevent debate after 10 p.m. they effectively increase the number of days that the business will have to come before the House and consequentially delay the implementation of the legislation which they would rather never reached the Statute Book anyway. On some occasions it will suit the Opposition parties to side with the rebels to prevent suspension of the 10 o'clock Rule, on others it will not. A calculation which Government has to make is whether by suspending the 10 o'clock Rule they risk being kept up all night or how often and for how long they can afford to keep the payroll (Government Ministers and Parliamentary Private Secretaries) on standby to try and force a 'closure', i.e. an enforced termination of that day's business if it threatens to be an all-night sitting.

On the first day of debate one of four speakers is Bill Cash who having spoken for $2^{1}/_{2}$ hours is still on his feet at 10 p.m. Perhaps fearful that he could go on for a further $2^{1}/_{2}$ hours and that we might have other speakers ready to follow him, the Government, on this occasion, does not seek suspension of the Rule and the House adjourns. It will not always be such plain sailing but we have to be ready for any eventuality. The one eventuality which we don't anticipate is Bill Cash's aberration to cry! 'I spy strangers' on the second day at a time when Tristan Garel-Jones, at the despatch box as Minister for Europe, is floundering. The subsequent division lets Garel-Jones off the hook, causes chaos amongst our own supporters who don't know which way to vote and makes James Cran and I very angry because this unplanned and completely maverick action will lose us some of the credibility so painstakingly built up over the past several months.

Acting as Whips for the rebel cause James Cran and I, assisted by Teresa Gorman and Roger Knapman, are left very much to our own devices. The leaders of the rebellion are seen to be Michael Spicer and Bill Cash but, initially at least, Michael seems to be somewhat 'semi-detached'. Perhaps he is waiting to see whether we've got it in us to organise and sustain the effort or whether, like so many other Parliamentary revolts, it will simply fizzle out. Having met to discuss tactics on day one little is seen of Michael until James and I pin him down over supper at Rodin a week later. At last he appears to be levelling with us but doubts remain as to whether or not we are all working to the same agenda. In contrast Teresa tells us not to keep flattering her because 'she is in it for the same reasons as you' and that 'we're fighting to win'.

Throughout the campaign there will be tension between Bill and Michael and my constant refrain will be that we need them both. Neither of them carries the full set of clubs that would make them the natural choice for leader but working together they have the potential to make our ragged army appear quite formidable. Michael's skills as a highly effective 'networker' combined with Bill's ability to pass the ammunition put us in a relatively strong position compared with the Government which is long on loyalty but extremely short on argument.

As 1992 draws to a close attention switches to Edinburgh where the European Community Heads of Government meet to resolve the 'little local difficulty' caused by the Danish 'No' vote. Unsurprisingly a compromise solution is proposed and the Danes are to be 'invited' to vote again. This may be the first time that the people of a Member State are being asked to vote again because they came up with the wrong answer first time but, as we shall see, it most certainly won't be the last. Democracy EC style does not brook dissent – the people must ultimately accept whatever the unelected and unaccountable Commission decrees, or else!

When the PM makes his statement to the House on Monday 14 December about the outcome of the Edinburgh summit the atmosphere is euphoric. Budgen, Cash and Gorman try to make their presence felt but such is the mood of the House that it is practically impossible for our side to make any runs. Major has 'agreed a solution to the issues raised by the Danish Government' that *'does not in any way change the Maastricht Treaty or require a new round of ratification in member states. It provides an interpretation of the treaty which Prime Minister Schlüter believes will enable him to hold a second referendum in Denmark in the spring.'*

In the tearoom afterwards I sit opposite an exultant John Major surrounded by acolytes being nauseatingly sycophantic. He asks me if I am a positive European to which I reply, 'Oh yes I'm a positive European but, as you know, Prime Minister, I'm against the Maastricht Treaty.' By and by I get the opportunity to ask him if he has considered that the effect of increasing Cohesion Fund payments will be to encourage the break-up of the United Kingdom when it is seen how much better Eire fares than the other regions of the British Isles. He responds by saying that he doesn't think that the Scots or the Welsh will be attracted to the high unemployment and high interest rates appertaining in Eire. When I say that the high unemployment and interest rates are a consequence of Eire's membership of the Exchange Rate Mechanism he retorts by saying that the ERM is not a bad system, it's just that we couldn't have anticipated the effects of German re-unification! This from a man who barely three months ago saw his Government's economic policy shredded to pieces as a direct consequence of being forced out of the system he still defends.

Before Parliament adjourns for Christmas, James, Teresa, Roger and I meet to discuss tactics for the New Year. We now know that the Labour Party will oppose suspension of the 10 o'clock Rule whenever Maastricht business is on the Order Paper and Willie Ross (Londonderry) tells me that the Ulster Unionists will do likewise. Willie is their Chief Whip and he says how pleased he is to have the excuse to demonstrate to Government that his Whip is effective. From now on in the Ulster Unionists will be solidly behind us right up to, but sadly not including, the final act.

The sage of Shropshire, alias John Biffen, agrees that the Edinburgh summit changes nothing but suggests that we need to adopt a rather more subtle approach than simply arguing that the proposals made to the Danes won't hold up legally.

In a particularly frank exchange of views with Party Chairman Norman Fowler (Sutton Coldfield) on the eve of the Christmas recess I tell him about my concern that the wealth-creating sector, particularly the private business sector, is not being listened to. I further instance the hazard of Government interference given the likelihood that additional regulation will tip many businesses into bankruptcy. The advice I am proferring falls on deaf ears. This is a Government that is arrogant in the extreme and the clear message that it is sending out is that it has neither learnt nor forgotten anything.

Norman asks me about feelings in the Ludlow constituency where I tell him there are, thanks to the diligence of the Member, not too many problems other than that more than a few people are expressing anti-Major sentiments.

I take the opportunity of saying that there is a pressing need for a greater sense of judgement and integrity amongst Government Ministers and that if they haven't got it then frankly they never will and they should therefore go. I realise that to a greater or lesser extent I am wasting my breath but believe that only a healthy dose of realism can possibly revive this desperately damaged administration's fortunes. Norman is also interested to know where I stand in the political spectrum, doubtless anticipating a left or right of centre answer. In this case the answer he gets is that in the sense that I do not believe that there are any problems that are incapable of solution if one is prepared to be radical rather than simply tinker round the edges, then perhaps I should be known as a radical. Notwithstanding that, I am and remain a Conservative although increasingly I feel that the Conservative Party is moving away from me and millions of others who share many of my traditional Conservative values.

CHAPTER TEN

1993

'It's people like you who are killing my husband.'

THE CHRISTMAS recess behind us, it is time to gear up for the impending battle. James Cran and I meet for lunch on Monday 11 January with a very relaxed Michael Spicer, just off the plane from Florida. The object of the exercise is, of course, to discuss tactics for the Committee stage of the European Communities (Amendment) Bill which will be taken on the floor of the House. The following day Roger Knapman reports that the Whips are looking to cut a deal and Michael undertakes to put out a few feelers. Personally I am not at all convinced that any such deal is on offer and James and I persuade Michael not to pursue the matter, not least because it will almost certainly be construed as a sign of weakness if we do. The fact that Roger is so keen on the idea and, leaving our meeting early, is later to be seen in earnest conversation with Government Whip David Lightbown (Staffordshire, South East) raises doubts about his loyalty to the cause. Because we are so nervous about his motives James subsequently has a few serious words with him about his meeting with Lightbown so that he is left in no doubt that playing both ends against the middle is totally unacceptable.

Much of our day is spent seeing and being seen and when the Government does not move suspension of the 10 o'clock Rule we feel that our tactics are paying off. Seeking John Biffen's opinion as to whether we are missing any tricks leads on to other things. He wants to talk about Constituency Association presidents as he is in danger of getting a relatively hostile Europhile. This sets me thinking about the Ludlow Association where both Michael Lumsden and Simon Kenyon-Slaney are bound to be strong contenders for President when Rosemary Hinwood steps down. In due course I shall come up with a name which will at least ensure that my flank is not exposed if it comes to fighting on two fronts – in Ludlow as well as in Westminster.

Wonders never cease. At a meeting of officers of the Conservative backbench Agriculture Committee in John Gummer's office at MAFF he confesses that he has come round to the Gill view on Beef Intervention, the EC system which takes top quality beef off the open market, freezes it – the inevitable effect of which is to reduce it in value – and then keeps it in cold store until such time as it can be disposed of at knock-down prices to anyone in Russia or the Third World who will have it. All this is at vast expense to the British taxpayer who in times of plenty under the old Deficiency Payment Scheme at least had the benefit of cheap meat, the result of which was that surpluses were eaten and enjoyed rather than frozen and forgotten. On another question, that of regulatory overkill, it is apparent that Gummer is not converted to the Gill view but when I explain to him how sales promotions in supermarkets are invariably at the expense of the producers' profit margin rather than the retailers', he promises to introduce a Code of Practice to be followed by retailers, including a stipulation about credit terms.

The fourth day's debate on the Maastricht Bill ends in uproar when the Government move a closure motion just as Deputy Speaker Michael Morris (Northampton South) has called the Reverend Ian Paisley (Antrim North) to speak. Ian Paisley dons the folding opera hat kept for such occasions and resumes his seat. The effect is to delay the voting procedure whilst 'Points of Order' are heard. These essentially come in two parts – Ian Paisley remonstrating about being called but not being allowed to speak and Bill Walker arguing that in a constitutional debate it is axiomatic that 'views from all parts of the United Kingdom' should be heard. The voting is 298 for the closure motion* and 240 against. This division is, as far as James and I are concerned, a gift because it is so obvious to all our pledges how they should vote. The consequence is that for the first time there is a full turnout of Conservative rebels with 27 voting against the closure and 29 in favour of the amendment (the substantive motion). Now that they are 'blooded' it will be that much easier to steer them into the correct lobbies when future divisions are called. From the Government's point of view progress of business is the most important consideration but, viewed from our perspective, their decision to stifle debate proves a significant boost to morale – the fact that the debate is now taking on the proportions of a David and Goliath struggle will strengthen our resolve and help to build a formidable camaraderie amongst us.

On day 5, by a majority of 307 to 271, the Government carry a motion to suspend the 10 o'clock Rule and debate proceeds throughout the night until 0702 the following morning. Assessing that there is unlikely to be another closure motion before dawn, after the one called at 2358, James and I draw stumps at 0230 leaving Teresa Gorman and Roger Knapman on duty as night watchmen and Messrs. Cash, Jessell, Spicer, Taylor and Walker at the crease.

On the following two days (6th & 7th on Maastricht) the Government are deterred from moving suspension of the 10 o'clock Rule for fear of being kept up all night and the risk of alienating the bulk of their backbenchers who would much prefer to be at home in bed than detained in the House for a vote that may or may not ever come.

---

*The purpose of moving a Closure Motion is to end the debate forthwith with a view to forcing an immediate division on the matter under consideration.

Whips are now in overdrive to obtain pledges from Fresh Start Group members not to vote against the Government when it comes to amendments dealing with the Social Chapter, one of the two opt-outs that the PM has obtained from the basic Treaty.

David Lightbown, the 'caring' Whip, points in my direction and grunts, 'Wanna see you.' I don't move and subsequently tell the Chief Whip that as a matter of principle I don't respond to that sort of treatment. Thereafter Lightbown becomes somewhat more biddable and taking a seat beside me in the Chamber suggests a meeting between us. I agree to meet him straight away but not in his office. Sitting on the benches in Members' Lobby outside the Whips' Office I tell him that I have absolutely no intention of revealing my voting intentions on the Social Chapter and am only listening to him out of politeness. Having taken the opportunity to tell him that he's a bully I consider that sufficient for one day but less than a month later when I meet his wife socially she tells me frankly that she has no time for the likes of me with our views on Maastricht and that 'it's people like you who are killing my husband.'

On 21 January Michael Spicer goes to the Chief Whip to complain about the bullying tactics which are being used against us but this I believe to be unnecessary since it will probably be construed as a sign of weakness. Throughout this whole saga I will have to keep reminding myself that I mustn't give any indication that anything that the Whips do or say concerns me in the slightest. To do otherwise will encourage them to think that with just a bit more pressure I will cave in. By and by I shall tell the Chief Whip that he has nothing in his gift that I want – neither title nor honours nor office – nothing. This shoots his fox stone dead because deprived of the power of patronage he is virtually impotent.

Whilst not usually in London on a Friday, 22 January is an exception because the House is debating the Sunday Trading Bill and this evening my wife and I have an invitation to attend a birthday party in the Tower of London. Amongst the other guests are Margaret Thatcher, Norman Tebbitt and other recognisably Eurosceptic figures and it is a relief to find the Portcullis still raised when it's time for us to leave. The time spent in the House that morning is not wasted because I am able to start canvassing colleagues on their views about Amendment 27* to the Maastricht Bill which seems to provide the best opportunity of scoring a hit. I also take the opportunity of striking a blow for less regulation by objecting to the Hedgerows Bill, a Private Member's Bill brought to the House by Peter

---

*Amendment 27 reads 'in page 1, line 13, after 'Community' insert 'with the exception of the Protocol on Social Policy'. Moved by Tony Blair (Sedgefield) the purpose of this amendment is to override John Major's opt out so as to get the Social Chapter reinstated. Whilst debated on 27 January the vote on Amendment 27, owing to the somewhat arcane procedures of the House, stands deferred until another day.

Ainsworth (Surrey, East) who will never forgive me for torpedoing his pet project. Everybody, it seems, wants less regulation but beyond that there is apparently no agreement as to what should not reach, or already be on, the already mightily inflated Statute Book.

Back in the House on Monday 25th Bill Cash reports that a senior Labour member has said that Amendment 27 is the only opportunity we shall have to actually win the vote – on all other amendments the Labour Party are simply playing games and by the simple expedient of slipping a number of their members each evening they ensure that the total votes cast in the 'Aye' Lobby are never quite enough to carry the day.

By the time the Fresh Start Group meet on 26 January it looks as though a mass abstention is the only course open to us because it is highly unlikely that the Liberal Democrats will vote for Amendment 27 if it is thought that we will too, for fear that the Treaty will be amended and thus rendered null and void. The arithmetic is such that 271 Labour members and 20 Liberal Democrats could combine with 24 other Opposition members and Ulster Unionist members to carry the amendment if there was to be a minimum of 22 abstentions amongst the 336 Conservative members.

Michael Spicer is in a bit of a spin as a result of our group meeting and I have to try and assure him that the group will, when the time comes, obey orders. The fact that he has upset Roger Knapman by suggesting that he is spying for the Whips' Office may be worrying him somewhat but as our de facto leader he is right not to pull any punches. We are playing for high stakes and we have to be prepared to be just as ruthless as our opponents.

On the 8th day of Maastricht (27 January) the Government move a closure motion at 1830 but with a majority of only 16 they are deterred from seeking to suspend the 10 o'clock Rule later in the evening. It will be a different matter tomorrow (9th day) when the Government win the 10 o'clock vote with a majority of 47 and the debate continues until after midnight. In the meantime there will have been further criticism of the Eurosceptics at the '22 Committee although James Spicer (Dorset West) gets as good as he gives from Nick Budgen who goes on to put in a plug for a Referendum on Maastricht as a means of resolving the Party's difficulties.

On 1 February Nicholas Soames and I attend Butchers Hall as guests of the National Association of Catering Butchers. In his speech to the assembled company Nicholas is fulsome in his praise for my efforts on behalf of the meat industry but rather less so regarding my activities in relation to the Maastricht Treaty! On one point we are all agreed and that is that the EC Beef Intervention regime has been, and continues to be, disastrous.

Returning to the House after a most agreeable lunch I am in time to put in an appearance at the Fresh Start Group meeting where I learn that elder statesmen John Biffen and Sir Peter Tapsell (Lindsey East) have paid tribute to the rebel Whips for our great efficiency and excellent organisation. We return the compliment by going on to record our highest vote yet when 31 Conservative members support an amendment concerning citizenship, the heads of state having, by dint of the Treaty, resolved *'to establish a citizenship common to nationals of their countries'*. The debate on this subject is first class and Charles Goodson-Wickes (Wimbledon) and other colleagues who stop to listen are clearly perturbed by what they are hearing. To their very great shame far too few colleagues have bothered to read the text of the Treaty and it appears that even fewer of them are minded to attend the debates where their minds would be opened to a whole raft of impositions with which it is hard to believe they would necessarily agree. If ever there was a time in British history when Members of Parliament should ensure that they are properly briefed, rather than relying upon the mendacious advice received from the Whips' Office, it is now. Sadly all too many of my colleagues will come to recognise the truth about the Treaty on European Union long after it is too late to do anything about it other, that is, than to vote to repeal the 1972 Act of Accession, a proposition that, regrettably at this stage, is just too fanciful to contemplate.

After no more than six hours of debate on the crucial issue of citizenship the Government move a closure motion which Michael Morris, in the Chair, accepts notwithstanding protests from Tony Marlow (Northampton North) and Sir Teddy Taylor, who complain that the debate should have been allowed to run on until at least 10 o'clock and that there has been no ministerial response to the debate. Ted Rowlands (Lab. Merthyr Tydfil & Rhymney) and Nick Budgen ask the Chairman, 'When will you refuse a closure motion from the Government?' and what the Chairman meant when he said 'that the question of the time was not within the discretion of the Chair'. The willingness of the future Lord Naseby to do the Government's bidding is widely regarded as being tantamount to debate being guillotined and suspicions are running high that the reason that the Government does not seek suspension of the 10 o'clock Rule on this particular evening is because of a deal with the Liberal Democrats to allow the debate on Regional policy, which follows, to take place in prime time on Thursday.

Having been in the House last Friday to object to the Hedgerows Bill* for the second time I am now sensing that the Government would like this particular Private Member's Bill to succeed. Government Whip Tim Wood broaches the subject with me in the Tearoom and when confronted by me as to the source of his information says that 'it's surprising what you can learn from people's telephone conversations.' This comment does nothing to allay suspicions that my home telephone is being tapped but by a judicious use of

---

*A Bill objected to on three successive occasions is automatically deemed to have failed and is removed from the Order Book.

the banks of unallocated telephones available to Members in various parts of the House rather than the phone on my desk, I can be reasonably sure that by no means all of my conversations are being listened to. Later in the week I have my second conversation with David Maclean (Penrith & The Border and Parliamentary Under Secretary of State at the Department of the Environment) who intimates that, whilst he would personally prefer not to have it, the Government are committed to the Bill by dint of various promises made at election time to pacify the Greens!

There is a very relaxed atmosphere when the House meets on Thursday 4 February for the 11th day on Maastricht. The Government Whips are saying that they are up to schedule, which may or may not be true, but they don't let on that the Nationalists (the 3 Scottish National Party and 4 Plaid Cymru members) may be tweaking their tail. When the House rises at 10 o'clock the Nationalists have not yet spoken about the Committee of the Regions and Alex Salmond, SNP Leader, tells James and I that his objective is to wring maximum concessions out of the Government on this issue after which they will be free to vote for Amendment 27.

The relaxed mood continues through the weekend and on Monday evening (8 February) the rebel Whips, Cran, Gorman, Knapman and I, together with our respective spouses, are to be seen dining together at the Carlton Club. This is not a secret meeting: on the contrary demonstrating to our colleagues that we are confident in the righteousness of our cause is all part of the psychology and might even have provoked the conversation at table in the Members' Dining Room the following evening when Archie Hamilton (Epsom & Ewell) is heard muttering darkly about withdrawing the Party Whip – presumably from the Maastricht rebels.

Amendment 27 is now the burning issue. At its Tuesday meeting the Fresh Start Group agrees to take further soundings but not to declare its hand. The following day Norman Tebbitt urges the Eurosceptics to vote for the amendment, the justification for this being that Douglas Hurd has stated that the UK will not ratify the Treaty if the amendment is carried. Privately James, Michael and I agree that voting for the amendment will be counter-productive because it will deter the Lib/Dems and others who really want the Social Chapter and that mass abstention is therefore our only option. Michael Howard who, as the former Secretary of State for Employment, negotiated the British opt-out, appears on the BBC 6 O'clock News saying that for Eurosceptics to vote for Amendment 27 would be disastrous. By keeping our powder dry we are keeping them all guessing and judged by the reaction of those present when I address the members of the Meirionnydd Nant Conwy Association on Friday evening (12 February) there is a growing awareness amongst party members that matters are coming to a head.

Over this same weekend there is speculation that the Government will ratify Maastricht irrespective of the outcome of votes in Parliament. By Monday (15 February) the picture is a little clearer when the Government announces that according to a new legal opinion obtained from Attorney General Sir Nicholas Lyell QC (Mid Bedfordshire) the carrying of Amendment 27 will not affect the integrity of the Bill. On the 17th Michael Lord produces a letter which he has obtained from the Library which, on the subject of Amendment 27, is much more favourable to our position but nonetheless the Group agree not to take up a common position nor to declare our individual intentions.

On Monday 22 February, the 12th day of the Maastricht debate, the Government is completely wrongfooted by an unexpected change of business. George Robertson (Lab. Hamilton and Shadow Foreign Secretary) moves a 'dilatory motion'* which Michael Morris, as Chairman of the Committee of the whole House, accepts. The effect of the motion is to subject to further debate the statement made by the Foreign Secretary last Monday relating to the legal position in the event that Amendment 27 is carried. Don Dixon (Jarrow, Labour Deputy Chief Whip) tells me that he is planning to move a closure before 10 o'clock but when he does so at 8 p.m. there is no vote because the Government decline to put in Tellers.† Neither does the Government seek to vote against the substantive motion 'that the House has made progress', because from their perspective, far from making progress, they have effectively lost a day's business and not a little face as a result of having been made to look rather foolish. Their efforts to play down the significance of Amendment 27 have seriously backfired.

By the time the Fresh Start Group meet the following day the dust has settled and Michael Spicer is full of praise for our own Whips in the light of yesterday's surprise turn of events. This is in contrast to the Government Whips who were to be seen running around like chickens with their heads cut off. At the instigation, I suspect, of Iain Duncan Smith (Chingford), Calum MacDonald (Lab. Western Isles) has tabled a new amendment which appears to offer the prospect of succeeding where Amendment 27 is said to fail – in wrecking the Treaty. Iain, possibly more than anyone else, understands how to undermine the Government position and will probably make a name for himself, deservedly, on this issue.

On the eve of the launch of his campaign to raise a petition to Parliament for a referendum on Maastricht, Bill Cash invites colleagues to a reception at 17 Great George Street where he and his wife Biddy have assembled a host of journalists and other converts to the cause. The converts, rather like religious

---

*A Dilatory Motion is a motion whose effect is to interrupt the business under discussion at the time. It can only be proposed by the Member speaking and is normally in the form, 'That this House may now adjourn.' If agreed to, all business for the day ends, and the House stands adjourned.
†Two Tellers, generally Whips, are deputed by each side of the House or each side of the argument to stand at the exit of the 'Aye' and 'No' Lobbies to count the number of members voting For and Against the motion.

converts, are infinitely more rabid than some of the original sceptics but one
is encouraged by the feeling that our movement is definitely spreading.
Needless to say we are not having it all our own way and a lynch mob
comprising Peter Bottomley, Winston Churchill, Sir Peter Emery, Sir
Michael Jopling, Sir James Spicer and Michael Stern awaits us at Thursday's
meeting of the '22 Committee. Michael Lord responds bravely to their
criticisms and in this he is assisted by Sir George Gardiner who, after an
ignominious start, appears now to have crossed the Rubicon in no uncertain
fashion.

On the 13th day of Maastricht we lose the 10 o'clock vote but instead of an
all-night session the Government draws stumps at midnight in accordance
with a deal they have done with the Lib/Dems. After the debate Teresa
Gorman tackles Tristan Garel-Jones, who has been at the Despatch Box in his
capacity as Minister for Europe, about his failure to answer my intervention
properly. He responds by saying that 'he doesn't need to answer the questions
of people who are so clearly opposed to the treaty'! Confirmation, if it be
needed, that no amount of reasoned argument is going to deflect the
Government from its determination to surrender the last vestiges of
Parliamentary sovereignty and for the UK to be fully integrated into the
European Collective. Somewhat taken aback by Garel-Jones' pathetic reply,
but never lost for words, Teresa tells him to take his hands off her shoulders
where he has so patronisingly laid them.

A 1-line Whip in the House on Monday 1 March affords me the
opportunity to attend the funeral in Lydbury North of Major Whitaker, a
long-standing member of the LCCA, and to take tea afterwards with my
Constituency Chairman, Mrs Jackie Williams, who lives close by. No one
could ever accuse the Ludlow Conservatives of being overly political and
having been brought up in the political hothouse in Wolverhampton it never
ceases to amaze me how totally apolitical the Ludlow Association continues to
be. After an hour or so with the Chairman I conclude that most, if not all, of
the problems that I am now beginning to experience with the LCCA stem
from a complete lack of comprehension of all things political to which I really
have no answer. If, as appears to be the case, the Chairman's horizon does not
extend beyond fund raising and social events then having a Member of
Parliament who is not prepared to show blind loyalty to a treacherous
Government is clearly going to be a problem for both of us.

Surprisingly the 14th day on Maastricht ends in a whimper. In spite of the
fact that Government supporters have been flown back from all over the
world the suspension is not moved and the House stands adjourned at
10 p.m. One wonders how long this can go on for though doubtless the
Government Whips will say they're on schedule but, unbeknown to any of us,
they're riding for a fall.

At Harrogate on Saturday 6 March the Government uses a meeting of the Conservative Party National Council as a platform from which to castigate the Eurosceptics. Simultaneously, but perhaps not entirely spontaneously, Nick Budgen's Chairman, Roseanne Williams, takes to denouncing Nick in the media. Talking to colleagues on the telephone I soon learn that the effect of all this is to harden opinion amongst my fellow Eurorealists to the extent that one of them, Sir Richard Body (Holland with Boston), says that what he really wants to do is to resign the Party whip. From all this I conclude that the Government will have a difficult run for their money when the House meets again on Monday.

Determined to have matters out with him I go to the House armed with a list of bullet points to make to the Chief Whip including a note of what the PM said when he addressed the '22 Committee on 29 October about not conducting the debate in the media. He had also stated that his 'door is always open' but that too has a hollow ring because I have requested a meeting and there has been absolutely no response.

Waylaying the Chief Whip, Richard Ryder, in the 'Aye' Lobby I invite him to be seated whilst I run through a few points with him. Regrettably our tête-à-tête ends shortly after it has begun when he gets to his feet saying that 'until you and others behave like Neil Marten* did in 1972, by not opposing procedural motions, you have no right to criticise the Prime Minister.' To me this seems a total non sequitur, quite apart from the fact that it misses the point entirely. Firstly, in opposing the Maastricht Treaty by all legitimate constitutional means, tempted though we may be, we are careful not to indulge in personal criticism or vilification of the PM, or anyone else for that matter. Secondly, my purpose in speaking to the Chief Whip is to explain that the Government's adoption of the technique evidenced at Harrogate this weekend is totally unacceptable and hugely counter productive.

Having been given this brusque treatment by the Chief Whip I am hardly sorry when the Government loses the very next vote by 314 votes to 292. I am not exultant that the Government has been defeated as a consequence of which I turn down an invitation to be interviewed for the BBC 9 O'clock News which is anxious to broadcast opinion as to why Amendment 28† has been carried by a staggering majority of 22. Whilst this vote is undoubtedly a defeat for the Government it is not an unqualified victory for us because the successful amendment does not alter the Treaty commitment to establish a Committee of the Regions, merely the method of selecting its members. Since this does not represent a defeat of the treaty provision it falls short of

---

*Conservative Member of Parliament for Banbury 1959-86.

†Amendment 28 ensured that the 24 members and 24 alternate members representing the UK on the European Committee of the Regions would be drawn from the body of elected local government representatives i.e. councillors, instead of being appointed by Ministers.

our requirement which is to carry an amendment that will alter and thereby derail the whole Treaty.

Michael Jopling (Westmorland & Lonsdale) adds his own commentary to the evening's proceedings by telling Nick Budgen and I that 'he never knew that there were so many shits in the Party'. Realising that Nick and I find this somewhat offensive he then proceeds to try and defuse the situation by saying that 'it takes one to recognise one' – a sentiment with which I cannot but agree.

When they meet on Tuesday (9 March) the members of the Fresh Start Group are obviously pleased with themselves after last night's coup but we have to listen rather too much to the loquacious Bernard Jenkin (Colchester North) who is not quite a paid up member of the club because he obviously feels that by consistently abstaining rather than voting he is keeping his future options open. His braver friend Iain Duncan Smith is equally talkative but he has earned his spurs by delivering his vote and not just talking about it.

At the end of our meeting Michael Spicer invites John Biffen to say a few words about whether or not we should reconsider our policy of invariably opposing the suspension of the 10 o'clock Rule. Apart from Bernard Jenkin there are no takers for any change but Michael is quite right to give the matter an airing not least because the Labour Deputy Chief Whip is warning that tomorrow's business (Wednesday) will run very late indeed unless the Government agree not to move suspension on Thursday, there being rumours that Government are considering running the business not just through Thursday night but also into the weekend, a prospect which has just as little appeal to us as it does to Don Dixon's people.

We must not let the euphoria of yesterday's hollow victory cause us to relax and over a nightcap in the Horse & Bower I warn Michael that this might be the high spot of our endeavours and that we need to take extra care hereon in. I am loath to spoil the illusion but I can't help feeling that his confidence in Jenkin and Duncan Smith, whom he describes as being 'very brave' which, as new members to the House, they undoubtedly are, is somewhat misplaced. This is rather borne out by evidence that Bernard has been approaching individual members of our group with suggestions about adopting different tactics, principally of doing deals with the Government on the 10 o'clock motion. Iain wastes my time with a similar proposition but the reality is that to date Bernard has only voted with us once and Iain three times.

It is not my place to tell the Chairman of the 1922 Committee what to do but when it is rumoured that the Europhiles have put together a letter with 100 signatures attacking those of our supporters who serve on the executive Committee of the '22 Committee, i.e. Vivian Bendall, George Gardiner, Ivan Lawrence, James Pawsey and John Townend, I suggest to Marcus Fox that he would do well to nip in the bud any move by the Europhiles to stir up further trouble at tomorrow's meeting.

On the 16th day of Maastricht Michael Spicer says that staff working in the Palace of Westminster have been warned that they may be required to work at the weekend which now seems improbable given the way in which Labour 'irregulars' wrecked yesterday's business by opposing each of 19 Statutory Instruments. One cannot but conclude that this is a shot across the Government's bows warning them that any attempt to detain the 'brothers' in Westminster beyond 10 o'clock tonight is going to have serious repercussions.

All in all 11 March turns out to be somewhat of an anti-climax – there is no drama at the '22 because for the first time in a long time the Whips demonstrate good judgment by saying that no good purpose will be served by debating the Positive European Group's letter: the 10 o'clock vote for which we have made a considerable effort to mobilise our forces is never called and, towards the end of the day, a number of Ministers appear to be happy to be seen talking to James and me in the lobby. Even the Chief Whip smiles so clearly the 'Dotheboys Hall' treatment appears to be giving way to a charm offensive, leastways it looks as though a thaw is setting in.

At the weekend I am encouraged to find the level of support for my stand against European integration holding up well. At the AGM of the Church Stretton branch of the LCCA the ratio of backers is 3 to 1 and only at the conclusion of the lively Question & Answer session do I discover that the really hostile questions are coming from a man who only joined the Association this morning, presumably for that very purpose. After the meeting Constituency Chairman Jackie Williams says that her thoughts on the matter are 'For £5 why not?' Comparing notes with colleagues back at the House on Monday it is gratifying to learn that both Walter Sweeney and Andrew Hunter have survived their Association AGMs unscathed and that the thaw, as evidenced by the willingness of Local Government Minister John Redwood and Paymaster General John Cope (Northavon) to share a table with Bill Cash and I in the Cafeteria, continues.

Any complacency that I might have had regarding my own situation vis-à-vis the LCCA is shattered when on the morning of 16 March Vice-Chairman Michael Wood telephones to tell me what he has just read in the Annual Report to be presented to members at the forthcoming AGM. The third paragraph of the Chairman's report leaves me speechless and incredulous. Michael is putting his copy in the post to me but if it's half as bad as he says then I've got problems. Upon receipt of the report the following day I immediately try to speak to the Chairman on the telephone, eventually making contact at 7.15 p.m. when I have to listen to some pretty bizarre comments.

Amongst other things Jackie Williams tells me that she doesn't know enough about the Maastricht Treaty to say whether she is for or against it.

When I suggest that she might therefore leave it to my judgment as indeed her counterpart in the North Shropshire constituency leaves it to John Biffen, she says, 'That's different because we all regard John Biffen as the elder statesman'! I am at pains to point out to her that I made a special journey to her home on 1 March to discuss these matters face to face and that she gave me no cause to believe that there was any kind of problem. I also remind her of the telephone call I have recently made to check that she is in agreement with the contents of my own annual report when again there was an opportunity to tell me if there were any problems.

Thursday 18 March is a long day. I am at my desk at 0445 drafting a letter* to Mrs Williams following on from our telephone conversation last evening and it is turned midnight before my head finally hits the pillow having in the meantime journeyed from Westminster for a meeting with former LCCA President David Hill, at Michael Wood's home in Shropshire. It is quite clear that the battle has moved on to the home front and Conservative Central Office's involvement is subsequently confirmed when on 30 March, Lightbown grunts that he wants to speak to me. His advice is that I should not take matters any further regarding my difference with the officers of the LCCA. Without in so many words saying so he hints that the Whip may be withdrawn from me if I don't see things his way, in response to which I tell him that whilst I don't start wars I am perfectly capable of finishing them. This provokes him to repeat the threat saying that 'life without the support of the Parliamentary Party can be most unpleasant!' Whilst not inconceivable, it is unlikely that the train of events which now follows is entirely at the instigation of the LCCA. Furthermore it seems improbable that the Whips' Office are so well informed unless they are in fact, from behind the scenes, orchestrating the lynch mob which is now baying for my blood in the constituency. One doesn't have to be a rocket scientist to work out that the change of attitude in the House – the thaw – is all part of a new strategy which now relies upon the constituency Associations putting the boot in where the Government Whips have thus far failed. Flattered by the attention that my Chairman is now receiving and puffed up by her new importance, this is a plot in which Mrs Williams and the equally apolitical President, Rosemary Hinwood, are willing accomplices. Sadly, from the Government's point of view that is, the two ladies and their acolytes are out of their league. They like the sound of this exciting new game but they don't know how to play it.

Early on Friday 19 March, the day of the LCCA Annual General Meeting, the Chairman calls and is somewhat nonplussed when I answer the telephone personally. By phoning my office early she had hoped to avoid speaking to me direct and simply to have been able to leave a message on the answerphone.

---

*Appendix D.

Caught on the wrong foot she says that she wants to talk about arrangements for the LCCA Annual Dinner, the Summer Party, the impending visit of Trade & Industry Minister Neil Hamilton (Tatton), and indeed anything other than the contents of my letter. When I insist on pursuing the matter of the letter her reaction is incomprehensible – far from recognising it as a rap across the knuckles she seems to be as pleased to receive it as if it had come from Buckingham Palace. Out of courtesy I call the President to make her aware of the contents of my letter to the Chairman and arrange for a copy to be delivered to her later in the day. She too appears to be relaxed and generally unconcerned and I can only conclude that the pair of them know something I don't know.

That evening's meeting of the Executive Council of the LCCA in the Prince Rupert suite at the Feathers Hotel passes off without a hitch and at 8 p.m. we move on to the business of the AGM. After the usual formalities the President proceeds to propose the adoption of the Annual Report whereupon up springs the Vice Chairman to say that it is not in order because it has not previously been put to and agreed by the Finance and General Purposes Committee, that if it had been he would have counselled using a different form of words, that he doesn't agree with it in its present form, that, not having been consulted, he is not prepared to take collective responsibility for it and that that being said he cannot support it. All hell breaks loose with all the usual suspects attacking my stand against Maastricht after which former President David Hill questions the propriety of putting forward an Annual Report which is defective for all the reasons given by Michael Wood. He is followed by Anthony Thompson who proposes and Clem Shaw who seconds a proposition that the offending paragraph be deleted. The President, from the Chair, having been at first reluctant to accept any amendment, puts the proposition to the meeting and deletion of paragraph 3 is carried by a convincing 2 to 1 majority.

Before the meeting ends the Bishop's Castle Area Chairman, Alan Screen, proposes a vote of thanks to the retiring officers which upon reflection I realise has been honed in anticipation of an altogether different outcome to this evening's meeting. The man from Conservative Area Office, for reasons which I shall only fully appreciate in the morning, leaves with a scowl on his face and the meeting is brought to a close by local farmer and Ludlow magistrate Bob Tilt, standing up to tell the assembled company of approximately one hundred members, including some surprise appearances, that he for one backs me to the hilt.

Not until Saturday morning does it dawn upon me that the whole of last night's meeting was a set-up. Lumpy, Simon Kenyon-Slaney (who served only two years of his three-year term as Chairman and quit at very short notice in 1991), District and later one term County Councillor John Wheeler and others of that ilk, realising that Michael Wood had shot their fox, had the sense to say not a word whereas other lesser lights blithely carried on acting out their allotted roles as though nothing had happened to alter the script.

Lunching at Eudon on Sunday, at the invitation of Bill and Margaret Crawford-Clarke, the plot thickens. Jimmy Goodall (his wife Ursula used to work for Enoch in South West Wolverhampton) tells me that someone stood at the entrance to our AGM handing out suggested awkward questions. To satisfy my curiosity Jimmy volunteers to find out who it was and later in the day telephones to say it was the Association Treasurer, Gerard Paris. Another guest at the lunch party, Margaret Williamson, a long standing and active member of the LCCA, says that she didn't receive a copy of the Annual Report in advance of the meeting and subsequent enquiries reveal that other members with close links to myself such as son Charles and Cleobury Mortimer farmer John Haywood were not sent their copies either. This is the subject of another letter, this time to the Association president, Rosemary Hinwood, requesting an investigation. Whilst I receive an acknowledgement by return of post a further week passes before she rings requesting a meeting at the weekend. Owing to prior engagements this is not possible and we arrange to meet on Saturday 10 April but not before she inadvertently lets slip that she is being advised by Area Office.

Returning to the House after an epic weekend I am bawled at in the Chamber by a highly disgruntled Lightbown who cannot subsequently remember when the vote on a 3-line Whip that he accuses me of missing was actually held. The fact that the Pairing Whip who keeps the records cannot do so either seems to indicate to me that Lightbown is becoming paranoid but the fact of the matter is that, with the exception of the Maastricht divisions, I have an excellent voting record and am deliberately refraining from defying the Party Whip on any other issues so as not to give the Whips or anybody else the excuse to accuse me of being a serial member of the awkward squad. On Bills such as that establishing the National Lottery (28 April) I would have much preferred to have voted against but in these troubled times the name of the game is maintaining consistency and credibility.

Unable to attend the Fresh Start Group meeting that day because I am confined to the Chamber hoping to be called to speak in the 2nd Reading debate of the Agriculture Bill, I am concerned to learn that in my absence my colleagues have apparently agreed not to oppose closure motions. This I regard as an unfortunate and unnecessary softening of our stance given that we have so little leverage anyway.

Michael Ancram (Devizes) who chairs our backbench Constitutional Affairs committee tells me that he is 'anti-Europe and pro-Maastricht', his argument being that signing the Treaty will hasten the end. It certainly will, but not the end of the European Community as he maintains: quite the reverse.

Here we are, less than one year into this Parliament, and I find myself sympathising with James who doubts whether he really wants to seek a third term. When the time comes I shall ignore my godfather's advice to do only two terms, the consideration being that having been such a nuisance to the executive in this Parliament I ought in fairness to put my views to the test in the only opinion poll that matters in British politics – a General Election.

Bill Cash telephones early on 24 March to warn against any softening of the Fresh Start Group line and to advise keeping a close eye on our 'troops' in the light of press reports that Ken Baker (Mole Valley) and possibly John Whittingdale (Colchester South & Maldon) have defected. In the division at 10 o'clock John, who has been a consistent abstainer, appears amongst the names supporting the suspension motion which is carried by precisely the number of the 17 Lib/Dems voting for it. At 0630 the following morning James and I hand over our watch to Teresa and Roger and the 17th day's debate continues until a closure motion is moved at 1148 on 25 March. The debate is resumed again at 6 p.m. but mercifully the Government do not move the suspension at 10 o'clock because, one suspects, the Lib/Dems are high-tailing it to Dunoon where their party is holding a Convention.

An accusation frequently levelled against the Eurosceptics is that we are voting with Labour. The truth of the matter is that we are voting to defeat the Treaty by all and every means at our disposal just as the Government, intent upon European Union, are doing deals and voting with the arch-integrationist Lib/Dems whenever it suits their purpose.

As the end of debate on Clause 1 of the Treaty looms James, Teresa, Roger and I meet for a working dinner at the Rodin where we decide upon the importance of getting the voting situation sorted out in advance of the outstanding votes to be put to the House in the not too distant future.

On 29 March the threatened revolt against Michael Heseltine's proposal to close 31 deep coal mines fizzles out with only four Conservatives voting against the final proposition which is to close 19 pits and keep the remaining 12 going. This helps to put the Maastricht rebellion into perspective. An enormous amount of heat and anger has built up regarding the future of the coal industry but when push comes to shove the rebellion is small beer compared to the Maastricht rebellion where the sceptics are, if anything, stronger now than at the outset and prepared to go through the lobbies night after night in opposition to the Treaty. As Alan Howarth (Stratford-upon-Avon) is to observe before he defects to Labour, we are holding the Executive to account in a way that is seldom seen these days. With the advent of the professional politician such action is becoming increasingly rare and may become virtually extinct as the Executive and the political parties themselves become more and more powerful at the expense of individual politicians.

At the commencement of the 19th day the Chairman announces that he will be selecting New Clause 75* to be voted on in lieu of Amendment 27. Instead of uproar there is so little reaction from the Opposition front bench that it is almost certain that there has been an agreement between the front benches but quite why Amendment 27, which stands in the name of the Leader of the Opposition, John Smith (Monklands), is being dropped from the voting list is unclear.

That night in spite of fielding 25 in opposition to the 10 o'clock suspension we lose by a mere 5 votes because Rhodes Boyson, Jim Pawsey and John Townend decide to vote with the Government instead of with us. The business then runs until 0405 the following day when Iain Duncan Smith is at long last able to introduce his Adjournment Debate about human rights in Burma.

On the last day of March Lightbown springs a surprise by saying that Amendment 27 might come back instead of New Clause 75. I suspect that this is simply a ruse to try and draw me out as to how the sceptics intend to vote. I tell him that I don't know pending our obtaining further legal advice but that he ought to know that some of our number are very gung-ho indeed. I have previously told him that I will not support the Government on a motion relating to the Common Agricultural Policy and that he should count himself lucky that we are not running a Whip other than on Maastricht business.

On 2 April we are all pleased to get away from Westminster at the commencement of the Easter recess but not before Roger Knapman tells me that his President, Sir Anthony Kershaw, previously the Member for Stroud, is after his blood. Judged by the efforts now being made to get their hands on the tape from the dictaphone that I had with me on top table at the recent AGM the President, Chairman and Treasurer of the LCCA are also still plotting to get mine. Subsequently at our meeting on 10 April the President's prime concern is to try to persuade me to hand over my tape recording.

The officers are clearly worried that a recording of that meeting might be rather embarrassing in the circumstances where their first attempt at censure has gone so horribly wrong on them. Little do any of them realise that in point of fact the tape is barely long enough to record my own contribution let alone the rest of the proceedings but far be it from me to put them out of their misery by telling them so. Having told me that at the AGM the Treasurer was merely handing over a press cutting to someone who had asked for it she then wants to know what can be done to patch things up between myself and the Chairman. The short answer to that is that through no fault of

---

*New Clause 75, proposed by Stephen Byers (Wallsend) proposes that 'No power transferred by this Act from the United Kingdom to European institutions shall be so transferred unless and until the House of Commons has had an opportunity to vote on a motion tabled by a Minister of the Crown relating to the incorporation or otherwise of the United Kingdom into the Agreement annexed to the Protocol on Social Policy.'

my own the trust and confidence that I previously had in the officers of the Association has been broken and that nothing she can say or do can mend it.

Knocking doors during the Easter recess to canvass votes for LCCA Vice Chairman Michael Wood who is standing for County Council reveals no evidence that my views on the European question are in any way unacceptable – quite the reverse. With this knowledge in mind and the little local difficulty with the LCCA temporarily behind me, it is time to head back to Westminster for the Summer sitting – always the worst one of the year owing to the inevitability of long hours as Bills come back to the House for Report stage and Third Reading; the probability that the weather will be hot thus making working conditions in the Palace of Westminster uncomfortable – only the debating Chamber benefits from air-conditioning; and the certainty that members' tempers, as a result of these factors, will in many cases be on a relatively short fuse.

Back at the 'shop' there is much talk about a vote of censure on Ways & Means Chairman Michael Morris, on account of his rejection of a vote on Amendment 27. Having discussed the matter with John Biffen, Bill Cash and James Cran and hearing that the Labour Party have no intention of moving such a motion we conclude that it's a dead duck.

Dining together at Rodin that evening James, Teresa, Michael and I agree to jointly fund a bright young Oxford graduate named Daniel Hannan* to act as our group research assistant. We further agree that when new Clause 75 is put to the House we should allow our group members a free vote, the reality being that the pressure that will be put upon them to support the Government will be so intense that any attempt to dragoon them into doing otherwise will be impracticable. Before we part Michael Spicer lets a cat out of the bag by saying that it was he, together with Chief Whip Richard Ryder and '22 Chairman Sir Marcus Fox, who devised the peace formula which had so effectively defused what had promised to be an ugly situation at the full meeting of the '22 Committee on 11 March. Telling us this a month after the event is, in my book, not playing the game and first thing next morning I telephone Michael to say that he really must level with the rest of the team if we are to continue working together in harmony.

Thursday 15 April is another lost day as far as the Government is concerned. A first class row erupts in the Chamber when Michael Morris announces in what is for the Chair an unusually long statement that he is 'not minded to alter my previous decision not to select Amendment No. 27 for separate Division', the Government having in the meantime stated that they will accept New Clause 75 without division. For reasons not entirely unconnected with

*Daniel Hannan went on to become Secretary of the European Research Group set up by Michael Spicer, James and me in the wake of the passage of the Maastricht Bill and a Leader writer for the *Daily Telegraph* before being elected to the European Parliament in 1999 as one of 6 Conservative MEPs for the South East region.

tomorrow's rail strike a vote is called at 1845 to 'report progress', in other words to bring this day's debate to a close forthwith, and by a margin of 556 to 9 Members vote to adjourn and head for the railway termini whilst the trains are still running. A sad commentary upon the current political scene is the sight of a solitary John Major walking in at one end of the Chamber and out at the other without a single Member seeking to catch his eye or engage him in conversation. When not a soul, apparently, seeks to attract the attention of the Prime Minister of Great Britain and Northern Ireland times are definitely not as they should be. From the Conservative Party's point of view it is difficult to anticipate when again they will be. Whilst out canvassing for the County Council elections one old soldier tells me that he will vote Conservative but only because of the stand I have taken over Maastricht. To be fair, another constituent says that he'll vote for the candidate but never for me whilst Ben Boot, a senior and respected member of the NFU hierarchy in Shropshire and himself a Europhile, concedes that I have a lot of support.

When the House meets on Monday 19 April to resume the European Communities (Amendment) Bill debate the Chairman of Ways & Means says again that 'I have decided that I should not alter my decision on Amendment No. 27 but that further debate on the social protocol, which the Government is to have, should be led by New Clause 74, with which New Clause 75 will be linked' to which John Cunningham (Lab. Copeland), leading for the official Opposition, says that he does '*not regard New Clause 74 as an alternative to Amendment No. 27*'. This is the nub of the ongoing controversy – the Opposition want the Social Chapter and the opportunity of a vote to reinstate it into the Treaty; the Government don't want the Social Chapter but neither do they want a vote which they risk losing because they do want the Treaty and we, the rebels, don't want the Treaty but neither do we want the Social Chapter any more than we want a Labour Government.

The business started on Monday 19th ends at 1.13 a.m. on Tuesday 20th but not before Teddy Taylor and Bill Cash have divided the House on Amendment 57 to omit Article 201,* Amendment 225 to omit '*the Protocol on the transition to the Third Stage of Economic and Monetary Union*' and Amendment 268 to omit '*Article 12.1 of the Protocol on the Statute of the European System of Central Banks and of the European Central Bank*'. Although not quite the last ditch the motion which then follows that Clause 1 'should stand part of the Bill' marks an important stage in the Bill's progress with far fewer opportunities for dissent or amendment to follow. James, Michael and I agree that we must now try to motivate their Lordships to continue the battle 'in another place'.

Although the end of the Maastricht business in the Commons is in sight

---

*The effect of Teddy Taylor's amendment would have been to starve the EU of funds by deleting 'the budget shall be financed wholly from our own resources' from the text of the treaty.

feelings are still running high as when Peggy Fenner (Medway) chides Bob Dunn for 'fraternising' with me. Although Bob has not yet voted with us he is anxious that I should know that he will be with us when it comes to a vote on the question of a Referendum on the Treaty.

Simmering discontent about Amendment 27 and the decision of the Chairman of Ways & Means not to allow a vote on it bubbles to the surface on 21 April when Tony Benn (Lab. Chesterfield) moves what is in effect a vote of confidence in the Chairman.*

After 3¼ hours of lively debate a Government Whip moves a closure motion after which the House proceeds to vote on Tony Benn's motion. The voting is 81 for the motion and 450, including 18 rebels, against. That business disposed of, the debate on Maastricht Bill amendments is resumed. The 22nd day's business eventually concludes at 2.20 a.m. the following morning, the Government having in the meantime obtained a healthy majority of 29 to suspend the 10 o'clock Rule. At 1.30 a.m. the Government move the closure motion and votes on New Clauses 10 and 12 standing in the name of Peter Shore (Lab. Bethnal Green & Stepney) and New Clause 49 in the name of Bryan Gould (Lab. Dagenham) ensue.

New Clause 49 which, if carried, would have the effect of obliging Government to put the Treaty to the electorate in the form of a Referendum, is the centre of interest and I am pleasantly surprised when the 120 Aye votes that I have forecast turn out to be 124, including 38 Conservatives. Those against a Referendum total 363 including Opposition Leader John Smith and 89 other Labour Members, a mere handful of Lib/Dems (5), 1 solitary Ulsterman, James Kilfedder (North Down) and 267 Conservatives. This effectively brings us to the end of the Committee Stage of this highly controversial Bill excepting only consideration of New Clauses 74 and 75.

With uncanny precision the Adjournment debate proposed by John Garrett (Norwich South) at the end of this day's business questions the use of the Royal Prerogative which, in all the circumstances, seems more than a little apposite. Under what is known as the Royal Prerogative the Government of the day can, amongst other things, make treaties with other nations without consulting Parliament in any way. That is not to say that a diligent Member of Parliament need be unaware of the treaties that have been entered into but the fact remains that Government are under absolutely no obligation to obtain the prior approval of the Houses of Parliament.

The only exception is that because they invariably impact upon existing domestic legislation the European treaties do have to be brought before

---

*'That this House regrets that the Chairman of Ways and Means, having selected Amendment 27...should then have decided, contrary to normal practice, not to permit a division to take place upon that amendment, thus denying the House an opportunity to reach a decision on an issue relating to the applicability of the Protocol on Social Policy, contained in the Maastricht Treaty, a protocol which Her Majesty's Government held to be so important that it sought and obtained a special opt-out from it for the United Kingdom.'

Parliament notwithstanding that any amendment to the agreed text will cause maximum embarrassment to the PM and his Foreign Secretary who will have already put their signatures to the treaty in question as though it was a 'done deal'. This is why Major has to get this wretched European Communities (Amendment) Bill through Parliament, without amendment, and why he is using every trick in the book to ensure that it emerges unscathed at the end of its Parliamentary passage. That being the case all eyes are now on the outcome of the divisions which must inevitably follow consideration of the two outstanding new clauses relating to the Social Chapter.

Whilst New Clauses 74 and 75 are put to the House on Thursday 22 April there are no divisions when the debate ends at 9.30 p.m. because the Government, as previously intimated, accepts that '*This Act shall come into force only when the House of Commons has come to a Resolution on a motion tabled by a Minister of the Crown considering the question of adopting the Protocol on Social Policy.*' During the course of the debate Foreign Secretary Douglas Hurd avers, in relation to the much vaunted Amendment 27, that 'its passage would not have prevented ratification of the Treaty' notwithstanding the fact that in February he had said the very opposite.

With the Government's acceptance of New Clause 74 in lieu of the New Clause 75 that has effectively superseded Amendment No. 27 the Committee Stage, after 23 Parliamentary days (not quite the same as calendar days owing to debates spilling over into the following day) finally ends and there will be a brief interlude before Report Stage commences on 4 May. That same evening John Major addresses a Positive Europe Group dinner in a West End hotel and John Gummer tells me that he will try to get the EC Council of Ministers to accelerate the decision on non-rotational set-aside because the Danes also want it and it will help the Danish Government to get a 'Yes' result in the re-run of their Maastricht referendum!

On St. George's Day, at the invitation of my colleague Iain Mills, I speak at the heart of England at a lunch organised by the Meriden Constituency Conservative Association. Slaying dragons is my theme – in this instance Regulatory overkill – and the questions which follow leave me in no doubt that the members present support me in my stand against European Union as indeed does a National Young Conservative gathering at Warwick Castle the following evening. The Young Conservatives are overwhelmingly and ecstatically on side and I feel sorry for the other Parliamentarian present, David Amess (Basildon), as he struggles to justify his own record but more particularly that of his boss, Michael Portillo, for whom he is acting as Parliamentary Private Secretary.

Earlier in the day I have told the AGM of the West Midlands group of Conservative Clubs that they presumably know my views on Maastricht but that they ought also to know that I believe in Queen and Country, the

Defence of the Realm, sound Money and the maintenance of Law and Order. The Secretary, John Corns, responds by saying that that is why he belongs to the Conservative Party and in short order I am elected President for the ensuing year.

Over breakfast on Sunday I tell my wife that I can't believe what is going on. Everywhere I have gone this weekend the audience have been overwhelmingly on my side, even to the extent that my views are perfectly reflected in the Leader in this morning's *Sunday Telegraph*. The Government, on the other hand, are seemingly hell bent on ratifying this deeply unpopular Treaty and Douglas Hurd is even today making statements to fuel the 'Yes' campaign in Denmark.

Whilst there is no formal Maastricht business in the House this week the battle continues. On Tuesday Bill Cash gets in at PMQs to put the record straight on Denmark. When I say how lucky he is to have been called he says 'not really' – he had tabled a Private Notice Question* and I am left thinking 'clever old Bill'.

Wednesday's meeting of the Fresh Start Group endorses the intention to seek a meeting with Madam Speaker to put pressure on her to allow a vote on Amendment 27 but not before we have taken time to consider developments in the light of the weekend speeches made by the PM and his Foreign Secretary. Those present spontaneously agree to support Bill Cash's Amendment 26 which is subsequently selected and Bill Walker's New Clause 9 which is not. By the end of the week 19 Members have signed Amendment 26 but 274 Members have signed the almost identical Labour Amendment No. 2, both of which will, to all intents and purposes, have the same effect as Committee Stage Amendment No. 27.

After dining in the Lords with Lord Pearson of Rannoch, Jessica Douglas-Home, Michael Spicer, James Cran and Toby Jessell, where it is agreed that we should hold a joint group dinner of sympathetic Peers and members of the Fresh Start Group, we repair to Speaker's House to talk about Amendment 27. Madam Speaker says that the decision relating to this amendment has been the most difficult that she has yet faced and anticipates that it may well be the most difficult one she ever faces.

Monday 3 May is a public holiday and though the House is not sitting it is business as usual. I talk to John Biffen on the telephone who wants to know how I read the situation. I tell him that it is my opinion that if Amendment 27 is put to the test the Government will accept rather than risk losing a high profile vote on the eve of the Newbury by-election not to mention the fillip it might give to the '*Nej*' vote in Denmark. John agrees with this analysis and, always the gentleman, seeks my permission to retail these views to the Editor

---

*A PNQ tabled before Noon on any Sitting Day on a subject that is both urgent and important can cause the Speaker to insist that the relevant Minister attends the Chamber to respond.

of the *Daily Telegraph*, Charles Moore, with whom he is dining this evening. My constituent Bill Cash comes down from Upton Cressett – 5$^1/_2$ miles as the crow flies but somewhat further by road – for coffee and a brief chat and we spend a useful 2$^1/_2$ hours going round the track on the eve of the Maastricht Bill Report Stage.

By 10 a.m. on Tuesday 4 May the opinion that I had expressed to John Biffen yesterday has become the received wisdom. At noon the Speaker publishes her selection of amendments which includes Amendment No. 2 (Amendment 27's successor). Meeting at 1500 that afternoon to consider the implication of the Speaker's selection the Fresh Start Group authorises Bill Cash to withdraw his New Clause 22 if it seems appropriate to do so in the light of Madam Speaker's opening statement. At 1555 the Speaker makes it clear that New Clause 22 and Amendment 2 are incompatible and meeting again at 1700, in the Cabinet Room behind the Speaker's chair, the group endorses Bill's decision to withdraw New Clause 22. By the time that Bill confirms that he has in fact withdrawn his new clause there is mounting press anticipation of a vote on Amendment 2 later tonight. Events take an unexpected turn when at 2100 Government Deputy Chief Whip Greg Knight (Derby North) proposes a deal. After due consideration we decide to accept the deal which is that in return for our not opposing the 10 o'clock suspension the Government will guarantee that consideration of Amendment 2 will not be reached tonight. This is a tactical victory as far as we are concerned because it ensures that instead of being debated and voted on in the dead of night the consideration of this critical amendment will be in peak time tomorrow afternoon.

By the time the Adjournment is reached at 0122 on Wednesday the daily newspapers have long since gone to press. The *Daily Telegraph*'s headline will be 'Major faces Euro Retreat or Defeat'. Everyone is on tenterhooks. Michael Spicer is jumping about like a bean and Roger Knapman is in a state of nervous excitement. Without a word to anyone Michael takes it upon himself to do a deal with the Government Whips whereby we will not oppose a closure motion. In the event the question of a closure never arises and shortly after 7 p.m. high drama changes to anti-climax when the Government accept Amendment No. 2 without division. Rather than 'defeat' the Government have chosen 'retreat' and by 8 p.m. the Report Stage is concluded without further ado.

As a final gesture I table Early Day Motion No. 1950* with the names of 21 colleagues in support. The following day I feel obliged to point out to John

---

*EDM No. 1950 states 'That this House asserts that ratification of the bilateral Treaty with the Russian Federation, laid before this House on 1st April, which requires that relations between the two countries be governed in particular by their commitments under CSCE documents, would be inconsistent with ratification of the Maastricht Treaty which requires Britain's external relations to be governed by the Common Foreign and Security Policy.'

Marshall (Hendon South) in his capacity as PPS to the Leader of the House, Tony Newton (Braintree), that my question about EDM No. 1950 at Business Questions was not flippant and that I did not therefore expect the Leader of the House to give me a flippant reply. When I subsequently encounter Tony Newton he is apologetic but in fairness I accept that had I given him advance notice of what I intended to say I might have got a better response.

Thursday 6 May is Polling Day in the English shires. It is also the day of the Newbury by-election and the House is on a 1-line Whip to debate the Royal Navy. Notwithstanding the fact that I am one of the very few Members to have actually served in the RN it is nearly 9 o'clock before I am called to speak and John Wilkinson, a regular contributor to Defence related debates, is kind enough to say that I spoke 'with the authority of someone who knows what he is talking about'. Dr John Reid (Lab. Motherwell North) winding up the debate for the Opposition, is equally complimentary but to say that I have been 'decorated for valour' is to rather exaggerate the significance of my being the holder of the Reserve Decoration.

The local elections and the high profile by-election in Newbury are the first opportunity that voters have had since last year's General Election to deliver their verdict on the way things are going. The results are unambiguous and the writing, as far as the Major administration is concerned, is clearly on the wall. At Newbury a Conservative majority of 12,357 is converted into a massive Lib/Dem majority of 22,055 and all over the country Conservative County Councillors are ousted, as indeed they are in Bridgnorth and Bishop's Castle in my own constituency.

Attending the AGM of the West Midlands Area Conservative Council at the weekend I am left in no doubt that many of the delegates feel that the Government is completely out of touch with popular feeling. Former Chairman Michael Price is very angry about it all and asks me 'where we go from here'. Sadly my response that 'our leaders will have to recognise that their policies are unacceptable' will prove to be so much wishful thinking.

The rest of the weekend is spent trying to kill off rumours, which appear to have started with Donald Macintyre of the *Independent on Sunday*, that I am allowing my name to go forward as a stalking horse when Major faces a possible reselection challenge as Party leader in the autumn. On Sunday, in an attempt to quash the rumours completely, I agree to be interviewed by BBC Radio 4's 'World This Weekend' programme. Mindful of the pitiful part that Sir Anthony Meyer played in the eventual demise of Margaret Thatcher, the role of stalking horse is one that has few attractions and even less chance of success. I conclude that this is a role for a maverick but not for me.

Before leaving for London on Monday I take a call from one of my 'saviours', Clem Shaw, who rings to say that every word of my address to the constituency AGM is now proving to be correct. That's as may be but, if I've learnt nothing else in the past six years, I've learnt that being right in politics is not necessarily the way to win and influence friends but, unlike my colleague Roger Knapman I am hardly disconsolate that the Whips are not speaking to us.

There is now talk of seeking judicial review regarding the Treaty but Bill Cash agrees that we must distance ourselves from this particular initiative which, it is felt, is more likely to succeed if it is not seen to be blatantly partisan.

The Fresh Start Group meeting on Tuesday 11 May is baying for blood but ironically fails to agree a common position in relation to the Government's Sea Fishing Licensing (Time at Sea) Order. The upshot of this is that there are a number of abstentions when the vote is called and whilst Fisheries has not yet achieved the prominence that it will eventually reach it is not, as far as I am concerned, the first, or by any means the last, occasion on which I fail to support the Conservative Party's adherence to collectivist policies. Once again James and I find ourselves discussing fears that Michael Spicer is all too anxious to do deals with the Government Whips. Concluding that he is after something we agree that we shall have to keep an eye on him.

There is good news on the home front this week. The new LCCA Treasurer, Charles Dickie, has made it plain that henceforth decisions will only be made by all the officers, acting collectively. This should prevent a repetition of the disgraceful shenanigans which occurred on and around the date of the AGM and make the President and Chairman understand that they cannot ever again act in such an arbitrary and high-handed manner.

On the eve of the Maastricht Bill's Third Reading the news from Denmark is not good – 56.8 per cent have voted *Ja* and 43.2 per cent *Nej*. Nevertheless there is an enthusiastic meeting of the Fresh Start Group which agrees to stick together, to battle on and to accept that this is only the end of the beginning. Never before have we had such a spontaneous and uplifting meeting – one that would have struck fear into the hearts of Government Whips had they been able to hear us and always assuming that Government Whips have hearts!

Canvassing support for a 'No' vote at Third Reading it is apparent that at least 40 colleagues, including one or two surprises, intend to vote against the Bill tomorrow. With any luck we might reach 50.

On the day in question (20 May) I start by making phone calls to a few of the 'wobblers' – Ken Baker is one of my targets but he is not giving anything away in terms of his voting intentions. On the other hand he does say that he has 'admired what you have done', that 'you've acted very honourably' and that 'I've put in a good word for you whenever I have had the opportunity' etc. The end result of this last minute canvassing is that by the time I leave home to go to the House I have received 41 pledges and in the event that is precisely what we poll when the vote is called later that evening. By now, of course, the official Opposition, which has been happy to vote with us to tease or discomfit the Government all through the Committee and Report Stages, has disappeared into the night and the Government carries the day. The voting is 292 for the Bill which includes 16 Lib/Dems, 4 Labour and 3 Plaid Cymru and 112 against which comprises 66 Labour diehards, including future Minister for Europe Peter Hain (Neath), 41 rebel Conservatives, 4 Ulstermen and 1 solitary Lib/Dem (Nick Harvey, Devon North).

Significantly the vote in favour of Third Reading is less than half of the total membership of the House of Commons (651) and 44 votes fewer than were recorded as being in favour of the Bill's Second Reading last year. Conversely the rebel vote has practically doubled from 22 at Second Reading to 41, taking the total 'No' vote from 91 at Second Reading to 112 today. There is no doubt as to who is winning the argument and although we have lost the vote all our people seem quite elated at the result which is in itself remarkable in the sense that whilst rebellions usually fizzle out this one most definitely hasn't. In point of fact our vote this evening is our best ever so we have the satisfaction of finishing the campaign with our heads held high and our position numerically stronger than when we embarked on this endeavour all those months ago.

With the exception of this evening only, the Vote Office have co-operated with James Cran and I by making the voting lists available to us as soon as the results of the various divisions have been announced. Immediate access to this information has enabled us to see who has or has not voted, how they have voted and more to the point, to gauge the prospects for the next vote. Sometimes we have been able to pore over the division lists and discuss tactics in the privacy of an office off the back stairs leading down to the East Cloisters. This office, although ostensibly allocated to the Deputy Chief Whip, appears to be unused or at least unoccupied whenever we have needed to use it. Doubtless it would have been kept under lock and key had the Whips been aware of the nefarious purpose for which it was being used but because of its situation off an unlit half-landing it is reasonable to suppose that our movements have gone undetected.

The House will have to return at some future date to the unfinished business of New Clause 74 but to all intents and purposes today marks the end of the Maastricht Bill's progress through the House of Commons. It now goes to the Lords for their consideration. When in due course the Bill returns from the Lords it will, in spite of our best efforts to persuade their Lordships to at least support an amendment to make the Treaty subject to a national referendum, emerge unscathed. In the meantime, on 24 May, 22 Fresh Starters, 14 Peers and Jessica Douglas-Home dine together at the St. Ermin's Hotel in an attempt to get a bandwagon rolling in the House of Lords. In spite of the Bill's huge constitutional importance the next few weeks will demonstrate that Conservative Peers have no stomach for challenging the recently re-elected Conservative Government although the appearance of the Government Chief Whip in the Lords, Lord Hesketh, as guest speaker at the LCCA Annual Dinner on 4 June indicates that there is more than a little sympathy within their ranks for what we have been trying to do. Without expressing outright support for my stance on Maastricht Lord Hesketh places great emphasis upon 'the privilege of speaking in the Ludlow constituency' and leaves the assembled company in little doubt as to where his own personal sympathies lie. Later that weekend I tell a branch luncheon party that the Conservative Government can no longer buy popularity because the money has effectively run out and that the best thing we can do now is to earn some respect by doing what the public recognises as necessary. Sadly, homilies of this nature are not what the Party hierarchy wish to hear – the death wish is upon them and nothing is apparently going to deflect them from the perilous course they have chosen.

A total lack of wind on 9 June means that the annual sailing race on the Thames between the Lords and Commons is little more than a drifting match and in spite of being the first Commons boat to cross the finishing line I am still too late to get back to the House in time to hear Norman Lamont make his resignation speech. Norman is not the first nor, I suspect, will he be the last to see a promising political career wrecked on the rocks of European integration but it seems self-evident that by putting ambition ahead of principle the danger of falling between two stools is ever present. Norman, it is widely believed, is far from being an enthusiastic supporter of Economic and Monetary Union and it is interesting to speculate how the course of history might have been changed these past twelve months had he and other ministerial colleagues, Neil Hamilton and Edward Leigh (Gainsborough & Horncastle) being cases in point, not to mention some of our more craven backbenchers, stood up for what they believe in against an administration which is leading the Conservative Party into political oblivion.

A lunchtime meeting with colleagues from both Houses presided over by Lord Rees-Mogg (*The Times* newspaper Editor 1967-81) assesses the current situation vis à vis progress of the Maastricht Bill in the House of Lords. Peers are interested to learn at first hand about the level of support for our cause as expressed in voting figures in the Commons. Later in the day (10 June) I chance upon Enoch Powell at the annual Ian Gow Memorial lecture who says that he thinks that we are doing exactly the right thing because, in his opinion, the European project is already starting to show signs of breaking up. Much as I should like to agree with Enoch I am mindful that in the commercial world companies continue to trade long after they are technically bankrupt and that the last people to accept that they are finished are those who are most deeply involved. The EC may be spiritually, morally and democratically bankrupt but sadly there are no signs that it will run out of money. On the contrary, as a consequence of the European Communities (Amendment) Bill now passing through Parliament there will have to be an European Communities (Finance) Bill in order to direct even more British taxpayers' money to the sink in Brussels. Already I know that I cannot and will not support such a measure but at this stage I have no means of knowing that it won't in fact come before the House for a further eighteen months.

On a not entirely unrelated subject I ask the PM at Question Time about the necessity for Ministers to be *'ruthless and arbitrary'* in the prosecution of the battle against regulatory overkill. This is the cue for John Major to say, *'It is not the first occasion in recent weeks that I have been invited to be ruthless and arbitrary.'* The unanswered question is at whom is his terse response directed – the rebels on his backbenches or those whose future in Government he is now weighing in the balance.

A mid-June reshuffle of Government Ministers sees John Gummer replaced as Agriculture Minister by Gillian Shephard (Norfolk South West). At our first backbench Agriculture Committee officers' meeting with the new Minister we whistle through the typed agenda that I have prepared in my capacity as Secretary of the group in a very businesslike fashion. This contrasts most favourably with Gummer's ploy of answering every question at such length that constructive dialogue becomes practically impossible. This technique is not unusual amongst politicians, it being generally easier to talk than to listen. The hallmark of this administration is that it simply refuses to listen but, post reshuffle and a more positive line from the PM, when I go home at the weekend I decide to take a more loyalist line. This does not go down at all well when I address the Alveley branch dinner dance on Friday night. On being made aware of the very real sense of anger that those present are feeling about our Government, I am cross with myself for having attempted to defend the indefensible and also conscious of the disappoint-ment that this must have caused to those who paid good money to hear something far more robust and sensible. Why I should put my own reputation and credibility on the line for such a crass administration is a question which I cannot answer. Hope springs eternal and on 29 June I meet the Chief Whip in yet another attempt to convey a few common sense views on current affairs.

Richard Ryder gives nothing away so that it is quite impossible to tell whether or not I have got through to him. Comparing notes with Bill Cash later in the day he tells me that he has it on the highest authority that the Government are seriously worried about being defeated in the final stage of the Maastricht Treaty Bill. It then transpires that Bill and Richard have lunched together and that Bill and I have covered much of the same ground in our separate conversations with him. What difference it will make remains to be seen but based upon past experience there are no grounds for optimism.

The focus is now on the important divisions that must inevitably be called before the House rises for the Summer recess and in this context I regret missing the opportunity to tell constituents at a Worfield branch supper party about the difficult decision that I am going to have to make before the end of this month. The following evening (9 July) I arrive to speak at a venue in the constituency of Paul Marland (Gloucestershire West) to find the Chairman of the Dymock branch in a state of nervous excitement. It transpires that earlier in the year another MP, one Hugh Dykes (Harrow East) had addressed a similar gathering and had been so rude and arrogant that the Chairman was fearful that I might be the same. Notwithstanding that Hugh Dykes is an arch integrationist he had apparently even succeeded in offending the Europhiles in the audience. The real bonus arising from this meeting is an interesting exchange of views with the only young person present. Having said that none of the political parties had anything to attract the younger voter he then went on to say that what he wanted to hear were politicians saying what they truly believed in as opposed to what they thought their audiences might like to hear. On that basis my young friend would then make up his own mind as to whether or not to support them. I couldn't agree more. For politicians to blame voter apathy for the current state of affairs is a travesty of the truth.

It is said that life is a search for the truth but often truth can be somewhat elusive as when I ask Defence Secretary Malcolm Rifkind (Edinburgh Pentlands) about plans to dispose of the four brand new and as yet unused Upholder class of submarines. He says that they are on the disposal list because Russian submarine activity is much reduced. Two days later, at a backbench Defence committee meeting, the First Sea Lord, Admiral of the Fleet Sir Julian Oswald, says, in answer to my specific question, that Russian submarine activity has not reduced. What Rifkind also tells me on 12 July is that the UK is obliged to furnish the Russians with certain classified information and that 'all we can do is to ask them to treat it as such and not to give it a wider distribution'. Who said that truth was stranger than fiction!

A surprising number of rebels are at 10 Downing Street on 13 July when my wife and I, together with our younger daughter Sarah, attend the PM's annual reception for Conservative Members, their wives and daughters under the age of 25. Rod Richards (Clwyd North West) takes the opportunity of telling me that he and others are very much of our way of thinking but with his foot on the promotion ladder as PPS to David Heathcoat-Amory that, sadly, is as far as it goes. He and the rest of the payroll know precisely what they will have to do when important motions are put to the House in ten days time – toe the Party line or else! For the rest of us the decision is going to be much more difficult – voting For something that we are intrinsically opposed to in order to prevent something we like even less or Against our own

Government at the risk of getting the worst of all worlds i.e. a Labour Government and the Treaty of European Union in spades.

As the day of decision looms Budgie advises me not to canvass John Biffen, saying that 'he will have thought it through and come to a conclusion in his own way'. That, in reality, is what we must all do because, as previously agreed, it is a forlorn hope that our group members are going to accept a Whip when the stakes are so high and the circumstances of each individual so different. When on the morning of the day in question, 22 July, Roger Knapman telephones me from the House to say that our people are being picked off by the Whips I politely suggest that it would be better if they simply kept out of the way rather than put themselves in the line of fire. Roger agrees and says that he will go home. Returning to the House later in the day he and I then spend all afternoon and evening nursing colleagues along and, figuratively speaking, rendering first-aid as colleagues emerge from meetings in the Whips' Office.

The motion standing in the name of the Prime Minister is *'That this House, in compliance with the requirements of Section 7 of the European Communities (Amendment) Act 1993, notes the policy of Her Majesty's Government on the adoption of the Protocol on Social Policy'* to which the Leader of the Opposition, John Smith, has tabled an amendment to leave out everything from 'That' to the end and insert: *'In the opinion of this House, Her Majesty's Government should not deposit the articles of Ratification of the Treaty of European Union with the Government of the Italian Republic until such time as it has given notification to the European Community that it intends to adopt the Agreement attached to the Protocol on Social Policy.'*

As the tension mounts it becomes increasingly apparent that what colleagues fear most is losing their jobs. I'm so taken aback and angry when Gillian Shephard says, 'You'll put us all on the dole, then what will we do?' that my reply is postponed to the next day when I tell her that her remark about putting us all on the dole is totally unacceptable and that instead of thinking about ourselves shouldn't we be putting the interests of the country first, not least because too many of our constituents already think that we are only in Parliament for what we can get out of it.

John Redwood and David Maclean, both Ministers of State at the Department of the Environment, tell me that we'll bring down the Government; Michael Jack, a Minister of State at the Home Office, also tries to talk to me but I can guess what he wants to say and tell him that I'm too busy trying to follow the debate. Assistant Government Whip Andrew Mackay (Berkshire East) eventually catches up with me in the Cloisters where I warn him that the Government will probably lose tonight's vote and that in those circumstances they need to think very carefully about how they word any subsequent Confidence Motion so that it is not made totally unacceptable to the rebels. At the end of this particular conversation I am left wondering why the Government have not used this technique before now. This is the first time since the beginning of the Maastricht debate that any of the Whips has even attempted to have any sort of rational dialogue, not that I'm sorry about that because if they had it would almost certainly have made it harder, not easier, to have remained so implacably opposed.

Even at this late stage in the proceedings there is still no indication as to which way the 9 Ulster Unionists will go but even if they all go over to the Government we can still win by 3 votes. In the event the Ulster Unionists do go over to the Government and the vote on the Labour amendment, which is put first, is tied with 317 for the Ayes and 317 for the Noes. On a free vote the Fresh Start Group has split down the middle with 15 voting in favour of the Labour amendment and 16 either abstaining or voting with the Government. In these almost unprecedented circumstances the Speaker announces that *'The numbers being equal, it is my duty to cast my vote. It is not the function of the Chair to create a majority on a policy issue where no majority exists amongst the rest of the House. In accordance with precedent, I therefore cast my vote with the Noes.'*

The House then proceeds to vote on the substantive motion which the Government carry with a bare majority of 8. The Government's majority is essentially the same 9 Fresh Starters who voted the ticket on the Labour amendment plus Warren Hawksley (Halesowen & Stourbridge) but less James Cran and Iain Duncan Smith. That Roger Knapman should have tried so hard to talk James Cran out of voting against the Labour amendment and then at the last minute joined him in the Government lobby is a huge disappointment. The three of us have come a long way together and the fact that we have finished up in different lobbies means that we have fallen at the final fence. We were favourites to win tonight but there is no disguising the fact that we lost and with it, the last opportunity to defeat the Treaty on European Union.

As soon as the result of the second division is announced the Prime Minister rises to say, 'On *a point of order, Madam Speaker. The House has not come to a resolution, as required by section 7 of the European Communities (Amendment) Act, and so the Act cannot come into force. We clearly cannot leave the matter there. Tonight's debate has shown that there is no majority in the House for the United Kingdom to join the social chapter; however, as we know, a majority of the House is in favour of ratifying the Maastricht Treaty. I therefore invite the Members of the Opposition parties who say that they support ratification, and that they respect the opinion of the House, to reconsider their position. We must resolve this issue; it cannot be allowed to fester any longer. I therefore give notice that the Government will invite the House to come to a resolution tomorrow in support of the Government's policy on the social chapter by tabling a motion of confidence in the following terms: that the House has confidence in the policy of Her Majesty's Government on the adoption of the Protocol on Social Policy.'*

The House meets at 0930 the following morning and, sitting on the green benches before the day's proceedings open with Prayers, I am got at by Patrick Cormack and Tony Durant (Reading West) who are mightily exercised that I will not support the Government in the vote of confidence. Lightbown wants to know how I am going to vote but, to the bitter end, I am determined to keep him guessing. These are the people who are giving away my country and I owe them precisely nothing.

After the front bench speeches at the beginning of the debate are concluded the Fresh Start Group convenes to take stock. In the light of the outcome of yesterday's cliff-hanger there is no stomach for opposing the vote of confidence and in any case, with the Ulster Unionists apparently bought off, the prospect of defeating the Government is at best tenuous. There is also an uncomfortable and somewhat embarrassing fact that each and every one of us was elected barely twelve months ago in the Conservative cause. The fact that the Government is now blatantly supporting policies which are entirely alien to its Conservative roots and traditions is something which rank and file Party members have yet to understand. It is therefore with heavy hearts that we choose to do the decent thing and live to fight another day. The Labour amendment *'That in the opinion of this House, Her Majesty's Government should not deposit the Articles of Ratification of the Treaty of European Union with the Government of the Italian Republic until such time as it has given notification to the European Community that it intends to adopt the Agreement attached to the Protocol on Social Policy'*, is defeated by 339 votes to 301 and the Government motion carried by the slightly larger margin of 339 votes to 299.

The House finally adjourns at 4.26 p.m. leaving me precious little time to get back to Shropshire to attend the LCCA cocktail party at Chyknell. Several of the guests are leaving or have already left by the time that I am able to get there which, after a 6.30 p.m. start, is hardly surprising. Two weeks later, at Burwarton Show, former South West Wolverhampton Conservative Association Chairman Ian Beddows tells me that the word is being put about that everybody left the party early in order to avoid meeting me. At the show itself there is massive support for my anti-Maastricht stance which rather confirms what Derek Bowden had said to me at the Ashford Carbonell branch function on 24 July – 'You've got some of the officers against you but I reckon 85 per cent of the others are on your side.'

After all the excitement and expenditure of nervous energy these past nine months the Summer recess comes as a godsend. Although we have failed in our objective to derail the Maastricht Treaty we have the satisfaction of knowing that we haven't missed a trick on the way and that our opposition has been at all times principled and in the finest tradition of British parliamentary democracy. Sadly the vast majority of the populace are little interested in the mundane details of international treaties – they leave that to their elected representatives – and the media have generally only been interested in our rebellion in so far as it might cause the Prime Minister to resign, the Government to fall, the Conservative Party to split etc. Any reporting of the very serious issues at stake has been minimal and to its lasting shame the Government itself has deliberately set out to obfuscate and deceive in the certain knowledge that had the truth been told the British people most certainly would not have approved. When, in the fullness of time, the people do realise what has been done in their name their retribution will be decisive and maybe, as far as the Conservative Party is concerned, terminal.

Returning to Westminster for the 'overspill' – the time between the Summer recess and the State Opening of the next session – I am accosted by Tony Durant who asks me if I will be supporting the Government from now on. By now well used to this sort of gibe I tell him that Europe is the only issue that we shall fall out about. At this stage I have no idea how big the fall-out when it comes is going to be nor even when it is likely to occur.

On a technicality Teddy Taylor manages to persuade the Speaker to allow a brief discussion of the European Economic Area (EEA) Bill to be included in the business of the House on 20 October. The Bill is due to complete all stages – 2nd Reading, Committee and 3rd Reading – tomorrow. One of its clauses affords EFTA (European Free Trade Area) nationals and companies equivalent treatment to that already given to EC nationals and companies. On the face of it this appears to be a relatively innocuous measure but I take the opportunity of pointing out that had the British people been consulted on another important matter affecting entry into this country thirty or forty years ago it is probable that we might have avoided one of the greatest difficulties that our society is currently experiencing. On one single day, with the connivance of all the political parties but without so much as a nod in the direction of the general public, Government will extend even wider the scope for foreign nationals to share the benefits of UK citizenship. Whether one likes it or not the fact remains that mass immigration and accession to what will henceforth be known as the European Union have fundamentally affected and changed the British way of life. In both instances the Executive has determined to give away that which was not theirs to give away in the first place and in both cases they have done so without any popular mandate from the people they are supposed to represent. I have little doubt that it will all end in tears.

Lightbown wants to know how I intend voting on the EEA Bill and whilst I tell him that I have no desire to pick another quarrel with the Government it is apparent that tonight's vote will be unopposed because the official Opposition is just as keen on the Bill as the Government. I do, however, take the opportunity of warning Lightbown that the European Communities (Finance) Bill, whenever it comes, is likely to be a sticking point and he undertakes to get me an appointment to see Ken Clarke, the new Chancellor of the Exchequer.* I also take the opportunity of telling Lightbown what I stand for, viz: Queen and Country, Defence of the Realm, sound Money and the protection of the Citizen and his Property. 'Oh yes,' he says, 'I heard what you had to say yesterday.'

The name of the game, as far as I am concerned, is consistency. Regardless of whether one is selling goods, services or political philosophies the prospective purchaser is far more likely to be interested in the product if it is invariably to the same standard. The same might be said of religion and it is in this spirit that I interest Michael Marshall, the Bishop in charge of the 'Evangelical Decade', in the proposition that whilst one can go into any Little Chef or Happy Eater anywhere in the country and purchase from an identical menu, nowhere can one go into church with any certainty of receiving a spiritual message. Indeed, in my experience, one is just as likely to have to listen to a political diatribe as to hear anything at all related to the Gospel. The bishop thinks that more of his kind ought to be hearing this message but somehow I doubt whether many of the clergy would find it acceptable as increasingly so many of them appear to be politicians *manqués*. In this context the attitude of the suffragan Bishop of Ludlow is instructive. His views on secular matters such as the siting of a Waste Transfer Site, the improvement of Road Safety on the A49 trunk road, the hazard of Organophosphate compounds used by farmers etc. are all well known but on moral issues such as abortion, divorce, homosexuality the church is strangely silent. Looked at in isolation this may not seem much to worry about but when, as legislators, we are hearing only one side of these contentious issues it makes it extremely difficult to hold the line against those whose panacea for all ills is greater liberalism and a more permissive society. Indeed the legislator might be forgiven for thinking that any concept of a moral or spiritual dimension to these matters was no longer of any relevance or importance.

When Parliament resumes, after the State Opening, the annual election of officers to the various backbench committees will be upon us and in anticipation of this a meeting of '92 Group members is held on 26 October. David Evans is keen to be nominated for election to the Executive of the '22 Committee and, if successful, will have to give up being PPS to his Minister,

---

*The meeting with Ken Clarke never transpired and when I retired from Parliament after fourteen years he was one of the very few Conservative Members that I had never engaged in conversation. Seizing what I thought was an opportunity to rectify this unfortunate situation I offered to buy Ken a drink when I spotted him at the bar of the Eastbourne hotel where the 'survivors' met for the so-called 'bonding session' after the cataclysmic 1997 General Election. Quick as a flash Ken parried my thrust and insisted on buying me a drink. Having bought the drink he passed it to me and without more ado turned his back on me to strike up an entirely fresh conversation with somebody else. Ken is well known for his Europhilia but like so many of his ilk does not like to be confronted by the facts. They advance their cause by making assertions which they simply cannot substantiate, hence Ken's reluctance to risk the possibility of engaging in a conversation which might just have alluded to the facts.

John Redwood. There is friction between the Chairman, George Gardiner, and Peter Hordern (Horsham) who is definitely 'not one of us'. George accuses Peter of activating his 'Progress Group' to put up a competing 'slate' against '92 candidates in retaliation to which Peter asks George if he intends to support the forthcoming EC Finance Bill! Another doubtful starter as far as our group is concerned is Ray Whitney (Wycombe) who is reported in the Press later in the week as organising the 'Loyalists' (for which read Lollards) to also oppose our nominations.

When the '92 Group was originally founded by James Cran's predecessor, Sir Patrick Wall, it was perhaps best known for its loyalty to and support for Margaret Thatcher. In those early days the big battles were about Trades Union reform and Privatisation. Now that the battleground is unquestionably Europe some of our members, Peter and Ray being cases in point, are becoming somewhat 'semi-detached' but that is, by the very nature of things, the way life tends to go in Parliament. One coalesces with certain colleagues on certain issues and as the business is disposed of the coalitions thus formed disband as colleagues move on to other issues.

At this time one such issue is the concern that colleagues have about our Government's policy on defence. I and others are happy to put our signatures to a letter on this subject drafted by Nick Bonsor (Upminster). This is on the clear understanding that the letter will remain private but unfortunately, as a result of somebody leaving a copy of it in one of the House of Commons' photocopiers, I get a phone call from the BBC at 0035 the following morning and headlines in the *Shropshire Star*: 'Gill joins Tory rebels on Defence', later in the day. On occasions such as this one can never be absolutely sure that the offending letter wasn't left in the photocopier deliberately thus almost guaranteeing that it would receive the 'oxygen of publicity'. On the other hand the colleague who was careless enough to leave his Bank statement in the photocopier must be relieved that the size of his overdraft remains, to this day, a secret between just the two of us!

As we move into November interest in the backbench elections is mounting and Roger Knapman, in his Mr Fixit mode, arranges a meeting between James Cran, Roger and I and Messrs. Boyson, Dunn, Gardiner, Pawsey and Townend. The 'famous five', having read reports in this morning's *Daily Telegraph* and *Times* newspapers that right-wing Members are being targeted, are seriously worried about their chances of being re-elected to the executive of the '22 Committee and are desperate for us to activate the Fresh Start Group Whip in their favour. The irony of this meeting is that it comes within twenty-four hours of the anniversary of their decision to accept John Major's blandishments instead of voting with us to reject the Maastricht Treaty Paving motion. Other colleagues who are seen to be 'putting themselves about' are Michael Portillo and John Redwood but clearly their interest is on a higher plane than the purely routine election of officers to backbench committees. The impression that they may not be entirely wasting their time is rather confirmed when John Hannan (Exeter) features on the BBC 'Today' programme saying that things are not looking too good for John Major and the Conservative Party. John's comments fairly accurately reflect Tea Room opinion and one can't help speculating that if this is what we in the House are thinking then whatever are our supporters and the country in general thinking? James Clappison (Hertsmere) confides that he wishes that he had voted with us on Europe – 'You were right but I will have to live with this on my conscience for the rest of time.' John Biffen's opinion is that this is a Government that has lost all authority and that after barely eighteen months into its 5-year term.

Contrary to expectations the centre-right are highly successful in the backbench committee elections notwithstanding that George Gardiner loses his place on the '22 Executive to David Evans. Paul Marland keeps the Chairmanship of the Agriculture Committee, Bill Walker gets the chair of the Aviation Committee, John Townend hangs on to the Finance Committee and John Wilkinson wins the Defence Committee chairmanship. Hopefully this 'grand slam' by the centre Right will send a clear message to 'the bunker' as to where the true centre of gravity within the Parliamentary party lies.

Meanwhile a meeting in Bob Dunn's room on 7 December to discuss the expulsion of turncoats from the '92 Committee concludes that Ray Whitney is the prime candidate but that there is insufficient evidence to expel Peter Hordern and Jim Spicer (Dorset West) at the same time.

Back in Shropshire a highly successful LCCA Area lunch at Bishop's Castle is only spoiled by the Area Chairman's determination to open up old wounds on Europe. Having heard me address the audience Alan Screen's plant says that he wishes to withdraw his question but nothing daunted Alan tells the assembled company of one hundred or more what it was that Mr X had been going to ask! I am obliged to respond with both barrels because I don't take kindly to troublemakers, nor to planted questions.

CHAPTER ELEVEN

1994

...a huge tactical error

TRAVELLING BACK to London at the beginning of the new sitting I find myself on the same train as my colleague John Biffen. He is of the opinion that Major is finished and goes on to say that he suspects that *The Times* newspaper has made up its mind to hasten the process. As far as we are concerned he agrees that having taken such an obdurate stand against Maastricht it is best left to others to kick the table over. Viewed from the Wolverhampton to Euston Intercity that Monday afternoon in January (10th) we could hardly have anticipated that Major would struggle on for a further 3½ years dragging the Conservative Party down to depths last plumbed in 1906.

In the voting Lobby next day I am somewhat surprised when Major himself bears down on me to wish me a Happy New Year and asks whether I am going to be voting with him this year. When I answer 'Yes' he says, 'That is the best New Year message I could wish for.' Seizing the opportunity presented by this entirely unexpected encounter I venture to offer the PM some advice. Dogged as he is by scandals surrounding the private lives of Government Ministers I venture to suggest that instead of trying to defend the likes of Michael Mates (he of Asil Nadir fame), David Mellor (and the actress) and Tim Yeo and his peccadillo it would be better for both the PM himself and the Conservative Party in general if he let it be known that any Minister causing either he or his Government this sort of embarrassment would, in future, be expected to have his or her resignation on the PM's desk by 9 o'clock the following morning and no questions asked. That would, at a stroke, obviate the necessity for the PM to have to get involved in wrangles as to whether the miscreant had acted honourably or dishonourably, honestly or dishonestly, morally or immorally etc. etc. – if he were to adopt a tougher line it just wouldn't be his problem. I conclude by telling him that we've been round this track too many times already this Parliament and that we can't afford any further repetition. What John Major made of that advice I shall never know but sadly by the time of the next General Election his administration will have been irredeemably branded as 'sleazy', with disastrous consequence.*

---

*Major's affair with Edwina Currie, revealed in September 2002, would perhaps explain his reluctance to take a stronger line.

It is perhaps symptomatic of the febrile atmosphere that when James Cran and I adopt our well-practised technique of sitting in the Lobbies, observing the scene, a surprising number of colleagues are apparently keen to talk to us, including Cabinet Minister Peter Lilley. Being invited to have a drink with Government Whip Sydney Chapman (Chipping Barnet) is a further indication that the ground is shifting. This time last year all attention was focused on the passage of the Treaty on European Union – now virtually the only topic of conversation is the question mark hanging over the Leadership.

Over dinner with David Evans on 18 January he tells me that his remarks to the '22 Executive about Tim Yeo had not been entirely appreciated but, notwithstanding that, he had been deputed to tell the PM a few home truths when the Executive met him last Thursday. David had weighed in by telling the PM that he appears weak and indecisive, fails to give leadership etc. but not before Geoffrey Johnson-Smith (Wealden) had congratulated the PM on this, that and the next thing! David and I agree, and so do many others, that Major is finished and we go on to talk about his former boss, John Redwood, as a possible successor – he's certainly bright enough.

There really is only one subject now – who succeeds John Major. Surprisingly, arch Eurosceptic Tony Marlow is clearly favouring arch Europhile Ken Clarke whilst closet Eurosceptics Neil Hamilton and Edward Leigh appear to be leaning in the direction of another arch Europhile, Michael Heseltine. Following his heart attack in Venice Hezza's physical fitness has been suspect but he assures John Biffen that 'I'm very well, I really am very well.' The old ambition to be Leader lives on!

On Friday 21 January I am scheduled to be guest speaker at the inaugural meeting of the Monmouthshire branch of the Freedom Association but the 'dirty tricks' department have been at work to stop the meeting going ahead. Long standing member of the Freedom Association Walter Sweeney (Vale of Glamorgan) has been leant on by the Conservative Party's Welsh Area Office not to attend and believes that the constituency agent acting for Roger Evans (Monmouth) is largely responsible for dissuading others from supporting the event. Word reaches me in the House that TFA Chairman Norris McWhirter is writing to the Party Chairman to protest but pending further evidence I decide not to confront either Party Chairman Norman Fowler or Chief Whip Richard Ryder. Things have come to a pretty pass when the Conservative Party has to devote so much time and energy to preventing its members from attending political meetings at which they might actually learn the truth.

On a more positive note Michael Spicer's guests at his Westminster home for dinner on 20 January, Nick Bonsor, James Cran, Alan Duncan, Bernard Jenkin, John Townend and I, agree to fund Daniel Hannan to develop our case in the run up to the next Inter-Governmental Conference in 1996 and to reach out to kindred spirits in other Parliaments.

In an attempt to sell him my ideas for Local Government – essentially divesting local authorities of the responsibility for Education and Social Services thereby cutting the umbilical cord that links them inexorably to central Government – I stand Local Government Minister David Curry (Skipton & Ripon) dinner in Mayfair. David agrees with much of what I have to say but half the problem, he says, is that they can't get a clear direction from the PM – he keeps shifting his ground! That figures because only this afternoon in the tearoom the PM has both disagreed and then agreed with me when I argued that an Independent Bank of England would achieve low inflation because, left to their own devices, they would treat their stock in trade, i.e. the currency, with the same care that other traders take to protect the value of their own stock in trade. Letting politicians use interest rates as an instrument of Government is not, in my opinion, the way to ensure sound money. What David tells me about the PM simply confirms what Rhodes Boyson has told me earlier in the day. Speaking as one ex-sailor to another he says that 'we are rudderless – the Government are inept and rotten (in the corrupt sense). All they can think of is hanging on to their jobs so as to pay the school fees.'

As interest in the leadership stakes increases Michael Spicer tries to interest James and I in the idea of putting Michael Howard forward but, not being persuaded that he is truly 'one of us', neither of us feels constrained to support this proposition. Clearly the runners and riders are being lined up but as to when and how the race will actually be started is anybody's guess – November is the usual time of year for dealing with these matters but that is a long way off. Whilst Michael Spicer is now in overdrive promoting Michael Howard others are busy advancing the interest of their own candidates. This turns out to be why I am invited to join George Gardiner for lunch at the Gran Paradiso. On 1 February George had led a deputation of the '92 Group to meet the PM but had apparently received short shrift and our lunch together is all about finding a successor to John Major. George's money is clearly on Michael Portillo but personally I have an open mind on this subject and haven't, for example, ruled out John Redwood as a possibility.

Out of the blue Lightbown says that he wants to talk to me about Local Government in reply to which I tell him that if he is serious I should be only too happy to oblige. Two days later the subject is debated in the Chamber and David Harris (St. Ives) is kind enough to say that my speech was 'as always, thought provoking'. For his part Lightbown says that he has found my papers on Local Government interesting but, as expected, is non-committal about the prospect of my ideas being adopted by Government.

During the course of a long conversation with Bill Cash at Upton Cresset at the weekend he expresses his concern about Michael Spicer's motives and also about the overtures which Ivan Lawrence is making to Government which may have the effect of splitting the Fresh Start Group. Bill has a point and on 8 February my patience with Michael Spicer is sorely tested at a meeting of the European Research Group* as indeed it is at a meeting of the Fresh Start Group which follows. Ivan Lawrence is still peddling the idea of making overtures to the Party Chairman and the European Election Manifesto Committee. After the meeting I tell him that he most definitely doesn't speak for me and that his initiative can only serve to weaken the group. James Cran and I corner Teresa Gorman and tell her not to convene any further meetings until there is really something to talk about. Any more meetings like today's will risk breaking the group up which may be exactly what the forces of darkness, working through Ivan and Michael Spicer, are trying to achieve. Subsequently Toby Jessel asks me what I thought about the meeting and goes on to say that 'he doesn't think that Ivan is up to mischief' but on the other hand the Boundary Commission is destroying his seat!

The following day I am warmly welcomed to a meeting with Michael Portillo in his office at the Treasury. In a surprisingly frank exchange of views Michael tells me, amongst other things, that in Cabinet Ken Clarke, Hezza and David Hunt (Wirral West) are for constant change whereas the PM is not. He says that the Left of the Party are trouble-making and that they have their candidate waiting in the wings. This is the one that I call the 'professional Managing Director' – one who goes from one company to another company, throwing everything into the air, but always taking care to leave before the jelly hits the fan.

Ken Clarke has been Secretary of State for Health, Secretary of State for Education & Science, Home Secretary and now Chancellor of the Exchequer. Successively he has alienated the doctors and nurses, the teachers and the police but soon he will be taking credit for a successful economic policy which, if the truth be told, is not his at all – it is in fact the one that the Government have had to adopt perforce in the aftermath of our unceremonious exit from the disastrous ERM.

Whether Michael Portillo is the man for the job remains to be seen. I tell him that for my money I want someone who will be radical and bold. Others, such as my colleague Charles Goodson-Wickes (Wimbledon), think that Michael Heseltine could be the person we're looking for on the basis that his hunger for power is stronger than his ideology. Charles is one of a growing number of colleagues who believe that there will be a change of Leader before the next election but when the opportunity presents itself next year it will be seen that a great deal of this seditious talk is just so much hot air and wishful thinking.

An appointment for Michael Spicer, James Cran and myself to meet

*The ERG was formed in the aftermath of the passage of the Maastricht Bill for the purpose of carrying out research in advance of the next IGC and to reach out to Euro realists in other EU countries.

Michael Howard is postponed to 23 February owing to difficulties in the House of Lords over the Police & Magistrates Courts Bill for which, as Home Secretary, he is responsible. We three repair to the Red Cow in Whitehall where Michael enthuses about the progress that he and Daniel Hannan are making with regard to politicians in other EC countries. Whether we shall be able to score any runs on this particular wicket is a moot point. Politicians elected in other countries on a party list system might well share our views privately but, in the circumstances where they must forever tip their caps to the political party that sponsors them rather than to the voters they purport to represent, it is perhaps a forlorn hope that they will make any waves against the prevailing trend. Under the British system the Member of Parliament is, in the final analysis, answerable to his constituents rather than the Party he stands for. That being the case I am anxious to ascertain whether Astley Abbots is the hotbed of Europhilia that it is claimed to be. Canvassing that village with the help of LCCA Vice Chairman Michael Wood, it is quite apparent that far from being opposed to my stance on European Union it is practically impossible to find anyone who disagrees with me.

On other issues I have to accept that I am in the minority as when, on 21 February, the House votes against capital punishment by 383 votes to 186 and in favour of lowering the age of consent for homosexuality by 427 votes to 162. That same day former Defence Secretary John Nott tells readers of the *Evening Standard* that current Foreign Secretary Douglas Hurd is the 'Weak Man of Europe'. Habitually seen wearing a full-length Loden overcoat one senses that Douglas Hurd would be equally content to adopt the 12 stars of Europe flag in place of the Union Jack and is only constrained from other blatant acts of Europhilia not by his own inclinations, but for fear of reaction from the backbenchers.

March opens with an invitation to join the Chief Whip for dinner in the Members' Dining Room. Extraordinarily there is no political discussion whatsoever at this particular dinner table but perhaps that is just as well because judged by his body language, Richard Ryder's nerves are in poor enough shape already. The following day I attempt to rectify the omission by telling the Chief Whip that, based upon my experience of whipping the 'rebels' on the Maastricht Bill, it is apparent that there are 50 Conservative Members of Parliament who are staunchly opposed to European Union with a further 80 undeclared fellow travellers. Against that there are fewer than 90 committed Integrationists and the balance of 130 will go whichever the wind is blowing. I suggest that because the figures in the country at large are even more decidedly anti-EU he would do well to bear this fact in mind when framing the manifesto for the European Parliament election later in the year. He thanks me for my comments but, once again, there is no dialogue.

On 5 February I had attended the Young Conservatives AGM in Southport where I had sat listening in wonderment to the utter hypocrisy of the otherwise excellent speeches made by Norman Fowler and Jeffrey Archer. Now it is time to warn David Willetts, in his capacity as PPS to the Party Chairman, that I shall hit the roof if there is any attempt to monkey about with the YCs (or any other Conservative youth groups for that matter) as a result of them having elected Adrian Lee and other members with sound Conservative views to be Chairman and office holders for the ensuing year. I am perhaps a little too frank with David in explaining why I think that it will be a complete waste of time talking to his boss, but based upon previous encounters with Norman Fowler I have concluded that he is unlikely to share my concerns.

A long conversation with Sir Jasper More's widow on Sunday 6 March leaves me seriously doubting whether we shall be able to speak to each other again. Three days later is the end of an era when news reaches me that Lady More has passed away, but not before signing David Hill's nomination to be President of the LCCA* in succession to Rosemary Hinwood. Having been an MP's wife for nineteen years Clare More was one of the few members of the LCCA who had any comprehension of the pressures of Parliamentary life or any understanding of the work involved. She has been a loyal friend and one that I shall greatly miss – not least at Election time when the hustings meetings in her local parish hall have always been packed to capacity.

Lunching as my guest at Simpson's in the Strand that day, journalist Simon Heffer is keen for the Fresh Start Group to prepare to field a stalking horse in the autumn – preferably announcing their intention to do so at 1 p.m. on the Friday of Conference week! He is very scathing about other Conservative MPs including, in particular, 'supposedly right wing' David Davis (Boothferry) who just happens to be sitting at another table nearby. At the conclusion of a very agreeable tête-à-tête Simon thanks me for lunch and also, more remarkably, for 'not lying to him'!

According to the size of their respective populations each EU member state is accorded a specific number of votes that they may cast in the various Councils of Ministers when matters are being decided by Qualified Majority Voting. A proposition has now emerged that means that the so-called 'Blocking Minority' is to be raised from 23 to 27. What this will mean in practice is that the UK, or any other country which objects to a specific proposal put to the Council of Ministers, will find it much more difficult to put together a coalition of member states to halt its progress. On 10 March the Fresh Start Group meets to discuss this latest piece of EU gerrymandering and resolves to send a message to Government, via the Executive of the 1922 Committee, to the effect that the proposal is totally unacceptable. We also give

---

*David Hill had previously served 1 year as President but declined to complete his full 3-year term in protest at the high-handed manner in which Lumpy had engineered the appointment of an Hon. Treasurer in 1988.

notice that we expect there to be an opportunity to discuss the matter further at next week's meeting of the full Committee.

Arriving late for Conservative MEP's Leader Christopher Prout's (Shropshire & Staffordshire) meeting with the backbench European Affairs committee I miss the excitement surrounding Norman Tebbitt's walkout. The question of the 'blocking minority' dilution is certainly hotting-up as evidenced by the midnight telephone call from the BBC's Emma Udwin seeking comments in advance of the 15 March 'Today' programme. Later that day the atmosphere in the House is electric pending the outcome of the Council of Ministers' meeting in Brussels. I explain to the Foreign Secretary's PPS, David Martin, that a compromise blocking minority of 25 will be no more acceptable than the proposed change to 27. Anything over 23 effectively precludes the UK and Denmark, plus one other small country, from being able to act as the blocking minority when and if circumstances demand it. After the vote at 10 o'clock David tells me that there is no decision and that Douglas Hurd is flying home. In the light of this latest twist in the European saga John Biffen appears to concede that there may after all be a leadership contest and says to keep a careful note of what goes on between 12 June and the end of July.

Earlier in the day I have attended a lunchtime meeting for visiting politicians organised by the European Research Group. The Spanish representative says that Maastricht is simply not an issue in Spain but the prospect of a formal Constitution most certainly is; the Portuguese representative says that it is quite impossible to express an anti-Maastricht point of view in their Parliament and the Norwegians, possible because of their non-involvement in Maastricht, are rather more woolly in their thinking although Norway's separation from Sweden at the beginning of the twentieth century is obviously still a potent factor in their overall outlook.

The following day (16 March) Douglas Hurd attends a special meeting of the European Affairs committee. Room 14 is as full as it would be for any meeting of the very much bigger '22 Committee but it soon becomes clear that the Foreign Secretary is almost certainly going to sell out completely, or at best compromise (on the question of the blocking minority) rather than risk postponement of European Union enlargement but, as Terence Higgins (Worthing) points out, not one of the Member States is opposed to enlargement anyway! The general consensus at a follow-on meeting organised by Bill Cash is that we should leave the running to others rather than be seen to act precipitately. That is not to say that we won't rattle the Whips' cage but, given that the level of opposition to this particular development appears to have a momentum all of its own, the necessity for us to take the lead, as at the time of Maastricht, is not quite so urgent.

Back in Shropshire we have a new Euro constituency Chairman who tries his best to persuade me to let my name be used in connection with the campaign for the forthcoming European Parliament election. I have absolutely no intention of endorsing the candidature of those that I regard as integrationists and tell Rupert Blum that the answer has to be 'No'! The fact that I have been invited to endorse the Conservative candidate in the first place is remarkable. It is indicative of the huge contradiction at the very heart of the Party's whole European policy. Those of us who have opposed European Union have been excoriated and vilified (and there's worse to come) but our endorsement is now being actively sought because it is all too apparent that our view is far more popular than that of the Government. In other words they want us to help Christopher Prout to get re-elected so that he and others of that ilk can continue to do their damnedest to liquidate both Eurorealist politicians in particular and Eurosceptic opinion in general. Such hypocrisy is breathtaking. When it suits them the Party is prepared to use us to enhance its electoral prospects but at all other times its prime concern is to bury us. Blum has better luck with my colleague in North Shropshire but it's going to take more than John Biffen's endorsement to save Christopher Prout from going down in June. Peter Tapsell (Lindsey East) tells me that he will go abroad for the duration of the European election – 'if I was at home how could I possibly vote for Newton Dunn?'!*

New Officers have taken over at 54 Broad Street, the Ludlow HQ of the LCCA. On 18 March, at a much less volatile AGM than last year, David Hill and Michael Wood have been elected unopposed to the position of President and Chairman respectively and Pam Twitchell has been elected Vice-Chairman by a large majority. The prospects, at least on the home front, now look set fair for the foreseeable future and David Amess (Basildon) is impressed when I tell him that already 360 tickets have been sold for the Constituency Dinner in May when his boss, Michael Portillo, is billed to appear as Guest Speaker. By the time the dinner is held on 13 May this number will have increased by a further third to little short of 500.

In Westminster the vexed question of the 'blocking minority' is still unresolved. David Martin tells me that matters at EU level have reached impasse – shorthand for saying that the Commission have not got their own way, yet – and that discussions will be resumed in Greece at the weekend. To the general public these subjects must seem somewhat arcane and so when Teresa Gorman congratulates me upon my 'lucid explanation of QMV and the blocking minority' on LBC radio I am naturally very flattered.

At Question Time on Tuesday 22 March John Major takes a robust stance in defence of British interests. On Thursday the 'Today' programme majors on the PM's meeting with members of the '22 Executive yesterday at which

---

*Bill Newton-Dunn, MEP for Lincolnshire 1979-94. Re-elected as Conservative MEP for East Midlands in 1999, Newton-Dunn defected to the Liberal/Democrats shortly afterwards.

Guest Speaker at LCCA Annual Dinner, Chief Secretary to the Treasury Michael Portillo, flanked by President David Hill, self and Chairman Michael Wood.

he sought to advance the case for a compromise on the 'blocking minority' and by Sunday there are reports of Douglas Hurd's capitulation. James Cran agrees that we should meet tomorrow to discuss this not entirely unexpected development but Michael Spicer seems to be much more laid back about it and opposed to taking any further action – we wonder why.

A Private Notice Question on Monday obliges Douglas Hurd to attend the House to address the burning question of QMV and its associated 'blocking minority'. There is intense speculation as to where we go from here – does the PM stand fast or does he go back to the position he took in the House last week? James and I agree that it would be best if he stuck to his guns and much of the evening is spent trying to get that message across to the Government Whips and the PM's PPS. Meanwhile Hezza is busy dining with Michael Spicer and Hezza's PPS, Richard Ottaway, is doing the business in the lobbies, including at least two attempts to beard James Cran. More in hope than in the expectation of winning I bet Iain Duncan Smith £1 that Major won't cave in but am not confident enough to raise the stakes to a bottle of champagne which, as things turn out, is just as well.

The next day I stand Paul Judge (ex-Premier Brands millionaire and, more recently, ex-head of Food from Britain) lunch in an endeavour to learn how the situation is viewed from Conservative Central office where Paul is

Director General. He agrees that the best decision that Major could make as far as the Party is concerned would be to reject the compromise on QMV but in the event he capitulates and I lose my bet.

Rather than sit in the Chamber when the House meets that afternoon I decide to sit in the Gallery so that I can study the reaction on the Government benches when the PM makes the statement announcing his decision – it is one of sullen acceptance with hardly anybody standing on our side to ask further questions. This makes it comparatively easy for Tony Marlow to catch the Speaker's eye whereupon he lobs a grenade into the proceedings by calling upon Major to resign.

Such is the mood amongst colleagues in the aftermath of this latest sell-out that when the Fresh Start Group meet later that afternoon there is no stomach to discuss either Major's craven capitulation or Tony Marlow's rather less craven reaction. Preferring to look to the future there are two schools of thought – either measured argument in the run-up to the next IGC in 1996 or, after the EP election on 9 June, direct action at every turn. In all the turmoil I almost forget to go to Michael Howard's room where Michael Howard himself, Michael Spicer and James Cran and I agree that, in the absence of any viable alternative, we have got to go on backing Major even though the harsh reality is that he's dead in the water.

When I vent my spleen on Major's PPS the following day Graham Bright defends his boss by saying that the sell-out was 'a Cabinet decision' and that in any case mine is 'a minority view'. He assures me that he really did pass on my views but says that 'unless we all get behind the PM now we'll all be swept away.' In response to that I suggest that the majority of the Cabinet would probably not be sorry if Major was swept away and that if he is to survive he'd best stop taking so much notice of the Foreign Office and pay more attention to the views of his own backbenchers. As a loyal PPS Graham has no alternative but to take the line he does but, whether he realises it or not, the reality is that he's whistling in the wind. Major's stock is at an all-time low and nothing short of a miracle can revive it. The 64,000 dollar question is why is he so beholden to the corrupt and totally undemocratic European Union and its venal advocates at the expense of alienating his supporters and destroying his Party at home.

Roger Knapman invites me to Tufton Court where, over lunch, we discuss the merits of John Redwood as a potential future leader but bumping into him later in the afternoon Norman Lamont tells us that many right-wingers are already going over to Heseltine. On this sad and sorry note the House adjourns for Easter.

During the recess things have taken a turn for the worse in Bosnia and once again Douglas Hurd is obliged to come to the House on its first day back to answer a PNQ tabled by the Opposition. Gone are the days when Douglas

Hurd would congratulate me on the content of my speeches and he is somewhat irritated when I ask him on this occasion if he is perfectly satisfied that 'it is both prudent and appropriate to use NATO forces in an offensive role' bearing in mind that 'NATO was founded as a purely defensive organisation'.

During the course of a long chat John Biffen seems to accept that there might yet be a leadership contest and appears quite attracted to the idea of John Redwood as a possible alternative to Major. In the meantime James Cran has spoken to Redwood's new PPS, David Evennett (Erith & Crayford) as a result of which it is agreed that we should meet JR. The fact that James and I have taken to re-occupying the benches outside the Whips' Office is paying off and Nicholas Soames, for one, is curious to know what is going on. Lunching with George Gardiner the following day James and I learn very little other than that George is promoting Michael Portillo as a leadership candidate.

Chatting to Michael Portillo I tell him that I'm fed up with reading about Douglas Hurd appealing for Party unity when, for the duration, many of us have been so restrained in terms of talking to the press about divisive issues. Douglas Hurd's public appeals for unity simply serve to perpetuate the impression that the Party is riven with disunity. Michael agrees and rather illuminatingly says that Hurd's intentions are always in the same direction, by which I presume he means European integration.

When Douglas Hurd attends the European Affairs Committee on 19 April, with Party Chairman Norman Fowler in tow, I take the opportunity of telling him that all his speeches about the need for Party unity simply confirm the impression in people's minds that we are deeply divided. To his credit Norman Fowler gives the meeting an undertaking to remove such references from the future script. This won't create unity where it truly doesn't exist but at least it will stop our people from crying stinking fish. Douglas Hurd is the real nigger in the woodpile – wherever we look, whether it be Bosnia, Hong Kong, Europe, South Africa or the old USSR the Foreign Office is getting it wrong. Perhaps his pronouncements on Party unity are simply a diversionary tactic. Whether they are or not is almost immaterial because all interest is firmly centred on the Leader and the prospect of him being put out to grass. Against this background Roger Knapman is more than a little excited to receive a letter from No. 10 inviting him to tea and a chat with the PM in seven days time. He is also amused when, upon going into the Marquess of Granby to buy a cigar, he is accosted by not one but three journalists who ask him if he is looking for Mr Cran and Mr Gill!

Attending the Institute of Directors Annual Conference at the Albert Hall I am amazed to hear the Lord Young of Graffham, speaking in his capacity as President, make an unprecedented outburst against the EC. This is a significant breakthrough and when I am subsequently befriended by another IoD Council member who announces himself thrilled to be meeting an MP who is both interested in industry and opposed to the EU I can hardly believe my ears. Up until this moment one has sensed that being sceptical about Europe was not a very respectable thing to be but the dam may be about to burst.

On 27 April His Excellency Professor Sergei Komisarenko, the Ukranian Ambassador, suggests to the backbench Defence Committee that 'maybe nobody now needs nuclear weapons'. He is somewhat taken aback when I ask him why we should believe that the 'former' USSR is now peaceable and benign given that the leaders are still the same people as held office prior to *Perestroika*, not least in Georgia where the former USSR Foreign Secretary, Edwarde Schevenardze, is installed as President. I also seek his comments about the situation in which former USSR republics who are not signatories to the Nuclear Proliferation Treaties are being used as conduits for passing on nuclear technology to Iran. I ask these questions not in the expectation of obtaining satisfactory answers but as a means of trying to interest colleagues in the proposition that *Glasnost* and *Perestroika* are not what they purport to be but rather that they are part of the ongoing Soviet dialectic which, with its long term objective of destroying the nation states, has a ready accomplice in the shape of the EU.

Monday 2 May is a Bank Holiday but I wake to the news that ex-Cabinet Minister and European Commissioner Leon Brittan has made some highly provocative remarks about the Single Currency. These are answered by Treasury Chief Secretary Michael Portillo, who, in turn, is roundly condemned by Agriculture Minister Gillian Shephard who chirrups on about Party unity. Treasury Financial Secretary Stephen Dorrell (Loughborough) joins the fray and David Evans caps it all by calling on Major to sack the Chancellor of the Duchy of Lancaster, William Waldegrave (Bristol West), Education Secretary John Patten (Oxford West & Abingdon) and Environment Secretary John Gummer. What a shambles – but to hear folk talk one could be forgiven for thinking that all the trouble in the Party was being caused by the backbench opponents of European Union.

Back in the House the following day I am pleased to exploit an opportunity to pull the Party Chairman's leg about Party unity in front of Gillian Shephard and am delighted when David Martin goes out of his way to say that I was right in the advice that I had previously given his boss (Douglas Hurd) on this very subject.

James and I spend time trying to analyse the events of the weekend but with so many axes now being ground it is difficult to come to any firm conclusion. Dining in the Members' Dining Room in the company of former Party Chairman Cecil Parkinson and Gerard Vaughan (Reading East), Michael Portillo insists on champagne all round to celebrate the 15th anniversary of

Margaret Thatcher's historic election victory in 1979. Whether this is an appropriate toast given the way in which the Thatcher legacy is now being squandered is a moot point, but with over four hundred people coming to hear Michael at the LCCA Annual Dinner next week all is not yet lost.

At today's meeting of the backbench Finance Committee Chancellor Ken Clarke, another contender for the crown, is careful to avoid being drawn on the question of the Single Currency but few of us are under any illusion as to where he really stands on this highly controversial and deeply divisive issue.

On 12 May fate gives the kaleidoscope another shake when the well respected Leader of the Opposition, John Smith, dies. Political hostilities are suspended until after the funeral on 20 May even to the extent that, at his adoption meeting, Christopher Prout declines to attack the Labour Party notwithstanding that the European Parliament election is barely three weeks ahead.

Amongst other Defence related issues I have been trying to interest colleagues in the existence of a whole raft of bilateral treaties between Russia and Western European countries whereby obligations are extant which effectively preclude individual nations from taking certain actions without first consulting Russia. Charles Goodson-Wickes, himself a Gulf War veteran, tells me that when he raised this question at NATO headquarters in Belgium, on a visit with the All-Party Defence Group, it caused quite a stir. The very next day Captain Richard Sharpe OBE RN (retired), Editor of *Jane's Fighting Ships*, in an address to the backbench Defence Committee recounts how, at the end of the Falklands campaign, a very senior civil servant at the Ministry of Defence had said that he 'very much hoped that Britain would never be in a position to do that again'! Understandably Defence is not an issue that constituents, particularly in peacetime, seem to concern themselves about but the fear that we are allowing the prospect of the so-called peace dividend to cloud our judgement and blind us to the realities of the post Cold War era is nonetheless real.

Before May is out James Cran, Michael Spicer and I have concluded that rather than be party to any attempt to oust Major it would be altogether more satisfactory if the Foreign Secretary were to be given the opportunity to 'spend more time with his family'. With such a committed integrationist in that key role it seems increasingly unlikely that we are going to be able to prevent the European juggernaut from completely crushing us. At an ERG lunch hosted by Chris Miller at his company's offices in Victoria Street on 24 May our guest is the Chief Whip. I take the opportunity of asking him to consider the thought that the Cabinet is unrepresentative of the Parliamentary Party and even more so of the Party at large. Richard Ryder retaliates by saying that Ministers are picked for their ability, not their views. I am then obliged to say to him that I picked my words very carefully and that whilst they were in no way personal the hazard is that if we carry on as we are doing then it will inevitably go very badly for us at the next General Election. At this point he begins to calm down but our exchange is yet further evidence that this administration cannot take criticism and, regardless of how constructive the criticism may be, regards it all as so much troublemaking.

After lunch there is a meeting of the Fresh Start Group to discuss tactics post the EP election on 9 June. Teresa Gorman says that she will simply say 'Bye Bye Brussels,' even if that makes her a crackpot. Dick Body takes the same line. Bill Walker says that the only reason that he will seek re-election is to defeat all this EU nonsense which is leading to the break up of the UK. Bill Cash says that he will provide briefs for Question Times so that we can all ask questions that Ministers will have great difficulty in answering but, as James Cran says, the reality is that this election is going to be a referendum on John Major's premiership rather than one fought on the European issues themselves. Meanwhile the question as to who, within Cabinet, is fighting the good fight remains unanswered – John Redwood has told one group of colleagues that he is virtually the only Cabinet Minister resisting further European legislation but James Cran says that he's heard that Michael Howard is the lone ranger consistently standing up for our point of view. The question remains – who to believe!

The 9 June is a bad day for Conservatives. Polling more than a million votes fewer than in 1989 the Party's representation in the European Parliament is cut from 32 out of 81 seats to 18 out of 87. The major beneficiaries of the Conservative collapse are the Labour Party with 62 seats (up from 45) and the Lib/Dems whose share of the votes cast is up from 6 per cent to 16 per cent giving them, for the first time, a small representation of 2.

Meeting at breakfast on 14 June, James, Michael and I discuss the EP Election results in advance of this afternoon's Fresh Start Group at which John Biffen tells colleagues that 'this Government is finished' and that the best we can hope for is a spell in opposition to reform. Not that the Party hierarchy will want to recognise this fact but the reality is that whilst the total number of votes cast for Conservative candidates in EP elections is consistently going down the total number of votes for Labour is going up. The simple truth is that Conservatives on the one hand are becoming ever more reluctant to vote for what is increasingly seen to be a socialist concept whilst, on the other hand, Labour supporters are shedding their reluctance for that very same reason.

Two days later I am contacted by Shropshire Radio to see if I will comment on Norman Fowler's resignation as Party Chairman. At this stage the news is embargoed until 5 p.m. But when I ask Norman's PPS, David Willetts, to confirm it he tells me that this is the first he knows about it! If this is typical of the level of communication amongst the upper echelons of the Party I can only conclude that we are in even deeper trouble than I thought. In similar vein the '22 Committee that afternoon (16 June) closes in record time without so much as a mention of the EP election results or the subsequent resignation of the Party Chairman. The tactic now seems to be to hear no evil, see no evil, know no evil – the whole Party seems to have gone into a mulch and one is almost envious of John Biffen who tells me that he has already informed the Chief Whip that he won't be seeking re-election.

The gloom that has descended is hardly lifted when the Chief Whip is guest speaker at the '92 Committee dinner held on 29 June. Richard Ryder fails to impress. He starts well and I get quite excited at the prospect of learning what he really believes in and, more to the point, where he thinks we are going, but I wait in vain. He concludes his address by threatening hell-fire and damnation if we fail to support the forthcoming Finance Bill. Walking back to the House with Angela Rumbold (Mitcham & Morden) I am amazed at the ferocity of her dissatisfaction with what we have both just heard. Surely as a Vice Chairman of the Party she is in a highly advantageous position to get her view across, I say. 'Not a bit of it – they just will not listen.' It is now more apparent than ever that the top brass have learnt absolutely nothing as a result of the past eighteen months and one despairs that they ever will.

The following evening the Duchess of Billericay, alias Teresa Gorman, entertains James Cran, Michael Spicer, Iain Duncan Smith and I to supper. Michael and James are serving notice that they are unlikely to oppose the EC Finance Bill and I get the impression that our hostess is more than a little disappointed that there is no real enthusiasm for her suggestion to produce a pamphlet articulating our views.* At the end of the evening's discussion Michael and James leave together in one direction and Iain and I in another. This gives me the opportunity to talk alone to a most unhappy and disillusioned Duncan Smith who can scarcely credit the way things are going and is deeply depressed about what he has, by entering Parliament, let himself in for. Standing at the intersection of Smith Square and Lord North Street trying to lift my young colleague's spirits on that June evening neither of us could have foretold that within seven years he would be challenging for the leadership of the Party of which we both despair.

Notwithstanding the fact that 2 July is my wedding anniversary I toil up to Blackpool to hear the PM address the centenary AGM of the Conservative Clubs Association. His long speech is more like an Auditor's report than a Leader's exhortation but nonetheless it appears to go down quite well with the rank and file. The local MP, Harold Elletson (Blackpool North), is in attendance and sitting next to him at lunch I soon come to recognise yet another disillusioned Member of the 1992 intake. Whilst Harold and I

---

*Acting on our own initiative Teresa and I will draft the text of a pamphlet entitled *Not A Penny More* during the Summer recess with a view to publishing it when Parliament re-assembles in the autumn.

establish quite a lot of common ground I am not a Heseltine fan and therefore cannot share his belief that selective state intervention is necessary and desirable. Where we are agreed is that there is nothing inspirational in what we have just heard from John Major.

Bill Cash telephones on Sunday to ask if I would like to join a group of colleagues to meet Margaret Thatcher tomorrow but not before both of us have heard James Cran make a most extraordinary recantation on Radio 4. When we meet on Monday Bill tells me that a number of our colleagues are extremely angry about James' outburst. Moving on to other things Bill says that he, like me, is frustrated by not knowing how we can rid ourselves of the 'pygmies' in charge of our Party's destiny but the essential difference between us is that he sees Major as a prime target rather than Hurd. We agree that all the fuss about Major vetoing former Belgian Prime Minister Jean-Luc Deheane for the EC Presidency is of no lasting significance. It is not difficult to think of other areas in which the use of the British veto would have been so much more satisfactory.

Payroll paranoia manifests itself again on 5 July when I join Barry Field (Isle of Wight), David Evans and Roger Knapman for supper at the far end of the Terrace. Barry says that, having regard to our respective reputations, it won't be long before we're joined by a Government Whip. Sure enough, within ten minutes we're joined by Irvine Patnick* (Sheffield Hallam) who sits himself down beside us. The Whips pride themselves on knowing everything about everybody but frankly there are more subtle ways of gleaning information than by intruding on private conversations.

Another Whip, my constituency neighbour, Derek Conway, tells me that my constituents Viscount Boyne and Simon Kenyon-Slaney are in line to succeed Sir John Dugdale as Shropshire's Lord Lieutenant. He also advises me that if I have anything to say on the matter, which I most certainly do, I'd best get my blow in soon because the decision is likely to be made within the next two weeks. Derek is livid about not being consulted and I'm not best pleased myself, particularly when he tells me that our County's NFU Secretary has been. Also relating to the Home Front I learn from a different source that Sonny Twitchell is serving a writ on Helen Mound† for libelling his wife Pam, our recently elected Constituency Vice Chairman.

---

*Irvine Patnick was a casualty of the 1994 re-shuffle at the end of July and returned to the backbenches as Sir Irvine Patnick.

†Helen Mound had been appointed LCCA Office Manager under Jackie Williams' chairmanship. She came highly recommended by Michael Mates as an efficient and conscientious worker dedicated to the cause although which cause that was didn't become altogether clear until some time later. The Europhile Michael Mates had gone out of his way to speak to me, for the first time ever, to commend Helen Mound to me for the vacant position at 54 Broad Street but whilst there is insufficient evidence to suggest that this person was definitely a plant her employment was terminated at the insistence of the incoming Association Chairman, Michael Wood, despite howls of protest from all the usual suspects. How the Member for Hampshire East knew of the vacancy in Ludlow is not recorded.

At 10 o'clock on 6 July Nick Budgen makes an objection regarding the EU (Accession) Bill which he and Bill Cash, Michael Spicer and I then follow up in the lobbies with Tony Newton, in his capacity as Leader of the House. We tell him that one day to debate this important Bill relating to the accession to the EU of Austria, Finland, Norway and Sweden is simply not enough, that to restrict debate in this way will be inflammatory and that all he will do by digging his heels in on this matter is antagonise his own backbenchers. To our surprise the point is conceded and next week the House will have two days to debate all stages of a Bill that Government need to carry in conformity with the corresponding Treaty obligations. The fact that Norway will have the good sense to reject the Treaty when it is subsequently put to a referendum of the Norwegian people is not a factor that we can at this stage anticipate.

When the PM addresses the '22 Committee on 7 July it is essentially the same speech as the one I heard him make in Blackpool last Saturday – once again he fails to inspire. Earlier in the day I had tried to waylay him on his way back to his office after PM's Question Time but unfortunately his PPS, Graham Bright, just managed to catch up with me in time to stop my gallop. Graham is just as reluctant to let me speak directly to the PM as Chairman Marcus Fox is reluctant for me to speak at the '22 Committee where I want to say that the Party's difficulties are as much to do with bad management – man management, day to day management and departmental management – as anything else.

Back in the constituency for the weekend I make a loyal speech at the LCCA annual Cocktail Party on Friday evening but with all the antis on parade I might just as well have saved my breath. That there is trouble on the line, again, is confirmed when on Sunday, John Morgan, the longest serving member of the LCCA Executive, tells me, amongst other things, that Kenyon-Slaney will be calling for Michael Wood's resignation as Association Chairman. John says that the President and Vice Chairman will also have to go. Later in the day our President David Hill, Chairman Michael Wood and I put our heads together to decide how best to deal with this latest seditious nonsense. On Monday the Vice Chairman receives a letter from Kenyon-Slaney expressing concern about the sacking of Helen Mound and calling for the Chairman's resignation. Not untypically the last person to hear about these machinations is the Chairman who might reasonably have expected to receive a copy of the letter himself.

With the greatest of difficulty I manage to make an intervention on a reluctant Douglas Hurd when he rises on 11 July to move that the EU (Accession) Bill be read a second time. He clearly doesn't relish my question about the reported remarks of the German ambassador in Moscow to the effect that national sovereignty is becoming irrelevant and meaningless. His reply is discourteous in the extreme – 'I feel sad for my hon. Friend the

Member for Ludlow after his intervention.' The Foreign Secretary's feelings are the least of my concerns – my job as a backbencher is to hold the Government to account for its actions and asking awkward questions is a crucial part of that process.

When I tell Lightbown that I shall not be voting with the Government on this Bill tonight he retorts, 'Don't bother to tell me what you're going to do, just go ahead and do what you like … it's people like you that are causing our Government so much difficulty.' That is debatable since it is not I, but Government itself, which has chosen to pursue this highly controversial and deeply unconservative course. In any case, I have no intention of bandying words with Lightbown in public outside Members' Entrance where to draw attention to our latest little spat he is raising his voice until he's almost shouting.

On 12 July the Honours/Appointments Secretary at No. 10 telephones in response to my letter to the Chief Whip about the choice of Lord Lieutenant. Reluctantly John Holroyd tells me that the names in the frame are Heber-Percy, Lady Forester, Lord Boyne and Kenyon-Slaney, one of which is, as far as I am concerned, totally unacceptable. Later in the day I am approached by Murdo Maclean,* who wants to talk to me about the same subject. I try to impress upon him that I am very serious in my objection to one of the candidates but not until the Chief Whip assures me that I am not going to be disappointed when the announcement is finally made do I have any confidence that my representations have borne fruit.

In a similar vein Health Minister Brian Mawhinney (Peterborough) assures me, yet again, that I will not be disappointed with the outcome of the review which has been conducted into the affairs of the Health Education Authority. It is now four months since I remonstrated with the Baroness Cumberlege, Parliamentary Under Secretary of State for Health, about the HEA's 'Best Sex Guide' telling her that it is an unacceptable use of taxpayers' money, that it sends entirely the wrong message to our supporters and that the people responsible for such filth should be disciplined. I came away from that meeting depressed by the impression that the Baroness was either unwilling or unable to grasp the nettle, notwithstanding it being on the record in Hansard that the 'Best Sex Guide' is 'not something that she would want to find in her own home'. As an everyday example of the abject failure of Government Ministers to control what goes on in their respective departments this incident takes some beating. A recurring question in my mind is why do we have Ministers when repeatedly it is demonstrated that the people who are calling the shots are not the Ministers themselves but their departmental civil servants.

---

*Murdo Maclean, a civil servant appointed to act as a 'go-between' to facilitate the progress of Parliamentary business, is colloquially referred to as 'the usual channels'.

Playing Monopoly with € 'funny money' – Teresa Gorman, self, Teddy Taylor and James Cran.

Having had a go at James Cran for 'selling out', Nick Budgen then proceeds to express the opinion that my constituent Michael Lumsden is probably one of those people who never had the bottle to stand for Parliament himself but is always 'agin' the sitting Member. Lumpy is well known to several of my colleagues and barely twenty-four hours elapse before Warren Hawksley, having given me the low-down on my constituency Chairman, Jackie Williams, avers that Lumpy is ' trouble'. To the extent that Lumpy almost certainly put the skids under my predecessor Eric Cockeram, is reputed to have previously sought the de-selection of Sir Jasper More and is now, I suspect, doing his best to get rid of me, my colleagues are probably correct. In politics it is after all a truism to say that one's opponents sit opposite but one's enemies are behind one.

The Foreign Secretary is our guest at the ERG lunch on 14 July. Douglas Hurd starts by gratuitously insulting our hosts, Jim and Chris Miller, by saying that all businessmen want a single currency, makes no attempt to hide his ongoing contempt for those who take a contrary view to his own and finishes by saying, in answer to a question about the effect of these important matters upon the future of the Conservative Party, that this is for our group to answer rather than himself or the Government. Our meeting is a deeply unsatisfactory experience and after our Right Honourable guest has left Jim Miller speaks for us all when he says that 'with clowns like that none of us can succeed'.

On that rather sour note the Summer sitting ends. At the usual 'end of term' reception at No. 10 on 19 July the PM says, 'Perish the thought,' when I enquire as to whether I am amongst those for whom 'he would gladly buy a ticket on the new roller-coaster at Blackpool'. The following day he reshuffles his Government as a result of which the officers of the Agriculture backbench committee, Paul Marland (Gloucestershire West), John Greenway (Ryedale) and I wait in vain for Gillian Shephard at her MAFF office in Whitehall Place only to discover that she has been moved to Education. Another consequence of the reshuffle is that on 21 July David Davis (Boothferry) finds himself at the Despatch Box, speaking at very short notice for the Government in his new capacity as Minister for Europe. It is hardly a surprise that there is no advancement for Eurosceptic colleagues but what is surprising is the report from Michael Spicer that Defence Secretary Malcolm Rifkind has told him that he would resign from Government if it was ever proposed to adopt the Single Currency. Whether or not we can persuade other colleagues to adopt the same stance is a moot point but Teresa and I leave Westminster for the Summer recess determined to have our pamphlet 'Not a Penny More' ready to launch at the fast approaching *moment critique*.

On the very first day back after the recess Teresa is approached not only by the Chief Whip and new assistant Whip, Simon Burns (Chelmsford), but also by the PM himself regarding the impending European Communities (Finance) Bill. Simon is anxious to find out whether we intend to oppose procedural motions during the course of the Bill's passage – clearly the management are worried that with their reduced overall majority* the outcome of the vote is far from assured.

On only the second day back the House is adjourned when the official Opposition raise the question of the two Ministers, Neil Hamilton and Tim Smith, named in tomorrow's *Guardian* newspaper as having received money from the Al Fayed brothers for asking questions in the House during the Harrods takeover struggle. In the circumstances I am mildly surprised that when I ask Major's new PPS, John Ward (Poole), for an appointment to see the PM he readily agrees to arrange it for me. I am also keen to arrange a further meeting with Michael Portillo. At this meeting on 31 October Michael and I have a very full and frank discussion during the course of which he seeks my opinion as to what he should do. I tell him that the decision as to

---

*The Conservative Party had not won a by-election since William Hague's victory in Richmond in 1989

whether or not to challenge for the leadership is essentially a personal one which only he can make. He alone will know whether he is equipped and confident enough to do the job. Michael says that whilst he agrees with the generality of my analysis of the current unsatisfactory state of affairs he does not accept the particular (for him to go for Leader) which he feels would split the Party irretrievably. He is however asking himself how he can continue to serve in an administration with which he disagrees. Amongst other things I point out that as Employment Secretary he will not be allowed to succeed because Jacques Delors (President of the European Commission) has already made it clear that the British opt-outs will not last. To help him resolve his dilemma I suggest that when he next looks in the mirror he should ask himself how he measures up to my seven C's – Capability, Courage, Conviction, Charisma, Competence, intellectual Capacity and last but by no means least, Conservative principles. Michael is not alone in being far from happy with the present situation but at this stage neither he nor I can anticipate the momentous events which lie ahead. His next appointment is the regular Thursday meeting of Cabinet which we later learn decides to abandon plans to privatise the Post Office. This, we are told, is because a number of colleagues are threatening not to support it. The irony is that in this instance Government are deterred from proceeding by mere threats of rebellion whereas on the European issue where rebellion is real rather than just threatened, they are pressing on regardless.

A thoroughly unsatisfactory meeting of the ERG on 1 November is followed by an equally frustrating meeting of the Fresh Start Group. At both meetings there is much discussion about membership of the groups but little or no concentration on the real issue – the impending EC Finance Bill. In this respect I am glad that I made my own position clear to the Fresh Start Group a fortnight ago when I said that I would neither act as Whip nor be Whipped. Rightly or wrongly I have decided that whilst there are no circumstances under which I will personally support the Bill I am not in the business of influencing how others might vote in the circumstances where the Government's overall majority in the House stands at 14. Later in the day Andrew Hargreaves (Birmingham, Hall Green) and John Horam both make it their business to tell me of their concerns about sending more money to Europe. As far as I am concerned they have the same option as myself – to use their vote in support of a principle or to use it in support of a Government that needs one.

Being particularly depressed about the current state of affairs and concerned about the future direction in which the Country is heading it has occurred to me that there is a former Parliamentarian who, in his own day, must have felt very much as I do now. With this in mind I make my way to 33 South Eaton Place to discuss my thoughts with my former Member of Parliament, Enoch

Powell. *Inter alia*, Enoch says that he never thought he would see public opinion on the European issue change as decisively as it has done these past twenty years. He tells me that the most important thing is to amend the Treaty of Rome so as to remove the European Union's right of jurisdiction over the Nation state and, on the domestic front, he advises that we should do all that we can to help Major to perform the necessary 'gyrations' to get ourselves into that position – a thing that Michael Portillo subsequently tells me Major will never do. All in all I am greatly encouraged by Enoch's comments about the sea change in public opinion and particularly by his opinion that, ultimately, 'the people will win', for the simple reason, he believes, that in the final analysis the politicians have to get themselves re-elected.

John Townend phones on 10 November in high dudgeon about a report in yesterday's *Daily Express* under the headline '12 Angry Men Out to Get Major'. John says that he, George Gardiner, Bernard Jenkin and Iain Duncan Smith will be issuing writs against the *Express*. The advice from my own solicitor is that the article is definitely libellous but having slept on it, I decide against taking proceedings against the *Express* for the very good reason that it isn't so much the newspaper that should be in the dock but the people in our own party who brief them.

John Townend is not the only one to be incensed by this scurrilous report. LCCA Chairman Michael Wood is also outraged by the Party's behaviour and quite apart from firing off a very strong letter of protest to Basil Feldman, Chairman of the Party's Executive Committee, gives the executive of the West Midlands area a blast when the matter is raised at their meeting on 12 November. I am ready to do the same at the full Area committee meeting later in the day but Chairman Cedric Insley, doubtless anticipating the trouble it will cause, studiously avoids any reference to the subject. As far as I am concerned that is not the end of the matter – if the Party, in its infinite wisdom, wants to start a war that's up to them, but if they expect me not to fight back then they've got another think coming.

At the State Opening of Parliament on 16 November I bump into former Speaker Bernard Weatherill who says that 'your Party has a terminal sickness'. He agrees that I shouldn't give in but on the other hand I cannot help thinking how much easier it is to say these things from the elevated position of the cross benches of the House of Lords than in a meeting of the 1922 Committee which is what I must now do.

During the course of a long chat in the Royal Oak with James Cran I tell him about my intention to speak out at tomorrow's meeting of the '22 and to resign from its membership. Whether that is the same as resigning the Party Whip I'm not too sure but one thing is for certain and that is that I'm not prepared to be treated like this by my own Party – they started this latest unpleasantness and they'll have to take the consequences.

Walking down Whitehall earlier in the day I fall into step with Government Whip Bowen Wells (Hertford & Stortford) and, seizing the opportunity, tell him that I am very angry about Marcus Fox's media pronouncements about the EC Finance Bill being a vote of confidence. In the first place it is no part of Fox's job as Chairman of the '22 to be doing the Government's dirty work and secondly, to elevate the matter of sending an additional £75 million of taxpayers' money to Brussels to a vote of confidence in the Government is an unacceptable abuse of power. Whilst about it I tell Bowen how John Major's open door policy hasn't exactly worked for me and can hardly believe it when he comes back to me later in the day to ask if it will be convenient for me to see the PM next Tuesday!

Back home in time to see the BBC 9 O'clock News I can hardly believe it when James Cran appears on screen saying that the EC Finance Bill is not important enough to make a fuss about and that he will be voting with the Government!

In spite of Marcus Fox's best endeavours to dissuade me from doing so, on 17 November I insist upon addressing the '22 meeting. Marcus had intended and would have much preferred that the meeting dealt simply with the usual formalities and so before the meeting starts, having reluctantly agreed to call me, he is obliged to leave the podium to tell David Mitchell (Hampshire North West) that, in the circumstances, he will call him too. In the event I am the only Member to speak other than Marcus himself who takes exception to my pointing out that he is a servant of the committee and that as such, his public pronouncements are out of order. I had deliberately refrained from calling him a lackey of Government but am confident that many colleagues will recognise him for what he is.

When I return home that evening, after speaking in the Debate on the Address (Queen's Speech) on the subject of the EC Finance Bill, Patricia tells me that she has heard from James Cran who reports that what I said at the '22 meeting has gone down well with our friends although, at the time, it was apparent to me that several of our other colleagues were more enthusiastic in their support for Marcus Fox.

Next Thursday I have Question No. 2 to the Prime Minister and waking up on Sunday 20 November I know precisely what my question has to be. In the meantime I shall be meeting the PM in his room at the House of Commons on Tuesday but before that happens, in the absence of the President, Norman Tebbit, and all other Vice Presidents, I am invited to take the Chair of the Annual General Meeting of the Selsdon Group. The feeling amongst the Selsdon Group members present is very hostile to what they perceive to be a non-Conservative Government and their particular *bête noire* is Marcus Fox who is spontaneously and unanimously voted off the list of Vice Presidents. Where their sympathies lie is apparent from the entirely

Photograph courtesy of Conservative Central Office!

spontaneous round of applause aimed in my direction when I have to leave the meeting for another engagement.

And so to the most bizarre interview of my life – my meeting with the Prime Minister at which I wanted to talk about Local Government in the light of the promised Review. Having explained my long held view that local government needs to be set free from the Whitehall machine and that only by giving them real authority can one reasonably expect to attract the right calibre of councillor etc., I feel honour bound to mention what I intend to say on Thursday. Up to this point our meeting has gone well but, as I am leaving, I ask the PM if he understands that I would rather resign the Party Whip than vote for the EC Finance Bill next week. At that he dismisses his Secretary and his two PPS, John Ward and Lord McColl of Dulwich, and we spend the next half hour alone being singularly unimpressed by each other's arguments. Soon the PM is in a state of nervous agitation, pacing up and down and round and round, first this way then the other. Meanwhile I simply stand rooted on the spot at the apex of the PM's relatively large L-shaped office, letting him do the walking and indeed, most of the talking. First he paces up and down the length of the lounging area and then round and round the boardroom table in the other area. Tellingly he admits that he is boxed into a corner to which I respond by saying that not only has he boxed himself into a corner but that he's also boxed me into a corner and that it's a great pity that they are opposite corners, otherwise we could, figuratively speaking, put our arms round each other's shoulders and agree on a way to fight ourselves out of the corner. The Prime Minister then tries another tack. He says that he knows more about me than I realise – that I am financially independent, that I have a stable marriage, that I'm my own man, that I'm not hungry for office etc. Clearly he has not forgotten what he learnt in the Whip's Office a decade ago – he is reciting, aloud, a check list that will hopefully reveal some weakness in my character or circumstances that will allow him to establish some hold over me. No such luck. I tell him what my father says which is that even the Bank of England doesn't have enough money to buy me and we move swiftly on to other things. I suggest that the way out of the impasse on the European issue is a Referendum. He says he cannot do that – 'Ken Clarke would never agree' – but he promises that he will get a good deal for Britain at the next IGC in 1996. Why, I ask, should I believe, that come 1996, the 'deal' won't be rammed through Parliament just like the Single European Act (guillotined), the Paving Debate with colleagues literally carried into the Aye Lobby, Maastricht on a vote of confidence and now the EC Finance Bill on a pre-announced vote of confidence. There is no answer to that and I feel that there isn't any point in prolonging the meeting. The spectacle of the Prime Minister of Great Britain and Northern Ireland in such a spin is one that I never thought to see but there's worse to come. As a parting shot I tell him that I have Question No. 2 to him at PMQs on Thursday. The colour drains from his face completely and he goes as white as the proverbial sheet. He then sets off again, rotating round and round the boardroom table, saying that I don't have to tell him what my question will be. To this I simply say that there really is no need to tell him what my question will be because it will be very much as I indicated earlier on – that I would rather resign the Party Whip than vote for the EC Finance Bill. At this he halts in front of the large gilt-framed mirror at the end of the room and studies his reflection, deliberately and intently. Face to face it is as though his eyes don't exist and that one is looking beyond them into a huge empty cavern that is cold, dank and eerie. The abiding impression is not of a person but of an automaton. I suggest that we should adjourn whereupon Major says that I have already caused him to miss his appointment with the Chancellor and am in danger of making him late for his audience with the Queen!

Leaving the PM's office I feel that I have had quite the best of the argument and that Major himself has demonstrably not been in control of our meeting. My other impression is that he is not in command of his Ministers, particularly D. Hurd and K. Clarke, and that, in spite of all his protestations to the contrary, he really isn't on our side of the European argument at all. All in all an extraordinary, revealing and deeply depressing meeting but at least the PM knows what is in store for Thursday.

At a meeting with Teresa on Wednesday 23 November she tells me about a telephone call that she has had from Michael Portillo who says that the Government is not bluffing and that if it loses the vote on the EC Finance Bill it really will go to the country. Portillo also says that with the Royal Family in its present state the Queen is bound to agree to Dissolution.

That evening I host a Freedom Association dinner at the Grosvenor House Hotel at which John Redwood is the guest of honour. John does his best within the constraints imposed upon him by dint of the collective responsibility of Cabinet but I am personally disappointed by what he has to say. Judged by the paucity of questions he hasn't struck a chord with the other members either. The benefit of the evening is when John, on our way back to the House together, quashes the rumour that there has been a resolution of Cabinet to the effect that none of its members would stand against Major if the Queen agreed to dissolve Parliament.

After the vote at 10 o'clock approximately fifteen colleagues gather in Committee Room J where all the talk is about amassing 24 names to trigger a leadership challenge. Contrary to popular opinion I am not much interested in insurrection and I leave the meeting early in the belief that what I have to do tomorrow may be far more significant in terms of getting an actual result than all the nebulous plotting behind the scenes.

In the morning it becomes apparent that the Press have also concluded that talk of a collective Cabinet decision about the succession, should the occasion arise, is moonshine but Major's problems are real and today's resignation of Party Vice Chairman Patrick Nicholls (Teignbridge)* is a further setback.

My question to the PM† – actually more of a statement – is heard in

---

*Patrick Nicholls' resignation is the culmination of continuing adverse Press reports and comments following his being 'shopped' for drink driving by, it is suspected, a Bournemouth taxi driver at the time of the Conservative Party Conference.

†Mr Gill: Does my right Hon. Friend understand that I for one would rather resign the party Whip than vote for a Bill with which dozens of his right hon. Friends and hon. Friends do not agree and for which there is no popular support? Will he recognise the absolute folly of imposing a highly unpopular tax for the purpose of paying the subscription to a highly unpopular and increasingly expensive club?

hushed silence. Toby Jessel and John Biffen are kind enough to go over to Patricia, sitting in one of the seats at the back of the Chamber under the Public Gallery, to offer their congratulations and there are plaudits from other colleagues too. John says that my question is in the best traditions of Parliament; Peter Shore (Lab. Bethnal Green & Stepney) and Dale Campbell-Savours (Lab. Workington) are both very generous in praise of my 'bravery' as is my Labour pair, Jeff Rooker, who congratulates me on a 'tough' question.

As far as I am concerned this is not a stunt. I meant what I said and said what I meant. It is unambiguous and there is no need to elaborate in press and media interviews which, with the exception of the *Shropshire Star*, I decline to do. John Biffen agrees that, tempting though it may be, my case is not enhanced by a surfeit of media appearances and sagely adds that I should always remember that 'the Press are not in it for any other reasons than their own'. I also decline to go to 11 Lord North Street where the plotters are meeting to talk again about precipitating a leadership challenge. I tell Roger Knapman and Norman Lamont that I've done my bit by smashing the door down, now it's time for others to show a little bit of courage when the opportunity presents itself next Monday. Apparently I have not made myself sufficiently clear because Roger Knapman telephones at the weekend in an attempt to persuade me to become one of the 24 signatories to a letter to the Chairman of the '22 requesting a leadership contest. I tell him firmly that this is 'not my bag' – I've done my bit and it's up to others to do theirs. I don't need to tell Roger how I intend to vote on Monday and least of all do I seek to influence how he should vote. My intention is already known and firmly stated on the public record – others must come to their own decisions in their own ways but of one thing they can be certain and that is that, if they do decide to kick over the traces, they most emphatically will not be alone.

Exceptionally I return to Westminster on Sunday so as to be on parade in time for the Press Conference which Teresa and I are sponsoring on Monday to launch our pamphlet 'Not a Penny More'. After trouble enough getting the final text agreed with our professional adviser, Russell Lewis, we now find ourselves launching on the very day that the Government has chosen to bring the EC Finance Bill to Parliament for its Second Reading. This ensures a huge press attendance and an unbelievably fortuitous platform for us to expound our views in advance of this evening's vote.

Roger Knapman has phoned me again earlier in the day to ask me to attend a meeting at 0930 but anticipating that it's all about a leadership challenge I tell him, once again, that the answer is 'no'. Arriving too late for the Fresh Start Group meeting that afternoon I am told by Tony Marlow that 'there are 9 Abstainers for tonight, including yourself'. In the event this proves to be a slightly optimistic forecast because only 7 of us sit on our hands when the vote is called – Budgen, Gorman, Marlow, Shepherd, Taylor, Wilkinson and myself although there are rumours that Richard Body, having voted the ticket, has gone straight to the Chief Whip to tender his resignation. The debate is opened by the Chancellor, Ken Clarke, who advises the House that *'the Bill will ratify the highly successful deal negotiated by my right hon. Friend the Prime Minister and my right hon. Friend the Member for Kingston-upon-Thames (Mr Lamont)* [the then Chancellor of the Exchequer], *in Edinburgh in 1992.'* Winding up for the Government is David Heathcoat-Amory who, as Deputy Chief Whip at the time of Maastricht, had little sympathy for Eurorealists and who now, as Paymaster General, commends the Bill to the House on the basis that it is merely 'about an extra 700ths of 1 per cent of gross national product at the end of seven years. It is worth more than that to stand firm and fight for the European Community we want and not sell out to the opposition parties.' Whether the strength of argument deployed merits 330 votes, against 303 for the Opposition amendment, is beside the point. The point, as far as those of us who didn't vote the ticket is concerned, is that retribution is soon on its way. We seven who had abstained, together with Michael Carttiss (Yarmouth), who had voted with the Government against the Labour amendment but abstained on the substantive motion, were soon to be advised that the Whip had been withdrawn and would only be restored upon certain conditions.

Having left home very early the following morning to hold discussions in Munich with the German CSU Party on behalf of the ERG my letter from the Chief Whip was somewhat delayed in reaching me and so it was that I only learnt that I was no longer a member of the Conservative Parliamentary Party upon returning to the House late on Tuesday 29 November. Albeit I had spent the day in Munich but the 'scraps of paper' that I received when I got back were not 'peace in our time' but frantic messages from the Press and media asking me to make contact.

Adjusting to our new status and weighing up what to do next is a somewhat daunting prospect but meeting together at 1600 on 30 November we agree neither to form a breakaway group,* nor to crawl back on our bellies, but to steer a middle course – in John Wilkinson's words 'High profile, Energetic and Authentically Conservative'. We also agree to meet regularly each Thursday at 1700. In the meantime we suddenly find ourselves on the receiving end of a huge number of letters, messages and telephone calls and even being stopped in the street by people all saying the same things – 'Thank goodness someone is at last standing up for what we believe in,' 'You're right,' and 'Don't give in.' There was, however, one curious reaction of which for many years I was unaware. According to members of his staff at the European Foundation, Bill Cash, upon hearing that nine of his colleagues had lost the Whip, immediately instructed all personnel at the Foundation to have

---

*With the benefit of hindsight perhaps this is precisely what we should have done but at the time we continued to labour under the mistaken belief that the Party could even yet be brought round to our point of view.

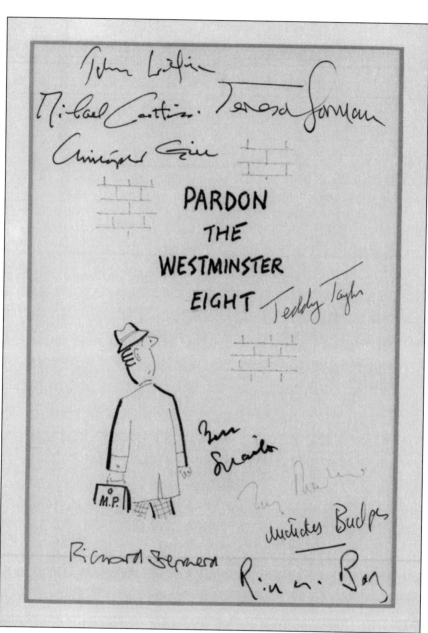

All the usual suspects!

absolutely nothing at all to do with us, not to assist us in any way and not to condone what we had done.

Thinking to test the water I take myself off to a reception in the City that evening reconciled to the fact that I might find myself persona non grata. Quite the opposite – everybody I speak to, without exception, thinks that we've done the right thing. Amazingly, back at the House, colleagues who haven't spoken to me since the beginning of the Maastricht debate two years ago are approaching me with smiles on their faces and I can scarcely believe it. As each day passes this feature of reaction by our colleagues becomes more pronounced and, unbelievably, doesn't alter even when we fail to support the Government in its bid to increase VAT on fuel. Speaking at Warwick University at the end of a highly charged and eventful week I am amazed at the warmth of the reception extended to me and the unqualified support of the students for our stand on Monday night.

The focus now shifts to which Lobby we eight rebels will be in when the Chancellor brings his proposal to increase VAT on domestic fuel to the House next Tuesday. Roger Knapman phones me at the weekend acting, I suspect, as a Whips' Office nark to find out how I intend voting. In reply I tell Roger that he should tell the Whips that they can count on my 100 per cent support, just as soon as we have got a truly Conservative Government – what it is to be free!

Whilst liberated from the necessity of obeying the Party Whip we are far from free in terms of the incessant demand for Press and media interviews. My excellent, supportive and politically astute constituency Chairman, Michael Wood, gets swept up in the media frenzy and journeys to London where we are interviewed and photographed together both before and after his meeting with National Union chairman Basil Feldman. Subsequently in a television interview at his home in Beckbury Woody tells the media that 'if we had wanted a sheep to represent us in Parliament we could have gone to Ludlow livestock market and bought one.' The press are desperate to know how the Whipless will vote because, having effectively excommunicated his Parliamentary majority, Major now risks losing important divisions which he could previously have been confident of winning. At 1730 on Tuesday 6 December we 8 Whipless Conservatives meet to discuss our intentions regarding the VAT motion. In point of fact there is no consensus although we are later accused of plotting an ambush and then disappearing into the night. The reality is somewhat different in that Nick Budgen on the one hand votes with the Government whilst Michael Carttiss,* Tony Marlow and Richard Shepherd on the other hand vote against and 5 of us abstain. The result is that the Government motion is lost by 8 votes and Ken Clarke announces that the

---

*Michael Carttiss is with us but not of us in the sense that whilst he has, like the rest of us, lost the Whip, he is not interested in attending our meetings or being much involved in our future activities.

VAT increase will not now go ahead. He will instead come back to the House on Thursday with alternative proposals. Far from disappearing into the night I remain in the House throughout the evening, dining in the Members' Dining Room with colleagues and former colleagues, including a Government Minister, Robert Hughes (Harrow West), before abstaining in person! Dodging the 'Newsnight' cameras as I do so, I leave the House at midnight but can hardly avoid noticing that the person that they are interviewing is my former comrade in arms, James Cran.

More than a week after we are 'drummed out of the regiment' Teresa and I conclude that, as soon as possible, we should launch a nationwide roadshow to take the European issue to the people. That is not to say that we haven't been flat out in the meantime with media interviews and desperately trying to cope with the huge fan mail we are receiving by every post. On the other hand, without the Party Whip, we are free to come and go as we please and in this context we are content to treat the EC Finance Bill with total contempt when it returns to the House on 7 December for its Committee stage and Third Reading.

By now it is apparent that the Government have made a huge tactical error in chucking us eight out of the Parliamentary Party. Quite apart from the fact that they have destroyed their own Parliamentary majority they have made public heroes out of what Nick Budgen later describes as eight 'ageing romantics'. The whole affair has thrown into sharp relief the poverty of the Conservative Party's foreign policy and the crassness of their day to day management. Doubtless the thinking inside Cabinet is that by withdrawing the Whip they are consigning us eight to outer darkness and that we will sink without trace, never to be heard of again. They couldn't be more mistaken! Under the British system of Parliamentary democracy, unlike the continental list system where the politician's loyalty is primarily to the parties without whose patronage election to any political office is nigh on impossible, the Member of Parliament owes his first allegiance to his constituents. Unceremoniously cast out of the Parliamentary Party we are now being sustained by our constituents and thousands of others, from every corner of the globe, who are making it abundantly clear that they consider us to be right and the Government to be just plain wrong. Under the continental system undoubtedly we would never have been heard of again – we would have been struck off the Party list and that would have been that. Quite unintentionally the Government have created an object lesson in constitutional democracy. Our case illustrates the strength of the British system of Parliamentary democracy which allows dissenting voices to be heard in a way that the continental system simply does not and long may it last.

Tam Dalyell (Lab. Linlithgow), himself from time to time a dissenting voice on the Opposition benches, helps me to illustrate the point. On 8

December he stops me to say that notwithstanding his total disagreement with my standpoint both he and his wife thought how 'powerful' my interview on the 'Today' programme had been. I presume that he is referring to the interview I gave on 28 November, the day of the EC Finance Bill Second Reading, but the point is well made. As a British Member of Parliament, regardless of whether anyone agrees with me or not, regardless of whether my Party likes it or not, I am at liberty to speak my mind in the certain knowledge that, always excepting the effects of the Party's 'dirty tricks department', the only people who can dismiss me are not the Party bosses but the people who elected me in the first place, i.e. my constituents. This is the priceless feature of our democracy which we give up at our peril. Proportional representation, for example, is not for the people, it's for the political parties and the political hacks who inhabit them.

Not willing to be a pariah nor wanting to create the impression that I am in any way ashamed of what I have done I continue to attend Conservative meetings as though nothing has happened to alter my status. I am still a Conservative, I am still a member of the Conservative Party and I am still the duly elected Conservative Member of Parliament for Ludlow. The fact that the Conservative Party in Parliament no longer requires my services is their problem, not mine. I will never deny that I disobeyed orders by failing to respond to a 3-line Whip and, as a former Royal Navy officer well used to discipline, I accept that my punishment was well deserved and I accept it without any feelings of rancour or resentment. Faced with the choice of voting for my Party or my Country I have chosen the latter. Many of my constituents will be content with the decision I have made and I am in no doubt that in the fullness of time my implacable opposition to Economic & Monetary Union and the Political Union which must inevitably follow will prove to be correct.

On the way to Richmond House, where Secretary of State for Social Security Peter Lilley is meeting with Conservative backbenchers, it occurs to me that my presence may be resented by some of my former colleagues. On arrival Peter Lilley's PPS Piers Merchant (Beckenham) urges me to stay and Peter Bottomley (Eltham) passes me a note to say that as I was invited I should definitely stay. Others clearly think otherwise and later in the afternoon Roger Gale (Thanet North) raises the matter at what I gather is a stormy meeting of the '22 Committee from which I am now, of course, excluded.

At a similar meeting sponsored by Secretary of State for Employment Michael Portillo, he is quite relaxed about my attendance but when the conversation turns to the question of the Whipless 8 tact indicates that I should leave.

At the weekend I get a mixed reaction from the Church Stretton Conservative Ladies when I address their Christmas Tea Party and can only conclude that my challenge to the orthodoxy and the received wisdom is difficult for them to come to terms with. Government Ministers in their infinite wisdom choose Saturday 10 December to announce their intention to launch a campaign to sell the idea of the Single Currency and on Sunday I am still countering Press allegations that the Whipless 8 are 'pledged to act together' and having plotted to ambush the Government last Tuesday simply vanished. The moral to the tale is clear – never let the truth stand in the way of a good story!

News that certain Government Ministers are going to go flat out to sell the Single Currency is hardly what we want to hear but on Tuesday 13 December it is apparent that Government generally is in some difficulty with another EU policy when it fails to table a motion in relation to the annual Fisheries debate. The Agriculture Minister's PPS Oliver Heald (Hertfordshire North) is anxious to know how I intend to vote when the issue is debated tomorrow but given that the Government has yet to table a motion it is hardly a question that I can answer, always supposing that I am minded to do so. The Whipless 8 give Teddy Taylor *carte blanche* to table a fiercely critical Common Fisheries Policy (CFP) amendment but reach no decision about how we shall vote owing to the absence of a Government motion. In the meantime David Harris (St. Ives), an animated oxymoron who purports to be the fishermen's friend whilst at the same time supporting the CFP, has shown me the text of an amendment which he has given to junior Agriculture Minister Michael Jack but which he can't table either because of the paralysis inside Government. Eventually the Government tables a motion for the House to 'take note of' the usual EU gobbledegook which, come the day, is carried by a majority of 28, with the Whipless 8 abstaining. A myth that will be perpetuated for years to come is that the Whipless voted against the Government on the EC Finance Bill when, as a matter of fact, we did no such thing. Nick Budgen is now mightily exercised about getting both the *Mail on Sunday* and the PM to apologise for repeating this 'terminological inexactitude' but obviously it suits Government to peddle this myth as long as possible to justify what can now be seen to have been an ill-considered over-reaction.

Waiting for my host at the Naval & Military Club (the In and Out) – Ian Beddows is actually standing me lunch at the Army & Navy Club but that's another story! – I encounter my constituent Pat Thompson of Dunval Hall. Pat is far from being onside as far as I and my views on Europe are concerned and so the opportunity to tweak his tail is irresistible. When I ask him how he's getting on with his efforts to unseat his Member of Parliament he is utterly speechless. Another member of the club tells me that he was in MI5 and that in 1940, with two battalions, he had planned to take over Parliament and install Clem Attlee as Prime Minister!

Before leaving Westminster for the Christmas recess I join Malcolm Pearson for tea in the House of Lords to progress the idea of a Euro Roadshow. Lord Mancroft expresses the opinion that the only way to solve the Government's difficulties is to persuade Sir James Goldsmith to tell John Major that he will pay off all the Conservative Party's debts in return for the PM adopting Eurorealist policies. The Party, I fear, will not be susceptible to such blandishments but we certainly haven't heard the last of Sir James!

CHAPTER TWELVE

1995

...we are determined to secure arrangements
which will safeguard the interests of British fishermen

AT BRIDGNORTH LIVESTOCK MARKET on Monday 9 January there is massive
and spontaneous support from the farmers for the stand I have taken on
the European issue. The following day a meeting of the Westminster 8 decides
to make common cause with the fishing industry. It is Teresa's idea but, telling
my colleagues that I know just the man to contact, I hurry home to telephone
John Ashworth, spokesman for the Save Britain's Fish campaign. John had
first come to my attention when he came to the House of Commons to give
evidence to the Agriculture Select Committee's investigation into Sea
Fisheries in 1993. He spoke good sense and clearly knew his subject inside out
which was all the more reason why the committee should hear more of what
he had to say rather than that he should have been given the short shrift with
which our Chairman, Jerry Wiggin (Weston-super-Mare), would otherwise
have dismissed him. As a Europhile and a former junior Agriculture Minister
perhaps Jerry sensed that John Ashworth was getting too near the knuckle and
as events unfold it will become ever more apparent that the last thing MAFF
Ministers and officials want is someone shining a spotlight on the British
fishing industry's problems post Ted Heath's betrayal of it in 1972.

Racing home as quickly as I possibly can I pick up the telephone and, even
before taking off my overcoat, dial John Ashworth's number. Answering the
phone Mrs Ashworth says that John is just about to board a plane in Canada,
where he has been advising the Canadian Government on fisheries
conservation, and that if I get off the line as quickly as possible she will try to
make contact with him before he takes off. At 0930 the following morning
John and I are sitting enjoying a cup of coffee together in the House of
Commons and we are bound to conclude that this is a meeting that was
destined to happen – if I had stopped to take off my coat before telephoning
last evening I would have missed him and he would, by now, be nearly home
in Yorkshire. The upshot of our meeting is that John is enthusiastic about the
prospect of a joint press conference in Lowestoft and we agree to take the idea
a stage further.

The Government are now trying to dig themselves out of another hole of
their own making. As a consequence of withdrawing the Whip from some of

their own supporters, i.e. the Whipless 8, thereby destroying their notional majority, they fear that their right to a majority of members on committees will be open to challenge. To obviate this risk they bring a motion to the House stating that unless Government loses its majority 'either as a result of by-elections or through secession of Members to another party' it should continue to nominate the majority on any committee. Having intervened on the Leader of the House to point out that the answer to the problem is self evidently in the Government's own hands and that by the simple expedient of restoring the Whip to myself and my seven colleagues there would be no need to seek approval for today's motion, I am content, when the vote is called, to abstain. The Leader of the House, replying to my intervention, says that I can't expect him to *go beyond what the PM said in his widely publicised interview on Sunday*' whereupon I am reminded that in his 'Breakfast with Frost' interview John Major was indicating that he might be moving marginally in our direction but there's still a long way to go in terms of renouncing the single currency to which other members of his administration pledged their support barely four weeks previously. The sequel to this afternoon's machinations is that it isn't long before the Government are offering to restore the Whip to those of our colleagues who vote with them on this motion but not to Carttiss, Gorman, Marlow and myself who didn't – a classic case of divide and rule. Hopefully the gentlemen's agreement between us that it's 'all for one and one for all' will hold but just in case it doesn't I decide that it's perhaps best to keep 'radio silence' this weekend and not to give any interviews.

On Saturday 14 January Daniel Hannan telephones to say that he has just found out that Ken Clarke is involved with a Committee, largely comprised of Europhiles, to promote the single currency. From that piece of information one concludes that the Parliamentary Party is working to dual standards – if one is Chancellor one can paddle a divergent view but not, according to my experience, if you're a humble backbencher. As if things were not bad enough already I arrive in Broseley this morning to discover that campaigners are out in force distributing leaflets against so called Local Authority 'cuts' – endorsed by the Conservative group at Shirehall! According to friends, former LCCA Treasurer Gerard Paris is still going round bad-mouthing me but generally speaking opinion in the constituency is overwhelmingly on my side, to the extent that a television crew sent to Ludlow to sound out opinion fails to identify anyone who is against. At a subsequent meeting of the LCCA Finance and General Purposes Committee on 23 January it is apparent that had I had somebody primed to make the proposition I could almost certainly have obtained a vote of confidence which would have been a comforting trophy to have up one's sleeve against the coming of the proverbial 'rainy day'.

Being part of a deputation to meet David Maclean in his capacity of Minister of State at the Home Office on 17 January I am amazed at the good natured reception that I get from my former colleagues. John Biffen says that it is either because they think I'm right or that, alternatively, they're afraid of me. Either way I tell him that I will have the Party in an entirely different mode by the end of the year or die in the attempt.

The Chairman and Vice Chairman of the Scottish White Fish Producers' Association, Tom Hay and John Thompson, are over the moon when Teresa Gorman, Tony Marlow, Teddy Taylor and I pledge our unqualified support for the Save Britain's Fish campaign. During the course of the day our group of eight has struggled to get an agreement on a mission statement and eventually accepts a draft prepared by Richard Shepherd and Teddy Taylor. On the Fisheries issue though we are unanimous and in advance of tomorrow's Opposition Day debate, Tony Marlow goes into overdrive to obtain 25 signatories to our amendment to the Labour motion. Not surprisingly the Speaker, acting in accordance with precedent, chooses the amendment tabled by the Government rather than our own but nonetheless we have put down a significant marker that more than a few backbenchers are far from content with the CFP and its effects upon the British fishing industry. The Government amendment congratulating itself on 'securing the exclusion of Spanish fishing vessels from the Irish Sea and the Bristol Channel' etc., is moved by the Minister of Agriculture, Fisheries and Food, William Waldegrave (Bristol West), who, whilst at the Despatch Box, admits that the root cause of the industry's problems goes right back to the deal done by Ted Heath at the time of Britain's accession to the European Economic Community, as it was then called, in 1972. This is precisely what SBF (Save Britain's Fish) contend and so it is music to their ears to have the fact confirmed by no less a person than the Minister himself. What is less satisfactory is that it subsequently transpires that what we all distinctly heard the Minister say on that specific and important point is not recorded in Hansard. In other words, by speaking the truth, the Minister has blown the gaff and behind the scenes the Hansard reporters have been leant on to omit the incriminating evidence.*

The Whipless have no compunction in voting against the Government amendment which will permit 40 Spanish vessels to fish in British waters from which they are presently excluded, i.e. the Irish box, but the Government win the day and their amendment is carried by 310 votes to 301.† Notwithstanding

---

*A continuing feature of Fisheries debates will be the Government's determination not to concede the point that the industry has been sold down the river and that on 1 January 2003, under the principle of 'equal access to the common resource' implicit in the CFP, fishing vessels of all other EU countries will have the absolute right to fish in what have previously been exclusively British waters – right up to our very beaches! Regardless of which Party is in power departmental officials will brief Ministers to procrastinate and obfuscate so as to perpetuate the deception upon which acceptance of the iniquitous CFP depends.

†In this division we are joined in the 'No' Lobby by Rupert Allason who is also without the Conservative Whip but for a rather different reason. Back in July Rupert had absented himself when the Government called the vote of no confidence following the tied vote on the Social Chapter but it was only after the House had adjourned for the summer recess that the news broke that he had had the Party Whip withdrawn.

we lose the vote, the SBF representatives who have travelled to London to listen to the debate are absolutely delighted with their new 'friends at court' and the new alliance that we have forged with them to fight for the fishing industry. We are now all looking forward to our visit to Lowestoft this time next week.

When the day arrives we are minus John Wilkinson who can't get away because of prior engagements but plus the local member, David Porter, and, on this occasion, his pal Michael Carttiss who represents the neighbouring port of Yarmouth. Thanks to Mike Penning who is now working for our group as our PR officer we leave Liverpool Street in a blaze of publicity which is replicated both at Norwich, where we have to change trains and rendezvous with SBF's John Ashworth, Tom Hay and John Thompson, and again at our final destination, Lowestoft.* Our highly successful and worthwhile day which includes visits to trawlers alongside the quay and a packed meeting in the Fishermen's Mission attracts excellent press reports and we are, so to speak, in business!

On 30 January I wake to the not so dulcet tones of John Gummer extolling the virtues of the Hedgerow Protection measures to be incorporated in his Environment Protection Bill. I might have guessed that the defeat of Peter Ainsworth's Private Member's Bill would not be the end of the matter!

Not being a reader of the *Irish Times* I am at somewhat of a loss when Willie Ross ventures the opinion that reports in today's edition are very significant. He goes on to say that he thinks we should be ready for an election in three months time. Would that it were true but the reality is that we are barely half way through the permitted lifetime of this Parliament and John Major is nothing if not stubborn – he is unlikely, as we shall soon see, to give up the top job without a struggle.

The following day the Westminster 8 decide to keep up the pressure on the European Commission for a meeting† to discuss fisheries pending which we plan to go to the West Country to meet more fishermen. As a result of the Press Release‡ issued by us earlier in the day we are reported on the BBC 9 O'clock News and in the morning, to our great surprise, the 'Today' programme announces that our statement has been welcomed by Paymaster General David Heathcoat-Amory. Subsequently I agree to be interviewed for

---

*With the Colne Shipping Company's decision to lay-up its fleet of 7 beam trawlers, with effect from the middle of August 2002, Lowestoft has now ceased to be a deep-sea fishing port but in 1995 we still believed that political pressure could result in changes to the CFP that would obviate the otherwise almost certain demise of huge swathes of the British fishing industry. Sadly we were wrong in this belief and the fishing industry has continued to be used simply as a pawn in the bigger game of European integration and has paid a corresponding price.
†It is practically unknown in Westminster for a Minister to refuse to see an elected representative but such efforts as we made to gain an interview with the unelected and apparently unaccountable Commissioner responsible for Fisheries were simply shrugged off. From this experience alone it is fair to conclude that democracy within the EU is, in effect, a dead letter.
‡Appendix E.

the 1 O'clock News to tell the nation what message the Westminster 8 have for the Government. The importance of what we are doing lies in the fact that, quite apart from standing up for what we believe in and also, thereby, articulating the views of millions of our fellow countrymen, we are acting as a strong counterbalance to the likes of Clarke, Heseltine and Hurd whose enthusiasm for the EU appears to know no bounds.

Over a cup of tea in the Smoking Room David Evans asks me when we eight are going to take the Whip back. Before I can answer, Norman Lamont, who is just about to join us, says very firmly, 'Stay out.' This is the former Chancellor who not so long ago was to be seen defending Britain's membership of the ERM and who, later in the year, will go on record at the Conservative Party Conference saying, 'As a former Chancellor, I can only say that I cannot pinpoint a single concrete economic advantage that unambiguously comes to this country because of our membership of the European Union.'

The day's hat trick is complete when Anthony Steen (South Hams) says that he will be pleased to welcome the Westminster 8 to Brixham, in his constituency, when we make our next foray to show solidarity with the fishermen in three weeks' time.

On the home front all is not well. The battle against so called Government 'cuts' is gathering momentum as Local Authority teachers incite parents of school children to participate in their propaganda campaign. The classic example of the LCCA's total lack of political nous occurs on 3 February when, at the end of the formal proceedings of the Lydbury North branch AGM, the Chairman, David Waters, orders the doors of the village hall to be thrown open to admit the general public. Local landowner and long standing member of the Association Billy Plowden, seeing what is going on, rises to his feet, tells the Chairman very firmly that he 'thought this was a Conservative meeting' and bids him goodnight. He's the lucky one – I have to remain to face the brickbats from a village hall which is by this time packed to the gunwhales with disgruntled teachers, Lib/Dem councillors there for the sport, disaffected Tories and anybody else with a bone to pick. To cap it all, on 8 February, I arrive at a television studio to take part in a programme about Local Authority funding and find myself idly chatting with the Labour Council Leader of the London Borough of Southwark, prior to us both going on air. During the course of our brief discussion he tells me that in the matter of Revenue Support Grant the Government (Conservative) have looked after them (Labour) quite well. 'The problems will be in the Tory shires,' he says – as if I don't already know it!

Whilst addressing a fringe meeting at the Young Conservatives Conference in Southport on Sunday 12 February I am somewhat surprised at the appearance of a BBC TV crew but it soon transpires that what they are interested in is my reaction to the breaking news of the resignation of junior Home Office Minister Charles Wardle (Bexhill & Battle). Ostensibly Charles has resigned in protest at the Government's immigration policy but subsequently Richard Body tells me how Charles, whilst serving as the Parliamentary Under Secretary of State at the Home Office, had gone to his boss, Home Secretary Michael Howard, to seek his support in a battle he was having with the department's civil servants concerning discarded office furniture. Chancing upon a quantity of apparently serviceable furniture stacked up awaiting collection Charles was angered by the refusal of civil servants to give him a reasonable explanation and information about its intended disposal. The view of the mandarins was that it was none of the Minister's business to be monitoring such matters and disappointingly it was the view of the Home Secretary that Charles should immediately let the matter rest.*

Back in Westminster at the beginning of another week I arrive in Pall Mall to find a phalanx of cameras and reporters outside the Reform Club where journalist Christopher Booker, former junior Trade & Industry Minister Neil Hamilton and I are scheduled to address over 100 members of the Bruges Group.† The audience are highly appreciative of what we have to say but on the way back to the House the taxi driver volunteers the information that neither he nor his brothers could ever vote for 'im – 'im being John Major – and that at the next election they will simply sit on their hands, along with 4,489,901 others as it turns out.

Voting in the House is on a motion standing in the name of the Liberal Democrats *'that this House believes that the popular assent of the people of the United Kingdom should be sought through a referendum before any substantial alteration of the present constitutional settlement between the European Union and its Member States.'* The fact that it is carried by 47 votes to 3 makes not the slightest difference because both the official Opposition and the Government boycott the division for reasons which future Lib/Dem leader Charles Kennedy (Ross, Cromarty & Skye) correctly 'assumes was based on collusion for their own purposes'. Question: when is a vote not a vote? Answer: when neither the Conservative Government nor the Labour Opposition want it put on record

---

*This incident illustrates the reluctance of Ministers to protect the interests of taxpayers by involving themselves in the day to day supervision and efficiency of their respective departments in the way that the head of any self-respecting commercial undertaking might reasonably be expected to do in order to protect the interests of the shareholders. Charles Wardle, having been chairman of a substantial group of companies in manufacturing industry before entering Parliament, fell into the second category but was one of only a tiny number of Members with this sort of experience, which accounts for a further defect in the system. Given their total lack of experience at running any sort of enterprise Ministers are often as not mere ciphers for their departments and are increasingly reluctant to challenge the departmental brief for fear of being exposed as inadequate or, more to the point, of finding their erstwhile promising political career brought to an unscheduled and ignominious end.

†Margaret Thatcher's speech in Bruges in 1988 was widely acclaimed as the defining moment in the ongoing debate about Europe and prompted the formation of the Bruges Group which continues to campaign to this day against European integration.

that they are both opposed to giving the British people the opportunity to deliver their own verdict upon the political elite's headlong rush towards European integration.

Our guest at an ERG lunch on 14 February is Minister for Europe David Davis, who convinces me that he is prepared to dig his heels in at the forthcoming IGC, particularly on the question of immigration.* After lunch Michael Spicer tells me that he has been to see the PM who has finally agreed to put his signature to the foreword of a 40-page pamphlet entitled *A Europe of Nations* which the European Research Group will now proceed to publish. This publication has been quite some time in gestation but will be launched at the end of the month as 'the conclusions of the ERG' in an attempt to offer an alternative vision to that of a United States of Europe. On the day in question (27 February) our pamphlet gets extensive press coverage but not surprisingly the headlines are stolen by the collapse of Barings Bank. Our press launch has one entirely bizarre and totally unexpected side effect. In the Families Room, back at the House, I am attacked by Bill Cash's wife, Biddy, who says that she will no longer go on taking my side in Shropshire – 'after all she and Bill have done for me, speaking up for me, helping to get me selected as the candidate, telling people what a loyal Eurosceptic I am' and 'now you've sided with Michael Spicer who is in cahoots with the Government which just wants to discredit the Eurosceptics and destroy Bill.'

I cannot believe that I'm hearing this and tell her so. When I ask Biddy if she has read our pamphlet (*A Europe of Nations*) she admits that she hasn't and I suggest that it might be helpful if she did.

Suspecting that there might be an ulterior motive my Chairman, Michael Wood, and his wife, Rosemary, accept John Major's invitation to drinks at 10 Downing Street on 20 February and are mildly surprised when it turns out to be a purely social occasion rather than an operation to suborn the chairmen of the Whipless MPs. On the contrary, Major pointedly tells his guests that he doesn't want to waste their time talking about political philosophy! Some interpret this as being the root cause of the Party's ongoing problems and it comes only a few days after Young Conservative National Chairman Adrian Lee has asked me, perhaps slightly tongue in cheek, whether Major is trying to close the whole country down. A week later I interview Adrian with a view to engaging him to organise our 'Roadshow' which in the meantime Teresa and I have concluded isn't going to happen unless we do it ourselves rather than relying upon other groups or committees to come up with the goods. We discuss this at some length on the journey from Paddington to Newton Abbot where Captain Portus and others are waiting to meet our train when the

---

*Events will demonstrate that there is generally little political will to tackle this issue in any meaningful way and one of the first acts of the Labour Government elected in May 1997 was to relax the entry rules, the inevitable consequence of which has been to attract even higher numbers to these shores.

Whipless descend upon Brixham in a further attempt to draw attention to the iniquities of the CFP and the disastrous consequences which must inevitably follow.

Notwithstanding that I am no longer obliged to deliver my vote in response to the Party Whip I continue to attend the House as usual from Monday to Thursday, returning to Shropshire each Friday where, quite apart from the usual constituency workload, it is necessary to bat down those still intent upon causing mischief. Attending a Ludlow Supper Club event on 24 February I am delighted to hear Graeme Stevens point out that 'those who have never had to earn a proper living themselves are the only ones to be consistently opposed to Christopher Gill's views.' That says it all and as a rule of thumb guide as to where I can expect to encounter criticism Graeme has hit the nail right on the head. Before the month is out however there is some good news on the home front as when Michael Wood reports that Lumpy has agreed to be kicked upstairs and will henceforth be Association Patron rather than a member of the LCCA Executive and that Mrs Lumpy has similarly agreed to be side-lined as a Vice President. The fact that former Chairman Jackie Williams has declined the opportunity to head up the Ladies' section is a further welcome indication that the antis are prepared to retire to lick their wounds – at least pro tem!

The 1 March is another Opposition Day and the new Leader of the Labour Party, Tony Blair (Sedgefield), tables a motion *that this House does not support her Majesty's Government's policy towards the European Union and does not believe it promotes the interests of the British people.* The 8 Whipless and doubtless, if the truth were told, many of our former colleagues, are naturally attracted to the wording of this resolution which is, of course, precisely why Blair has tabled it – in the vain hope that he will defeat the Government in the division lobbies when the vote is called later this evening. The Whipless are much in demand by the press and media who scent blood but with Body, Budgen and Shepherd voting the ticket the Government scrape by with a majority of 5 notwithstanding that Bendall and Cash have joined Gorman, Marlow, Taylor, Wilkinson and myself in abstention and that Norman Lamont has gone the whole hog by voting with Labour! Ken Baker's observation is that 'the chair has become even more rickety'! After the vote I have to take time out to explain that all talk of splits in the ranks of the Whipless is just plain nonsense – we are not operating a Whip and each of us is more than capable of deciding for themselves how we should vote, or not vote, as the case may be.

During the course of the debate I intervene on Ted Heath to remind him that in 1971, whilst he was PM, he wrote to fishermen in the West Country stating quite categorically that 'for our part, as the White Paper said, we are determined to secure arrangements which will safeguard the interests of British fishermen.' Replying to my question Ted says that if I look up what happened in the negotiations and examine the agreement that was reached I would see that 'the fishermen got complete protection'! One of the ironies of Parliamentary life is that whilst one Member may not accuse another of telling lies there is no compulsion, beyond the convention that we are all 'honourable' men and women, to speak the truth. If Ted Heath chooses to ignore the overwhelming weight of evidence that refutes the truth of what he has just said that is the end of the matter, notwithstanding that he may possibly be in a minority of one. I thought that my intervention on 'the Grocer' might be my sole contribution to the debate until, approaching the Chair to 'pull' my name, Michael Morris says how pleased he is to see me because he can't see Richard Shepherd in the Chamber and he is due to be called next but one on the Conservative side. Because he wants to call one of the Whipless, Michael suggests that I stick around. Finding Richard in the Library I pass on the information whereupon he goes immediately to tell the Speaker that he wishes to withdraw his name because the spirit no longer moves and by and by I am called in his stead. I appreciate the opportunity to put on record my reaction to the current situation and suggestions as to how the Conservative Party might best improve its appeal to the general public but, as evidenced by a chance encounter with the Chief Whip, the Government are still not prepared to listen.

When I go to the Smoking Room the following afternoon for a cup of tea who should be sat there, entirely alone, but Richard Ryder. I offer to buy tea for the two of us but he insists on doing the honours and thereafter we talk about everything under the sun except the big issue – Europe. I do, however, manage to ask him whether it is his opinion that the PM is enjoying being pushed in a Eurosceptic direction but answer comes there none. Former Chairman of the '22 Committee Cranley Onslow (Woking) puts his head round the door and concluding that the Chief Whip is spelling out how many beans make five – which he isn't – beats a retreat. The ongoing reluctance of the top brass to engage in any sort of meaningful dialogue is extraordinary but perhaps they realise that this is an argument that they cannot win. In that case the question is why Major doesn't accept that public opinion is over-whelmingly on the side of the rebels and that instead of throwing us out of the Party the sensible thing to do would be to embrace us and by so doing make a political virtue out of an electoral necessity. During the course of a very positive meeting of the Group of 8 Teresa says again that we really should have a candidate in mind to replace Major – she says that she has spoken to Norman Tebbitt who confirms that he would be willing to stand if the circumstance arises. The next day (8 March) Andy Stewart, formerly the Member for Sherwood and now heading up the Agriculture Training Board, tells me how impressed civil servants at the Welsh Office are with John Redwood.

In the Cloisters, Michael Trend, 'Badger' Glyn's successor at Windsor & Maidenhead, voices concern about the state of Party morale. He exaggerates – there is no Party morale! The only question is for how much longer this totally unreal situation can continue. There is ongoing pressure upon the Whipless for them to seek the restoration of the Party Whip but the 'management' does not seem to understand that firstly, we are not unhappy with our present status and, secondly, that we have absolutely no intention of coming back with any sort of strings attached. George Gardiner has been putting out feelers in our direction but I guess this is because he is trying to maximise the voting strength for his preferred candidate as and when there is a leadership challenge.* Over an agreeable dinner at Simpsons in the Strand with James Cran and Michael Spicer on 15 March Michael works hard to influence me to rejoin the fold but as always it is almost impossible to define his real motives. Speaking for myself I can only say that I am treating all talk of a challenge to the leadership with supreme indifference – my present situation is a direct consequence of objecting, on principle, to Government policy with which I fundamentally disagree and not in any way an expression of animosity towards John Major. I accept that he has thrown me out of the Parliamentary Party but in no way am I 'out to get him'. That is business that I am perfectly content to leave to the 'plotters', of which there are many, and the 'malcontents', of which there are more than a few.

At a meeting of the '92 Group, where the Whipless are still very much persona grata, there is no suggestion that we are in any way responsible for the Party's disastrous opinion poll ratings. James Pawsey strikes a chord when he says that 'we're all wasting our time if the man at the top isn't getting it right' and Edward Leigh gets a round of applause for saying that the most important thing for the Party to do is to get back to true Conservatism. As if to reinforce the point, two days later, on 22 March, I bump into Sir Arthur Hill and Sir Pat Lawrence in Central Lobby who both pump my hand vigorously, congratulate me on what I am doing and urge me not to give in. The significance of this endorsement of my action is that Arthur and Pat are both former Presidents of the Federation of West Midlands Area Conservative Associations and Pat is also a former Chairman of the National Union. These are men who have given a lifetime of service to the Conservative Party and whose views the leadership would do well to heed. Gerald Howarth, formerly the Member for Cannock & Burntwood, telephones to say that the councillors at Aldershot, where he is now PPC, are incensed by a critical article written by their member Julian Critchley in the *Mail on Sunday*. Everywhere and at every level support for our stand is genuine and rock solid. For those with eyes to see and ears to listen the message is clear, except, that is, to the 'management' whose

---

*Deprived of the Whip we are barred from attending backbench committees and disqualified from voting in Parliamentary Party elections including, of course, leadership elections.

siege mentality precludes any consideration that they might just conceivably have got it wrong.

Michael Wood tells me that West Midlands President Michael Price presided at the lunch with Arthur Hill and others in the House yesterday and that he was deputed by the meeting to seek a personal interview with the PM to 'put him straight'. In terms of putting people straight I do my best to enlighten Agriculture Ministers in a debate on 21 March. A week later there is a sudden flurry of activity from William Waldegrave's office, the upshot of which is that I get to meet him that evening (28 March). I am not overly impressed by his flattering 'spiel' about my knowing so much about the Abattoir industry etc. and lose no time in telling him that his Department has acted appallingly with regard to the introduction of the new Meat Hygiene Service and that that is not the only example of poor performance. I instance our correspondence regarding the Transport of Live Animals (Poultry) Regulations where he has actually lied to me. Amazingly he makes no attempt to refute my accusation and I conclude by telling him frankly that, like many other Ministers, he is being run by his Civil Servants whereas, of course, it should be the other way round.

The next day (29 March) it is Gillian Shephard's turn to be put through the mangle although to give credit where it is due she has been far more sympathetic than other Ministers in my battle to get a fairer deal for the shire counties in terms of local authority funding. The Prime Minister has replied to the letter I wrote to him following my encounter with the Labour Leader of Southwark Council without actually addressing any of the issues raised; Local Government Minister David Curry has told me that both he and his boss, John Gummer, are opposed to 'rate capping' but that the 'High Command are incapable of making a decision' and now the Secretary of State for Education is telling me that all our problems can be laid at the door of the Chancellor, Ken Clarke, whom she says is arrogant, doesn't listen, doesn't study his briefs etc. Gillian agrees with everything I say about Shropshire's financial difficulties and urges me to write to John Gummer, which I will do, with a copy to the PM, the Chancellor of the Exchequer and just about anybody and everybody who might be the least bit interested in the problem.

At an ERG lunch on 4 April our guests are Cabinet Ministers Aitken, Howard, Lilley and Portillo. They are given a fairly uncompromising message – no more fudging on the European issue. Sadly their views are much less robust which only serves to reinforce the impression that there is indeed a paralysis at the heart of Government.

For the first time in several years I fail to speak in the Third Reading debate on the Finance Bill. My theme has consistently been that taxes on capital are an anachronism in a capitalist society and that Inheritance Tax and Capital

Gains Tax, which after all the available Reliefs & Allowances actually net the Treasury relatively small amounts of money, should be abolished. Not only is the principle of capital taxation wrong but the cost to the nation of engaging the country's finest financial brains in devising schemes of tax avoidance and the financial consequences of decisions based upon tax considerations rather than market opportunities must surely outweigh the very few billions that the Treasury might otherwise forgo.

Yet another backbencher joins the growing list of former colleagues who want the Group of 8 to resume the Party Whip. This time it is Terry Dicks (Hayes & Harlington) who corners Teresa and I to ask whether he should approach the PM regarding our rehabilitation! He says that he agrees with us but none of this squares with his unpleasant behaviour towards us at the time of Maastricht – not that that made him any different from the vast majority of our colleagues at that time!

On Easter Monday (17 April) I receive a telephone call from Home Secretary Michael Howard, asking me to use my influence to dissuade the Group of 8 from coming out against Identity Cards. He assures me that they will not be used as an excuse to dismantle border controls and would be useful in fighting crime. This is the usual departmental line and tomorrow we will issue a press release in which we express our own views which go beyond the rather simplistic approach adopted by the Home Office.

With local elections looming I am pleased to have the opportunity to go canvassing on behalf of Conservative candidates in the Bridgnorth area with the admittedly ulterior motive of gauging the strength of feeling amongst my constituents for my stance on Europe. There are no adverse reactions and I am rather encouraged at the weekend, when, in Clun Parish Church for a St. George's Day service, I am told that the whole of the Clun Valley is firmly on my side.

That afternoon Michael Spicer telephones to say that all the Whipless he has spoken to so far have told him that they would accept the Whip back if it was offered. Not being so keen on the idea myself I tell him that I couldn't possibly give him any commitment unless and until I have had the opportunity to discuss the proposition with my other colleagues. At 10 p.m. *Times* correspondent Nick Wood, with whom Michael Spicer is on good terms, phones to quiz me about the possibility of the Whip being offered back to the rebels tomorrow. All that I can tell him is that the rumours of such a possibility are stronger than usual but when he mentions Michael Spicer's name I decide that, he knowing more than he's letting on about, it's time to change the subject. Scarcely have I put the phone down when it rings again. This time it's Teddy Taylor to warn me that Nick Wood is on to something!

The following day (24 April) a meeting of the Group of 8 in Committee

Room J is in very real danger of rushing its fences to the extent that I feel obliged to tell my colleagues that I'm going to go home, that I am not going to speak to the Press and that I will see them again at 0900 tomorrow if in the meantime the Chief Whip has indeed put a letter on the board inviting me back. At this, Teddy Taylor, one of the kindest souls ever to have crossed the Westminster portals, says, 'What about poor old Michael Spicer who is waiting outside the room for our answer?' The meeting then agrees that I should convey our conclusions to Michael for it is he, after all, who, acting as the Government's emissary, has delivered the proverbial olive branch. Michael is incensed at this rebuff and insists upon going back into the Committee Room, even though our meeting is ended, to tell us that we're a bunch of shits, how he has worked so hard to get us back into the fold, how he thought we were all on the same side, fighting the same battle etc. and that the least we could do is accept the offer whilst it's on the table. Mercifully the majority of my colleagues agree that it's 'no dice' until the offer is received in writing and we adjourn until the morrow. Richard Shepherd kindly offers to drive me home where we exhaust my supply of whisky poring over the entrails of an altogether fascinating and completely unexpected turn of events.

Having collected the Chief Whip's terse two line letter early on Tuesday 25 April I make my way to 7 Millbank in time for the Group of 8 meeting at 9 o'clock. The meeting readily agrees that we have to accept the offer to rejoin the Parliamentary Party* and adjourns to the canteen for a cup of coffee prior to holding a spectacular Press Conference at 1015. Speaking for myself I tell the serried ranks of reporters that we will not abandon all that we have fought for these past five months and repeat the pledge to carry on supporting the Save Britain's Fish campaign. I say that we have achieved four significant things – we have given hope to thousands, if not millions, who thought their views were being ignored; we have demonstrated that there are still a few people of integrity inside Parliament who are prepared to put the National interest first: we have stimulated a wider debate in the country at large, and

---

*In arriving at the decision as to whether or not to accept the restoration of the Party Whip there were several factors to be taken into account and the consideration of each one of them would inevitably vary according to both the circumstances and the inclination of the individual Member. Whilst not exhaustive the following list of questions sprang to mind:

1. What will be the reaction of rank and file Conservative Party members if the rebels are seen to throw the Government's offer back in its face?

2. Having dramatically awakened public opinion and stimulated Eurorealist thinking what more can eight 'ageing romantics' hope to achieve on their own?

3. If, for their own reasons, the majority of the group wish to return to the fold what ongoing influence can two or three expect to have on their own?

4. What are the prospects of reselection if, when the time comes, we are still without the Party Whip?

5. Does perpetuation of the current split help or hinder the Conservative Party to defeat the real enemy which is socialism?

6. Will the general public regard acceptance of the Whip as a sell-out or, to paraphrase Shakespeare, is this a time which taken at the flood leads on to greater things?

Victory is ours! Teddy Taylor, self, John Wilkinson, Teresa Gorman, Nick Budgen and Richard Shepherd.

we have served notice that the UK is not going to be pushed around inside the EU in pursuit of objectives which are not in Britain's interest.

We get excellent and extensive coverage in the press and media and our refound colleagues welcome us back with warm words and beaming smiles. We have had the Whip restored unconditionally and everybody recognises that we have won but, of course, it doesn't do to say so! If we have won then it follows that the management have lost but simply rubbing their noses in it is not our style.

It soon becomes apparent that in the eyes of the public the fact that we are all now once again fully fledged members of the Parliamentary Conservative Party makes no difference to how we are perceived – we are still in great demand for interviews and speaking engagements, we are still being stopped in the street by well wishers and none of the opprobrium with which the Party itself is now so firmly saddled appears to be attached to ourselves. On the contrary our reputation for having the guts to tell it how it is seems undiminished and in the circumstances we decide that we must stick together and battle on. We have made it clear to the Government Whips that we have commitments which we intend to honour but, not that the gesture is appreciated, that we would be only too pleased to share some of our experiences with the 'management' in an honest endeavour to help them to attract the popularity which they so obviously lack.

On 11 May we journey to Truro for a public meeting in the City Hall under the auspices of the Freedom Association. My research assistant Adrian Lee has been despatched to Truro in advance to make sure that all the necessary arrangements are in hand and to meet Sir Louis Le Bailly* who will take the chair. An audience of approximately 270 people awaits our arrival and after we have all spoken and answered numerous questions from the floor the proceedings are brought to a close with a standing ovation but not before a young man from Brixham has told the assembled company how he had doubled his majority at last week's local elections as a direct result, he claimed, of taking a leaf out of our book and telling his electors precisely where he stood on the issue of Europe.

A couple of days later my Chairman, Michael Wood, enlivens the proceedings of the West Midlands Area Conservative AGM by moving a resolution instructing the President to convey in person and in the strongest possible terms the angry sentiments expressed at the meeting about Party direction to the PM himself. Michael Price now has two mandates to seek a meeting with the Leader and I take this as my cue to tackle Major's PPS John Ward, for the second time, about the possibility of the Group of 8 meeting the Leader to pass on the benefit of our experiences. John is adamant that the PM is not prepared to meet us as a group but only as members of other deputations. I take the opportunity of saying to John that asking the public for policy ideas, which is what the Party is now doing, and meeting, as Central Council did only recently, to debate how to win back 'Middle England' sends out entirely the wrong message – it simply tells the public that the Party has lost its way and hasn't a clue as to where it is going and in any case the Party should know instinctively what 'Middle England' wants and expects of a Tory party. John assures me that he really does pass on the messages he receives, however unpalatable, and I remind him that no man can make the right decision unless he is given the correct information. In spite of the desperate situation there is, however, one message that the Party hierarchy just doesn't want to hear and that is the message which the Group of 8 have been picking up loud and clear wherever we have gone and with daily reminders in our postbag not just from our own constituencies but from all over the country and all over the world. People simply cannot believe, let alone accept, that a Conservative Government is so hell bent on surrendering our sovereignty to Brussels and little wonder that the question of a leadership challenge is never far from the surface. On 17 May George Gardiner stands me a lunch, the object of which, it eventually transpires, is to sound me out as a possible 'stalking horse'! I am no more attracted to this idea now than I was previously but in any case it is all rather academic because, over a beer in the Marquess,

---

*Vice Admiral Sir Louis Le Bailly KBE CB DL is a Council Member of the Freedom Association living in Cornwall and a former Director General of Services Intelligence.

Guest Speaker Secretary of State for Wales John Redwood at LCCA Annual Dinner flanked by self and Chairman Michael Wood.

Roger Knapman tells me that he will be coming back to me soon with the name of somebody acceptable to ourselves who will resign from Cabinet to stand against Major. John Redwood is the guest speaker at the LCCA Annual Dinner at Ludlow racecourse on 19 May and gives a good account of himself when called upon to address an audience of nearly three hundred. Whether this is the person alluded to by Roger I do not know but what is clear is that the issue simply isn't going to go away.

At the beginning of June at a meeting of the LCCA Finance & General Purposes committee there is an unusually full and frank discussion of the contemporary political scene and I come away thinking that the penny has at last dropped and that those present perhaps now realise that the Party's biggest problem is not their own Member of Parliament but the man at the top. More and more John Major's performance reminds me of the brief time I spent in HMS *Modeste* on the Far East station in 1956. Captain Claude Dickens, great grandson of the famous author, had inherited a happy ship which, remarkably for one with such a small complement, had won the Fleet Games at Singapore at the beginning of the commission and would have continued to give the Captain their best shot if they had ever actually known what it was that he required them to do. Time and again we would go into a situation badly briefed or in total ignorance of the object of the exercise and, not surprisingly, foul up. At this point it was Captain Dickens' regular practice to give the ship's company a thorough dressing down for their supposed failings which inevitably gave rise to feelings of deepening resentment on the lower deck. It did not help that few if any of the other officers had it in them to arrest the rapidly deteriorating situation – it was as though the Admiralty had deliberately posted all the commissioned bad hats to this one poor frigate – and the writing by the time I joined the ship was very much on the wall. Sailors would come to me 'dripping' (naval slang for complaining) about the way they were being treated and I soon found myself 'pig in the middle' between what I judged to be a good crew and a thoroughly bad wardroom. As a junior officer I knew that my loyalty had to be to the Captain and Officers but on the other hand my sympathies were with the ill used crew. What to do? As a mere National Service Midshipman I was in a quandary. I had already concluded that the crew would ultimately be driven to mutiny; the Captain, quite apart from being the root cause of the problem, was totally unapproachable and the other officers seemed to be completely detached from the reality of everything that was going on around them. Salvation lay in the voluminous pages of Admiralty Fleet Orders from which I discovered that there was a dearth of junior officers for an aircraft direction course starting in the autumn at HMS *Harrier*, a shore establishment in Pembrokeshire. My application for the course was accepted and on the eve of the Suez campaign I was winging my way back to 'Blighty' but with strict instructions from Captain Dickens, who had been at the gangway to see me off, not to open my 'flimsy'* until I was safely aboard the aircraft! This said it all. Consistent with his practice of keeping his subordinates completely in the dark Captain Dickens, who should have been prepared to discuss personnel matters man to man, chose to send me on my way without a word. Many years later, whilst attending a training course at the Royal Naval College, Greenwich as an officer in the Royal Naval Reserve, I bumped into a Regular Officer who, as a Lieutenant, had been the Navigating Officer in *Modeste* all those years ago. Until he told me what had happened I had no idea that my premonition of a mutiny had come true approximately six weeks after I had left the ship at Singapore. All this happened three decades ago but Captain Dickens' incompetent command of HMS *Modeste* and John Major's ill-starred leadership of the Conservative Party bear a striking resemblance. At the top of the Party there is, according to all reports, a paralysis of decision-making; the Leader's Lieutenants in the form of the Cabinet appear to be unwilling or incapable of doing anything to improve matters and the crew in the shape of the backbenchers is in a pretty ugly mood. I do not predict wholesale insurrection on the backbenches because courage is in very short supply but when it comes to the next General Election I feel almost certain that the

---

*The 'flimsy' is a small form printed on remarkably thin paper upon which the Commanding Officer writes a précis of the confidential report that he must submit to Admiralty upon an officer leaving his command.

electorate will mutiny in no uncertain terms.* In the meantime the 'management' soldier on like Mr Micawber in the hope that something will turn up.

The Fresh Start Group is scheduled to meet John Major on 13 June but attending their meetings for the first time in six months I cannot help noticing several new faces. Prior to having the Whip withdrawn I had always objected most strongly to widening the membership of the group beyond those of us who were genuinely opposed to European Union for fear that others would use it as a bandwagon for their own purposes. Predictably there are now colleagues in membership of the group who are using it to further their aims in relation to the Party leadership and so when we meet Major in the large Ministerial Conference Room in the basement below the Chamber there are more than fifty colleagues in attendance. Major appears oblivious to the fact that this meeting is crucial to his own personal survival and by refusing to come off the fence simply increases the sense of discontent that his leadership arouses. It is a deeply depressing experience which leaves us all feeling utterly frustrated. In spite of some fairly direct questions and very blunt expressions of opinion one senses that the meeting hasn't achieved anything. There has been no meeting of minds, no grounds for believing that the air has been cleared and generally no feeling that matters will improve.

At a meeting of the ERG earlier in the day our guests have been Leader of the House Tony Newton and Scottish Secretary Ian Lang. It is a constructive meeting at the end of which Ian says how good it is to have the opportunity to concentrate on these important matters for a while, the inference being that Cabinet never does!

In the meantime the Group of 8 has continued to meet and on 6 June approves the arrangements for a series of fringe meetings at the Party Conference in October as well as an event in Nottinghamshire to counter the pro-European rally which Adrian Lee has discovered Conservative Central Office are staging in that city on 7/8 July. After the meeting Teresa and I discuss at some length the merits of canvassing support for a 'stalking horse' who would run on a Referendum ticket as a means of pressurising Major's eventual successor into adopting that as a policy commitment. It's an interesting idea but I suggest that before swinging into action we'd best sleep on it, not least because Norman Lamont is now emerging as the most likely colleague to perform this somewhat unenviable task.

The day after the calamitous meeting with Major I am less than comfortable at the prospect of being interviewed on TV about my voting intentions on the Rate Capping motion that will come before the House tomorrow but against that we are probably at the stage where it's now a case

*In the event the Conservative vote was down from 14,092,891 in 1992 to 9,602,989 in 1997, a net loss of almost 4$\frac{1}{2}$ million votes.

of every man for himself as this rotten administration founders. Quite apart from the fact that John Biffen and I feel that all our representations on the subject of Local Authority funding have been totally ignored and that our county of Shropshire has been particularly badly treated we are also at loggerheads with Environment Secretary John Gummer, on the issue of the Local Government Review. Letters to him on this subject written in March and April remain unanswered and when we meet Minister of State David Curry on 15 June in yet another attempt to make our voice heard he launches into an apologia about the Revenue Support Grant settlement. We are at pains to point out to David that what we want to talk about is the Review and not least the cavalier attitude of his boss (John Gummer) in not having the courtesy to consult us about matters of great importance to the county we represent, nor even the manners to reply to our correspondence. Nothing that David says does anything to allay my suspicion that a deal has been done behind the scenes and that Telford & Wrekin will be granted Unitary status despite opinion in the rest of Shropshire being strongly against it. John Biffen and I both speak in the debate on Rate Capping and vote against the motion which, in all the circumstances, is no more than the Government deserve. Significantly there are no repercussions from the Government Whips who presumably recognise that John and I have been flagging up the problem for a long time and that our case is almost unanswerable.

Major's PPS, John Ward, wants to know what question I will ask the PM at Question Time next Tuesday and facetiously I tell him that I think that something along the lines of 'if he intends to have a reshuffle next month will he, instead of simply re-arranging the deckchairs, change the officers on the bridge…Or does he intend to go down with the ship?'

There is a prompt reply from the Pairing Whip, Andrew MacKay (Berkshire East), to my letter advising him that six of the former Whipless will not be available to vote next Thursday (22nd June). This is because we will be addressing a previously arranged public meeting in Malvern. News that the Government intend to have 3-line business in the House that day is their problem, not ours, least of all when they plan only 2-line business on Tuesday and Wednesday.

According to the early morning news bulletins on Friday 16 June last night's meeting of the '22 Committee must have been quite seminal – according to the BBC, messages are being delivered to Downing Street telling Major to get his act together and to get back to old style Conservative principles. The pressure upon Major is building up to an unprecedented extent but it is anybody's guess as to how he will respond.

On the eve of our public meeting in Malvern Douglas Hurd tries to lay the blame for all our European ills at the door of Margaret Thatcher. This strikes my visitors in the Public Gallery that day as being disingenuous in the extreme as indeed is the advice from former Minister Tim Sainsbury (Hove) who, 'as an old hand', tells me that 'now is the time for restraint'.*

Prior to setting out for Paddington station on Thursday 22 June I agree to be interviewed by Central TV who are naturally interested in tonight's meeting in their area, at Malvern. The questions keep returning to party unity, a possible leadership contest and the future of Douglas Hurd. In spite of their importance the answers to any of these questions have not been forthcoming for what seems like a very long time but unbeknown to any of us and indeed before we are very much older we shall at least have the answer to one of them.

As I take a seat aboard the Paddington/Worcester train a man leans over from a seat on the opposite side of the gangway to ask me if my name is Christopher Gill. His is Sebastian Hamilton and when I ask him where he's going he tells me that he is going to our meeting in Malvern. Mildly interested to know why the *Sunday Times* consider our meeting worth reporting he tells me that it is because his editor is fascinated to know whether the public meetings we are holding in different parts of the country are the beginning of a revival in this rather old-fashioned mode of political campaigning. He goes on to say how much he admires the fact that we don't just address our audiences and disappear but actually take questions. Realising that my five colleagues Body, Budgen, Marlow, Shepherd and Taylor must be in a different part of the train I move to another carriage which is where, an hour or so later, Sebastian finds us all chatting, completely oblivious of the news he now imparts. 'Major has resigned.'

The news is staggering – it is barely credible – but Sebastian, who has the benefit of a mobile phone, assures us that it is only too true. Major has told the world that his critics must 'put up or shut up' and it looks as though he has deliberately chosen this very day to drop his bombshell so as to make the Group of 8 the scapegoats. He certainly has caught us on the hop. Within a very few minutes we must disembark at Worcester where John Farbon and Marcus Wilesmith are waiting with cars to take us on to Malvern. There is barely time to consider how we should react to this new and entirely unexpected situation but there is no escaping it. Arriving at the Winter Gardens we are immediately besieged by the army of journalists and cameramen who are already assembled there, with more on the way. Thanks to the tireless efforts of local entrepreneur John Farbon who has handled all the publicity for our meeting, as well as all the other necessary arrangements, our meeting was always going to be newsworthy but now suddenly we are thrust, once again, into the limelight. The question they all want answering is whether we will support Major in the contest that he has just precipitated.

*Tim Sainsbury's son-in-law, Shaun Woodward, might have better profited from this advice. Two years after being elected as the Conservative Member for Witney in 1997 he defected to Labour.

Not knowing any of the detail surrounding his shock announcement nor, indeed, at this stage, whether anyone will have the courage to put up against him, the question is not quite as straightforward as it looks. Were it the case that our objective all along had been to unseat Major then doubtless our reaction would have been one of jubilation but consistently we have eschewed getting involved in this aspect of Party politics and, so as not to detract from our core message, have conscientiously avoided name calling or personal denigration – which is more than can be said for those who oppose us.

Inside the Winter Gardens an audience of close on a thousand people welcome us with rapturous applause. The atmosphere is electric. Suddenly this long scheduled meeting is in the cockpit of national politics and the sensation that history is being made as we speak is inescapable. With six of us all wanting to add our own pennyworth the Chairman, Councillor Martin Jolly of Malvern Hills District Council, is relying upon each of us to be brief so that there will be ample time for questions from the floor. When it comes to questions it is apparent that not quite the whole of the audience is on our side but that is a bonus in the sense that preaching to the converted and answering anodyne questions does not make for the best of meetings, whereas a little bit of controversy livens the occasion and stimulates audience participation. The meeting is an unqualified success and leaving to a standing ovation we are once again confronted by the battery of cameras and microphones which is still drawn up outside the auditorium. For programmes like 'Newsnight' this is a scoop. The timing is perfect, the circumstances are unprecedented and a live audience of 980 people is something that most politicians would die for. Still there is no news as to whether or not John Major has a rival and so the question as to who we will all vote for remains hypothetical. At this stage there is no indication that anyone within Cabinet will break ranks and it appears that Major, regarding this as a straightforward vote of confidence, is defying them to do so. After a long but exciting day we shall simply have to wait and see what the morning brings.

In the morning I wake up feeling that I've missed an opportunity. Last night, instead of telling the media that I would stand by Major, I should have told them that I would stand against him but all is not yet lost. Shortly after breakfast George Gardiner telephones to see if I will agree to be the 'stalking horse' and after consulting the 'kitchen cabinet' and reasoning that my standing in the first round could set the agenda that would then have to be picked up by a challenger in the second round, I ring George back to say that I will do it.

Next on the line is Norman Lamont asking if I will nominate him. In view of what I have just said to George I am obliged to play for time and it is agreed that Norman will phone me again at 1700 for an answer. In the meantime I speak to Teresa Gorman who tells me that she has already agreed to second

Norman and is telling the world that if nobody else will stand, she will – that lets me out! As I walk back to my office at 1652 the phone is already ringing and it's Norman Lamont wanting my answer. I tell him that in my candid opinion it would be in his interest to get someone who is less obviously Eurosceptic, and a rebel to boot, to nominate him, particularly as I understand that he has already got Teresa to second him.

On Saturday morning (24 June) I ring Roger Knapman to see if he can tell me what is going on. Roger is very cagey and learning nothing that I don't already know I put in a call to David Evans. David encourages me to believe that John Redwood is seriously minded to make a move and we agree that I should speak to JR personally with a view to putting him in touch with Norman Lamont. David tells me that Ian Bruce (Dorset South) and Ian Twinn (Edmonton) have also been in touch with him so I am not alone in identifying JR as Major's most plausible challenger. When I speak to JR he is mildly enthusiastic about talking to Norman and suggests that I invite him to come to JR's office in the House at 1100 on Monday or, if he wants to, to give him a ring at home over the weekend. When I contact Norman later in the day, to suggest a meeting in JR's office on Monday, there is a short pause after which Norman says that he thinks he'll give JR a call now but not before I have spoken to JR again myself to report NL's reaction.

On Sunday (25 June) the newspapers are full of speculation that Redwood will pick up the gauntlet that Major has so petulantly thrown down. My first call is to David Evans to tell him that I have put NL and JR in touch with each other whereupon David tells me that Julian Brazier (Canterbury), Ian Bruce, Barry Field (Isle of Wight), Roger Knapman, David Martin (Portsmouth South) and Ian Twinn will be meeting in JR's room at the earlier time of 1000 tomorrow morning. For my part I undertake to contact Iain Duncan Smith, Barry Legg (Milton Keynes South West) and Michael Lord (Suffolk Central) but warn David against inviting Bill Cash to the meeting simply because his verbosity is inclined to make it difficult for others to get a word in edgeways and for meetings to make constructive progress. David is particularly anxious for me to give him my assessment of Barry Legg and I am subsequently amazed when Barry is given a key role as JR's aide-de-camp. Much of my Sunday is given over to phoning other colleagues including members of the Group of 8 who are generally very positive in their support for JR with the exception of Teddy Taylor who continues to be pro Major. One or two colleagues are reluctant to declare their hand. Paul Marland says that he's on our side but would prefer not to attend tomorrow's meeting. Michael Lord's wife, Jenny, tells me that Michael is likely to be late back from a day's golf but sadly nothing further is heard from that quarter.

On Monday, despite the vagaries of the railway system, I manage to get to the House just in time for the start of the meeting in JR's room where I find

myself in the company of Jacques Arnold (Gravesham), Julian Brazier, David
Evans, Barry Field, Roger Knapman, Norman Lamont, Barry Legg, David
Martin and JR's special adviser, Hywel Williams. JR informs the meeting that
he will address a Press Conference at 1400 this afternoon. The meeting agrees
that David Evans should be JR's campaign manager and David suggests that
we reconvene in his office at noon. I undertake to provide the midday
meeting with nominal lists which will help us to identify potential supporters
but by the time I get back to the House, having in the meantime been home
to dig out the relevant information and make sufficient copies for our
purpose, the meeting is already under way and I discover that in my absence I
have been delegated to run the campaign office! The urgent necessity now is
to find premises, ideally not far from the Palace of Westminster, in which to
establish the campaign Headquarters. With this in mind Messrs. Evans, Field,
Williams and I go to inspect accommodation at 32 Queen Anne's Gate as
arranged over the telephone at our ten o'clock meeting. The premises are
more than adequate but our contact cannot authorise their use for political
purposes without first obtaining the permission of his superior landlord
which by 4 o'clock that afternoon is clearly not forthcoming. As one door
closes, fortuitously another one opens and when I speak to Patrick Robertson,
Director of the Bruges Group, at about 5 p.m. he says that there is accommodation 'all ready for you', that 'telephones can be put in' and that 'tables
and chairs etc., whatever you need, will arrive in the morning'. Later that
evening Barry Field and I go to run our eye over 164 Ashley Gardens and
deciding that it's a case of any port in a storm plan to move in as soon as we
possibly can tomorrow morning.

Meanwhile at 2 p.m. on Monday afternoon a packed Press Conference in
the Jubilee Room at the House of Commons hears JR tell a stunned world
that he is resigning from Cabinet to stand against Major. Without being
invited to do so Tony Marlow, clad in a highly colourful striped cricket blazer,
and Teresa Gorman, dressed in equally eye-catching garb, stand immediately
behind a seated JR for the duration of the proceedings thus affording his
detractors the opportunity to portray JR as a challenger whose support does
not extend beyond the maverick fringe. It is an unfortunate start and one that
could have been avoided had JR insisted on sitting at the centre of the top
table. After the Press Conference I bump into Mike Penning and ask him to
get his boss, Teddy Taylor, to agree to let him join the campaign team as Press
Officer, having earlier in the day contacted my own researcher, Adrian Lee,
and told him to get to the House as quickly as possible to lend a hand with the
thousand and one things that we need to do to get the campaign going from
an absolute standing start. When the Group of 8 meet at 1530 I tell them that
I've joined the Redwood campaign team but ask them to adopt a low profile
so as not to spoil JR's chances by 'frightening the horses' but in saying that I

Redwood rises to the challenge, surrounded by Teresa Gorman, Bill Walker, Edward Leigh, David Evans, self, Barry Legg, Norman Lamont and Hywel Williams.

am of course mindful that I'm attempting to shut the stable door after at least two of the horses have already bolted. Somewhat reluctantly I agree to be interviewed on the BBC Nick Ross programme tomorrow after it is pointed out that fielding Tony Marlow or Bill Cash will probably be counter-productive and that if Barry Legg is featured it won't be long before someone phones in to ask whether that is the same Barry Legg who is involved in the Westminster City Council housing inquiry. A long day ends in the Royal George public house where over a pint of beer with Barry Field, Adrian Lee and his girlfriend Samantha Davies we make plans for tomorrow before sending Adrian and Sam home to produce a Bulletin ready for the Press Conference at the Queen Elizabeth II Centre at 1030 in the morning.

At 0900 on Tuesday 27 June I am at the BBC studios at 4 Millbank for the Nick Ross show. Ann Widdecombe (Maidstone) appearing for the Major camp doesn't pull any punches – neither do I! At the end of the programme Nick Ross says, 'You must be very pleased that over 55 per cent of our callers support John Redwood,' to which I reply that less than twenty-four hours after the start of the campaign that isn't bad. This is followed by a highly successful Press Conference at the QEII Centre after which it's back to Ashley Gardens which is rapidly filling up with all sorts of people who are piling in to

Being interviewed on College Green.

help. I agree to allocate authors Robin Harris and Andrew Roberts a room to themselves so that they can get on with recording what goes on for posterity. Sir Alfred Sherman, co-founder of the Centre for Policy Studies with Keith Joseph and Margaret Thatcher, sits patiently but forlornly in the entrance hall but sadly before I can deal with him he tires of waiting and disappears. John Spiers hands me a note to say that he hopes that he can be used in a more productive writing role but is one of the unsung heroes who spend the rest of the campaign answering telephones and generally making themselves useful. Other volunteers are either employees of our host, Sir Benjamin Slade Bt., friends of Hywel Williams or a profusion of effeminate young men who mysteriously appear from nowhere to offer their services. There is an urgent necessity to establish an adequate communication system to cope with the huge volume of incoming calls as well as to facilitate contact with other members of the campaign team in different locations. BT engineers work flat out all day to get a telephone system installed and Sir Benjamin's assistant, the svelte Lucky, is despatched to acquire a consignment of mobiles. One of the calls received is from the TV studio where JR is supposed to be appearing live on the Richard Littlejohn programme. Disconcertingly nobody seems to know where JR is and I suggest to David Evans that he'd better get down to 4 Millbank pronto to sort the problem out. Richard Littlejohn's agreement to forget all about today and to have JR on his programme tomorrow is, in all the circumstances, very generous and further evidence that much of the Press is sympathetic to the Redwood cause. Although this is only the first full day of a ten-day campaign it is already becoming clear that Hywel Williams is going to be a difficult person to work with. For reasons best known to himself he is extremely reluctant for me to join a newspaper planning meeting attended by Norman Lamont, Andrew Roberts, Robin Harris and later, Edward Leigh. What Williams' 'locus' is in the overall scheme of things is never spelt out but he and I will soon find ourselves on a collision course.

Wednesday 28 June gets off to a bad start when Mike Penning phones at 0700 to say that he can't get into the HQ at Ashley Gardens. Arriving there fifteen minutes later I find Barry Field fulminating about not having left someone on duty overnight to prevent this sort of thing happening. Barry, Adrian Lee and I then put our shoulders to the door in an attempt to force an entry but the doors prove stronger than we are. What then follows defies explanation. At 0730, as if by prior arrangement, a photographer from *The Times* newspaper arrives to witness our predicament followed shortly by Hywel Williams who sees that we're locked out, sees the photographer and, without a word to anyone, disappears!* Of the Ashley Gardens caretaker there is still, mysteriously, no sign. By this time David Evans has arrived on the scene and he and I decide to go to the House, where at least we will be contactable, having in the meantime instructed Barry to drop everything else so as to concentrate on finding new premises. Later in the morning he collects me from the House and we go to inspect the vacant office accommodation that he has located on the ground floor of 78 Buckingham Gate. Having agreed that the premises will serve our purpose Barry undertakes to do the business with the landlord's agents and solicitors and to call me when 'the eagle has landed'. By the time the eagle does actually land the residents of Ashley Gardens are up in arms and Sir Benjamin is having to take steps to thwart their threatened injunction. The fact that their building is now practically under siege from hordes of affectacious young men who are coming up in the lift shaft faster than I can kick them down the stairs is clearly doing nothing to endear us to the neighbours and the sooner we're out of here the better. By evening time it is possible to tell our helpers, but only the ones we trust, that we intend moving at least part of the operation out of

---

*It later transpires that Hywel had made an appointment for *The Times* to meet JR but there is no explanation as to why he chose such a ridiculous time of day or why JR did not appear

Ashley Gardens whilst tomorrow's Press Conference is taking place and to have the Buckingham Gate premises up and running shortly thereafter. In the meantime my long suffering secretary, Vicki Stevens, has been instructed, for the second time in thirty-six hours, to make all the arrangements for telephones, furniture and equipment to be installed at the new HQ. Rather inconveniently I have a long-standing engagement this evening to dine with the Group of 8 and their spouses, together with our respective Association Chairmen and their spouses. This is by way of a thank you to our Chairmen for all the help and support that they have given us during the past particularly trying six months. En route to dinner in Dining Room A at the House of Commons I call in at Buckingham Gate to give Adrian Lee a cheque to cover the hire charge on office equipment that is due to be delivered within the hour only to discover that he and Huw Shooter have taken it upon themselves to interfere with the instructions previously given to BT regarding telephones. Subsequently I was glad that I didn't sack them on the spot but given the pressure we're working under and the deadlines we have to meet departures from the agreed plan simply cannot be tolerated. One of the day's more time consuming tasks has been that of agreeing the text of a letter and policy statement that Teresa Gorman's office will mail out on JR's behalf to all constituency Chairmen. This is no mean task but essential if John is to enlist the support of the voluntary side of the Party which, whilst not having a vote in these matters, may have some influence as to how our colleagues vote in six days time.

At 1000 on Thursday 29 June desks and chairs are delivered to 78 Buckingham Gate and with great relief at 1230 we are able to close the doors on 164 Ashley Gardens for the last time. Who has put them up to it we shall never know but today *The Times* and the *Daily Mail* reporters express the wish to meet some of our female helpers. So as not to be upstaged by the mother and daughter photograph of the Cash family which they have with them I summon my younger daughter, who is waiting in the wings, but the *Mail* reporter is suspicious because, being married, her surname is not the same as mine! Despite time spent on the lower deck I seldom swear and am therefore somewhat surprised to hear myself telling Hywel Williams to 'bugger off and don't come back' when I discover him changing all JR's media appointments after they have all been previously agreed. He provokes the altercation by criticising me for letting the media into the HQ where they might 'pick up sensitive information'. As much of the resultant TV programme features himself I can see what he means! That evening there is a campaign meeting in the House but, as it is mainly to do with number crunching – which Members have pledged their support and which others might be persuaded to do so – I conclude that my time would be better spent back at campaign HQ. Whilst I am still on the premises the Division Bell rings and so I decide to cast my vote. Exiting the division lobby with JR I tell him that I'd like a word but since he doesn't appear anxious to stop and talk we have to talk on the hoof as we walk towards New Palace Yard where he offers to give me a lift in the Jaguar car which he has been lent by a benefactor for the duration of the campaign. Going through the main gateway out into Parliament Square the boot of the car flies open and refuses to shut when the policeman on duty repeatedly slams it down. The chauffeur then gets out to attend to the problem leaving our potential PM immobilised on the pavement crossing with crowds, but fortunately no TV cameras, gathering on either side. After dropping JR and Barry Legg at 4 Millbank the chauffeur cannot get back into the car because the driver's door won't open from the outside! As I direct the chauffeur to our HQ, which he says he couldn't find yesterday, I cannot help thinking that somebody, somewhere, doesn't want us to win. Nevertheless, in our brief time together I have got JR to agree to appear on the 'Breakfast with Frost' programme on Sunday and possibly on one of the Dimbleby programmes. That evening I give my daughter and my secretary supper at the greasy spoon Italian restaurant next door but, as we go back into the HQ, JR and his retinue are just leaving – they exit so fast that Sarah doesn't even see JR!

On Friday 30 June our band of helpers is swelled by the arrival of Christopher Monckton who volunteers to telephone canvass Members of Parliament, many of whom are personally known to him. That is a bonus but on the other hand Mike Penning is absolutely beside himself because JR has now decided that he doesn't want to do either the 'Breakfast with Frost' programme or 'Panorama'. Deciding that the way the conversation is heading it would be best if we continue it out of earshot of the rest of the campaign team Mike and I adjourn to the greasy spoon where, over a cup of coffee, Mike voices his suspicions that the whole campaign is phoney – there have been just too many strange coincidences and unexplained occurrences for both his liking and mine. Not long afterwards, as if they had been reading our thoughts, David Evans and Barry Field arrive at campaign headquarters bearing gifts of chocolates and a bottle of House of Commons whisky. They try to smooth us over but the suspicion remains that we at HQ are not being told the truth. Mike's suspicions are shared by Adrian Lee and Samantha Davies who are becoming increasingly agitated about what's going on and once again, this time for supper, I repair to the greasy spoon to see if we can make any sense of things. The only conclusion we can reach is that we just have to stick it out and see how the final chapter unfolds but always at the back of my mind is what JR's wife Gail said to me when we chatted briefly earlier in the week.

On Saturday 1 July it's business as usual at campaign headquarters, but owing to a longstanding engagement I have to leave Westminster before 7 a.m.

to travel to Shropshire where I am due to present the prizes at Wrekin College Speech Day. My address to the parents, staff and pupils is all about Courage, Courtesy and Integrity but there is no time to find out whether or not my remarks are well received because as soon as the formal proceedings are ended I am heading for the railway station and a return to London, arriving back in Buckingham Gate at 1740. In my absence the team have successfully fended off calls about allegations of homosexual activity and, thankfully, there the matter rests. Adrian and Sam's friend Bunny Smedley has now also concluded that all is not as it should be but at the end of another long day none of us are any the wiser.

At 0800 on Sunday I open up the HQ but am not entirely surprised to be alone until other members of the team arrive having watched JR who, after all, appeared on the Frost programme. On TV, compared to his rival John Major, JR looks every bit the winner. Just after 10 o'clock I decide to go home for a late breakfast which is where I am when Barry Field telephones me to say that at 1245 David Evans is going to take us all out to lunch. Arriving at Members Entrance at the appointed hour I am met by Roger Knapman who escorts me to an office adjoining David Evan's office where he insists on making me a cup of coffee. Having made it clear that I am far from happy with the way things are going, at 1315 JR himself comes into the room and when we are alone I ask him whether this is for real and whether he really wants to win. He says, 'Of course,' in reply to which I tell him that it's not very satisfactory that we with the more positive candidate have the least positive campaign. Thanks to one of my constituents we even have the best campaign slogan – 'No Change, No Chance' – but in deference to colleagues who almost certainly won't vote Redwood anyway there is a diffidence about using even that to maximum advantage. At the conclusion of our private discussion we adjourn to the Savoy Grill where at lunch with David Evans, Barry Field and Roger Knapman I learn that plans for JR to be at St. Bartholomew's Hospital* at 1400 this afternoon have been aborted!

After lunch there is a totally different atmosphere. I can only conclude that I was kept waiting at the House en route to the Savoy whilst the rest of the gang decided that as there is now every prospect of winning they might as well go for it. Norman Lamont comes on the line insisting that we send out copies of today's *Sunday Telegraph* leader and cartoon to all our Parliamentary colleagues. Before doing so I insist that he clears this with JR himself because I am not prepared to waste any more precious time on plans which are subsequently countermanded or aborted. JR reluctantly agrees and we turn to to deliver the goods. This will be in addition to the personal letter from JR to all colleagues which my wife Patricia types out at home whilst we are en route

*With threats of closure hanging over this ancient hospital it was much in the news thus affording a potentially good PR opportunity for JR.

from the Savoy to HQ in David Evans' limousine. The reluctance to make a plan and stick to it or to commit wholeheartedly to an aggressive campaign to win is a worrying and inexplicable feature of the past seven days. Over a cup of tea in the St. James' Hotel opposite our HQ, Mike Penning tells me that he is convinced that the campaign is phoney but we agree that for as long as JR is in the running we'll carry on doing our best to get the result we want to see. The day ends with my bawling out Hywel Williams for, once again, countermanding my instructions. Whether or not he is a fifth column within our midst is a moot point but his propensity to cause dissension in the ranks is something we could well do without.*

Monday 3 July is the last full day of campaigning before tomorrow's ballot. During the course of the day my wife Patricia has spoken to JR's wife Gail who says that only last night did JR tell her that there was a real possibility that by Tuesday evening they could be the new occupants at 10 Downing Street.

The big day arrives and at 0645 I am picked up at home to be taken to College Green to do an interview for Radio 5 Live. Despite the hour the Green is positively teeming with colleagues giving media interviews but whether, at this eleventh hour, there are any more votes to be garnered is rather doubtful. The main thing now is to monitor the actual ballot to ensure that there are no dirty tricks. Arriving at a campaign conference in the House I am in time to hear Norman Lamont reciting some doggerel he has written about the contest after which we get down to the business of making a roster of tellers to stand guard outside the Polling Station. I volunteer to be on duty from 1100 till 1200 during which time Julian Critchley arrives in his wheelchair. Deciding that this is an opportunity not to be missed I tell him that his scurrilous articles in our local press are hardly the behaviour of an officer and a gentleman, let alone those of a colleague. At this he tries to move away but placing my foot firmly under one of his wheels I tell him that whilst it seems that he doesn't wish to continue this conversation, I do! I then go on to say that people who live in glass houses shouldn't throw stones, particularly if they have a voting record like his. Always quick with the repartee Critchley says, 'F*** off, Gill,' and propels himself into Committee Room 12 to cast his vote. Michael Brunson, ITV's political editor, and his BBC counterpart, Robin Oakley, and other reporters crammed into the Committee Room corridor sing out, 'What did he say?' They know precisely what Critchley has said but not until I tell them do they know the rest of the tale. On that day's 1 O'clock News Robin Oakley credits me with having tried to help Julian Critchley before being told 'to do something unrepeatable'! Taking advantage

---

*When, after the Leadership contest, John Redwood established the Conservative 2000 Foundation Hywel Williams was appointed Director. Subsequently he left the Conservative Party and in a waspish book published in 1998 attacked his former associates in a most extraordinary way.

of a lull in the proceedings I skip home to grab a bite to eat on my way back to campaign HQ only to find that JR has just left. How the boss always manages to visit HQ when I am somewhere else is yet another mystery in a campaign which, from the insider's point of view, doesn't quite ring true. Less than two weeks after it all began the final scene in the leadership drama is about to unfold. At 5 p.m. the result of the ballot will be announced in Committee Room 14. Realising that it will be standing room only I am far from being the only one to arrive early but my plan to stand by one of the doors so as to make a quick getaway after the declaration is thwarted by the decision to lock us all in whilst the Chairman of the '22 conveys the results to the Press in an adjoining room. The 'management' have clearly understood the importance of getting to the media first so as to put their own 'spin' on the result regardless of whether the total number of votes cast for Major is good, bad or indifferent. The result, when it comes, is just enough for the Majorites to claim victory. With 218 votes, equivalent to only two-thirds of the Parliamentary Party, it is a close call for Major. Had Redwood been the beneficiary of some of the votes of the 8 abstainers or the 12 who, incredibly, spoiled their ballot papers, a second round would have been inevitable but JR concedes and we are back to where we started, albeit with one or two significant differences.

When on Wednesday 5 June Major announces his new Cabinet and a reshuffle of other ministerial appointments it is apparent that the main beneficiary is Michael Heseltine who becomes Deputy Prime Minister, the suspicion being that this is the price he has extracted from Major for delivering the Heselteeny votes. There is nothing for the right of the party other than the promotion of Nick Bonsor (Upminster) to Minister of State at the Foreign Office which the cynics amongst us recognise as simply a ploy to prevent him challenging Marcus Fox for the chairmanship of the 1922 Committee later in the year. Walking part way home that evening with my old comrade in arms, James Cran, I cannot resist asking him why he voted for Major – 'To keep Hezza out,' he replies. Meanwhile Hezza has lost no time in ensconcing himself in Downing Street and is rumoured to be intent on even having his own Question Time too!

On the morning of 5 July my telephone scarcely stops ringing. The leadership contest is water under the bridge but now the focus is back on the Group of 8 public meeting scheduled for tomorrow evening in Nottingham. Because of my close involvement and identification with the Redwood campaign, others beside my constituency chairman are advising that it would be best if I sat this one out. Mike Penning is particularly anxious that I should give Nottingham a miss and so, whilst my colleagues Body, Gorman and Marlow are making their way north to join Freedom Association Chairman Norris McWhirter on the platform, Mike and I crack a bottle of champagne to celebrate how well we did to get such a substantial and significant number of

votes for JR. Meanwhile at PMQs JR congratulates John Major on winning
and expresses the hope that his policies, as extolled during the course of the
past ten days, will be 'useful' in the months ahead. The weekly meeting of the
'22 Committee passes off without a murmur after which we all repair to the
QEII Centre where, at 1800, John Major delivers his 'coronation' or 're-
coronation' address to the Members of the Parliamentary Party, other Party
members, CCO workers, helpers on the campaign team and, of course, a
throng of press and media reporters all anxious to record the final curtain call
on one of the most bizarre and unprecedented events in British political
history. The episode, as far as I am concerned, ends as it has begun, on a train.
Journeying from Euston to Shropshire on Friday 6 July Derek Conway tells
me that Roger Knapman is to be one of three new appointees to the Whips'
Office. He alone from the Redwood camp is to be the recipient of John
Major's largesse but the surprise is that the PM's largesse extends in our
direction at all given the level of acrimony that the contest has generated.

After all the excitement and hard work of the past fortnight, on Monday 10
July it's back to reality. We have fought and lost and as Richard Shepherd says
we now have a deeply integrationist Government. For JR to have attracted 89
votes is a creditable effort but it should have been and would have been more
if, for example, all the members of the ERG had voted in accordance with
their avowed convictions. The fact that they didn't persuades me that for the
foreseeable future the group will be regarded as no more than a paper tiger.
Concluding that I no longer wish to support a group which cannot present a
united front when faced with an almost heaven-sent opportunity to move
things on in the direction it purports to want to go, I write to James Cran
tendering my resignation. The following day I am pleased to have the
opportunity of explaining the reasons for my resignation to group secretary
Daniel Hannan and am just about to put a note on the letterboard for Michael
Spicer when I bump into him in Members' Lobby. Michael is anxious to get
me to change my mind but, assuring him that it is nothing personal, the fact
remains that last Thursday the group members went every which way with
the result that Major can now afford to ignore the group with total impunity.
Finding myself walking home with James Cran I offer to buy him a drink in
the Horse and Bower. He tells me that his benefactor David Caldow wants
nothing more to do with him – a fact that will be confirmed by John
Townend when we talk next Monday – and I conclude that he must be a very
disappointed man having lost friends, allies and credibility without so much as
a smell of a job in the administration.

On Wednesday I bump into Archie Hamilton in Abingdon Street. He tells
me that the group are not going to accept my resignation and subsequently
Dan Hannan says that the group were almost unanimous that I shouldn't be
allowed to leave – the dissenting voice being James Cran who felt that my

note of resignation was too curt. My note was indeed brief and deliberately so. I had purposely sought to avoid spelling out what I really thought of my colleagues in the ERG whom I hold responsible for delivering the Party into the hands of a Major/Heseltine coalition, a situation which is, if anything, worse than the one we had before.

John Biffen will not concede that he might have been wrong to vote for Major but Warren Hawksley makes no bones about it. In a voice loud enough for the whole dining room to hear he tells my visiting constituency President that he voted for Major but within twenty-four hours realised he'd made a mistake! David Harris is charitable enough to say that 'as a Major man' the margin was not sufficient for him to claim victory and that he thinks that the Redwood camp behaved very well indeed in the circumstances.

The general consensus on Thursday 13th is that the re-elected Leader's address to the full '22 Committee is good stuff – just like his recent letter to all Constituency Chairmen – but it's action we want, not words.

As the dust surrounding the recent leadership contest settles 10 Conservative Members meeting in JR's room on 17 July are told that Hywel Williams and Rollo Clifford are working on establishing a Redwood Foundation. The MPs – Brazier, Duncan Smith, Cash, Evans, Evenett, Field, Hargreaves, Legg, Martin and myself – agree to set up a cell structure amongst colleagues to multiply the level of support for JR in the almost certain knowledge that a further leadership contest cannot be long delayed.

Tomorrow Andrew Rowe (Mid Kent) is scheduled to introduce his 10 Minute Rule Bill 'to abolish the House of Commons'. Giving me advance notice of what he intends to say, Andrew invites me to become one of the Bill's sponsors. Whilst his proposal to abolish the House of Commons sounds extremely dramatic it carries the rider that he only intends to abolish it 'in its present form' and since his views are very similar to ones which I myself expressed in front of an outside audience as recently as last Wednesday I can hardly refuse to support him. It is all about making changes to curb the excessive power of the Executive although I recognise the irony of expecting Parliament to do anything about this problem when it is, in point of fact, Parliament that has created it – most obviously and most recently by agreeing to give away even more of its power to the unelected and unaccountable European Commission by dint of the Treaty on European Union.

Meeting on 18 July we finalise plans for our various activities at Party Conference in Blackpool. Tony Marlow is keen for us to undertake more public meetings and is very pushy about doing the wind-up at the conclusion of our big meeting in the MGM Cinema. I think that we should try to talk him out of this idea for fear that he might get carried away with his own rhetoric.

As we head for the Summer recess David Martin (Portsmouth South) is

SBF fringe meeting at Blackpool Conservative Party Conference with l-r Chris Venmore,
David Porter, Teddy Taylor and James Cran.

more than usually forthcoming. He confirms my view that Douglas Hurd is ideologically driven in a way that the new Foreign Secretary is not – 'Malcolm Rifkind's just plain ambitious.' Having been Hurd's PPS for four years David should know. Our mutual friend Charles Goodson-Wickes is very depressed about the current situation and fearful that there will be very few of us left in the next Parliament. Time alone will tell how true that prediction will prove to be but with less than two years to go to the General Election it is cold comfort to hear colleagues with bigger majorities than one's own talking in such terms.*

At Conference the Group of 8 meeting on the fringe is extremely well attended and the Party hierarchy could hardly fail to notice the crowds heading for the MGM Cinema at lunchtime on 10 October. Harking back to former times, at a separate fringe meeting, Lord Griffiths of Fforestfach tells me how, as head of the Prime Minister's Policy Unit, he was present when Margaret Thatcher, against his advice but at the insistence of the then Chancellor, John Major, made the fateful decision to join the ERM, the consequences of which will live to haunt the Conservative Party for years to come.

David Porter and I get a good response when we address a meeting organised by the Save Britain's Fish campaign. SBF meetings will become a regular feature of both the Labour and Conservative Party conferences and

---

*In 1997 the Conservative Party win only 165 seats compared with 336 in 1992. Charles Goodson-Wickes with a majority of 14,761 is but one of many to lose his seat.

working together in harmony we will raise the profile of the fisheries issue which is a living testimony to the disastrous effect of EU collectivist policies. In an attempt to get Government to recognise the strength of the SBF case I have earlier in the recess taken it upon myself, at my own expense, to wine and dine Fisheries Minister Tony Baldry (Banbury) in London. At this meeting he acknowledges the need to recognise the consequences of alienating the fishing industry so close to the next election and the necessity of representing their best interests in Brussels. By getting to him so soon after his appointment I hope to open his eyes to the realities of the CFP before MAFF civil servants suborn him into perpetuating the big lie first promulgated by Ted Heath in 1971.

Back in Westminster at the beginning of the Autumn sitting Teresa and I are stopped in the street by a group of young people on their way home from a party at CCO. They say how much they support our stand on Europe and go on to tell us that they've just heard Party Vice Chairman Jeffrey Archer say that he is against the Single Currency and right behind what Michael Portillo said at conference about EU defence policy. This is music to our ears not least because Jeffrey Archer appears always to be close to No. 10 regardless of who the present incumbent might be. As far as the European army idea is concerned Defence Secretary Michael Portillo himself has already told me that he received a letter from a very senior diplomat pointing out how disingenuous it is of European Commissioner Leon Brittan and former Foreign Secretary Geoffrey Howe to say that the prospect of a European defence force will never materialise when they both know perfectly well that it is an accepted part of the EU grand design.

Determined to do what I can to help SBF to raise the profile of the debate about the CFP I am extremely disappointed to find myself laid up in bed when Fisheries are debated in the House on 23 October. This is the first day in eight years that I have not attended Parliament owing to sickness but to avoid wasting the time and effort that I have already put into preparing a speech I decide to convert what I had intended to say into an open letter to the Fisheries Minister. What effect this will have is impossible to tell but the ongoing challenge is to find ways and means of forcing the Executive to sit up and take notice. It is in this spirit that on 2 November, in a speech during the course of a debate on what have come to be known as the Jopling reforms, I rail against the fact that Government is almost invariably persuaded not so much by the force of argument as by the very much more fundamental consideration of how many votes they can muster on any particular issue. Critical of the Jopling proposals in so far as they do nothing to enhance the power of the backbenches to hold the executive to account, quite the reverse, I am amused when the Leader of the House, winding up the debate, says that *'there is some irony in the fact that my hon. Friend the Member for Ludlow (Mr Gill) should have made the speech he did. I find it difficult to think of anyone who has demonstrated more clearly the effectiveness of the Chamber and the role of the Backbencher than my hon. Friend and some of his hon. Friends during our consideration of certain recent Bills.'*

The question remains, however, as to whether backbenchers will ever again hold Government to account in the way that we did over Maastricht or indeed whether the system will in future allow for such sustained opposition. Later that evening the '22 Committee receive my comments about the importance of Government itself making the tough decisions instead of sub-contracting them out to committees and commissions with such acclamation that I am stopped in mid flow. The current case in point is the Nolan Committee's report on members' interests, the adoption of which will forever change the relationship between the institution of Parliament itself and the elected representatives of the people, its Members. Up until now Parliament has set its own rules and established its own procedures for dealing with any transgressions in accordance with the principle that Parliament is the highest court in the land and that Parliament can do whatsoever it wants to do subject only to the will of the people from time to time expressed through the ballot box. The precedent is now established whereby Parliament shirks its responsibilities to decide matters which it should itself decide, choosing instead to hide behind the recommendations of 'impartial' and 'disinterested' outsiders. It is an abdication of responsibility and it is symptomatic of desperately weak leadership. The fact that we have been put in an absolutely no-win situation by our own Government is both depressing and deeply demoralising and so it is little surprise when Teresa tells me the following day that she's off to see Sir James Goldsmith.

For my part I have been asked to approach John Redwood on behalf of SBF to see if he would be willing to appear on the platform with Christopher Booker and I at public meetings at Exeter in the spring, Aberdeen in the summer and either York or Scarborough in the autumn. JR says 'No'! When I say that there's really no need to give me an answer straight away and that perhaps he'd like to sleep on it and let me have his considered opinion in due course he simply retorts by saying, 'I know my mind.' I explain that each of the meetings will be very well attended but it is all to no avail and the best I get out of him is an offer to send a message. His priority, he says, is to 'help colleagues here' but it is far from clear as to whether he means colleagues in the House or in London or even, perhaps, in the Home Counties generally.

Whilst I might have reasonably expected a favour from JR the time is long since past when I regard Julian Critchley as anything other than hostile. On 15 November he attacks me personally in an article published in the *Evening Standard* but he has counted without Christopher Booker who, taking my part in an article in the next edition of the *Sunday Telegraph*, puts Critchley down with devastating effect. The sequel to this is a letter from Critchley in next week's *Telegraph* telling the readers why he won't be voting for me at the next Election. As a Conservative MP he really shouldn't be saying this sort of thing about a 'colleague' but given his left of centre views and his blind devotion to the cause of European integration I suppose I should count myself lucky that Critchley is not actually endorsing me. Henceforth I refer to him as my 'recruiting sergeant' and can only imagine how irksome it must be for him that the other half of the Critchley household, Prue Bellak, is on my side of the argument, not his.

The 21 November is a red-letter day in the sense that for the first time in my eight years in Parliament I have managed to get myself onto the BBC 'Farming Today' programme. As one of the few MPs with an agricultural background and the only one with an active involvement in the meat industry the BBC's reluctance to let me loose on this particular programme is inexplicable unless it is that I am precluded on account of my implacable opposition to both the CAP and the CFP. A week later I wake to hear part of my interview being used again on 'Farming Today' in a discussion with NFU President David Naish. John Biffen who also heard the programme tells me that he made a point of getting to his office early that day purposely to pen a letter to Naish condemning what he said.

All the usual suspects are present at 2 Wilfred Street that evening for a reception to launch the Conservative 2000 Campaign, aka the Redwood Foundation. When I start to press Hywel Williams for an explanation as to how or why it was that 22 Lord North Street, having been equipped as a campaign HQ for Michael Portillo, was subsequently used by JR he breaks off the conversation and I am reminded of my meeting last week with Ian Milne and Keith Carson. They are suspicious about the real aims and motives of the 2000 Foundation and share my concerns about the apparent inconsistencies of the recent Redwood campaign. Subsequently David Evans tells me how hard he has tried to persuade JR that Hywel Williams is the wrong man for the job but without success. HW is now installed on the top floor at Wilfred Street as the Foundation Director!

By now Teresa has had her meeting with Sir James – lunch in his suite at the Berkeley – and he has undertaken to come back to her with his suggestions and/or proposals in due course. The next thing I know is that on Friday 24 November there is a message for me to contact the *Sunday Times*. The upshot of this is that Goldsmith has alleged that I and some other rebels – Gorman, Marlow and Taylor – are going to stand as candidates for his Referendum Party at the next Election! Never ever having met the man this is certainly news to me as it is, I suspect, to my colleagues. It is, as they say, a nice try but entirely without substance.

As November draws to a close the good news is that Richard Shepherd has been voted Parliamentarian of the Year. This is a great cause for celebration amongst the Group of 8 and a welcome reminder that the Executive don't always get it all their own way. Without fear or favour Richard will always speak his mind and his contributions to debate, particularly on constitutional matters, are object lessons in themselves especially to those who would otherwise have so little understanding of the workings and importance of Parliament and the frightful consequences that inevitably flow from its diminution.

At a regular meeting of Redwood groupies on 6 December JR tells me that No. 10 is constantly briefing against Cabinet colleagues – particularly if they appear to be doing well! There are no surprises in this as far as I am concerned because I have known for a very long time that this is a trademark of incompetents. Rather than risk being seen for what they are they will always seek to deflect criticism onto their subordinates. It is the very antithesis of leadership but an accurate summation of where we are today – rudderless!

On Sunday 10 December I telephone Roger Knapman* to ask why the Government are being so provocative in bringing forward another Fisheries motion a week tomorrow. On Monday my priority is to get an appointment to see the Fisheries Minister, Tony Baldry, and soon. This is arranged for Wednesday and in the meantime other members of the Group of 8 have expressed interest in coming along with me. Our meeting with Baldry is deeply unsatisfactory. He obstinately refuses to address the issue which we put to him, namely the political price to be paid for continuing with the absurd CFP. He refuses to express any personal opinion and constantly seeks to take refuge behind the treaties. Any hope that the investment which I made in him three months ago will pay dividends is dashed to the ground and we are obliged to tell him that we shall table our own amendment to his 'take note' motion. Baldry is desperate to know how we will vote next Monday and I conclude that, for all the use it's been, perhaps he only agreed to our meeting to find out the answer to that question. Whether or not as a result of our meeting, later in the day it transpires that the Fisheries debate has been postponed from next Monday to next Tuesday. Maybe this is to wrong-foot the Opposition who otherwise stand every chance of winning the vote.

Yesterday Paymaster General Heathcoat-Amory got a mauling when Eurosceptics piled in to European Standing Committee 'B' where the motion was to do with '*the practical arrangements for the introduction of the single currency*'. Only arch Europhile Quentin Davies (Stamford & Spalding) takes the Minister's part but not even Quentin is prepared to support Tim Eggar, when today the Energy Minister comes before the same committee to make the case

---

*Roger is the archetypal poacher turned gamekeeper. From having been a key member of the Redwood campaign as holder of the highly confidential list of names of colleagues who had pledged to vote for JR, he is now an Assistant Government Whip.

for EU subsidies to the loss-making Irish steel industry. He is totally isolated and when it comes to the vote, notwithstanding the support of SNP member Roseanna Cunningham (Perth & Kinross) the Government loses. I am by now thoroughly fed-up at seeing so many of our Ministers attempting to dance on the head of a pin – the only people who fail to see that the King has no clothes are the Ministers themselves, a point that I put to Baldry at our meeting this morning.

By Thursday (14 December) there is great excitement in the Lobby at the prospect of the Government being defeated in next week's Fisheries debate. Roger Knapman is anxious to know whether the rebellion will be limited to the Group of 8 which clearly it won't be because Michael Carttiss has already written to his Whip to say that he has no intention of voting with the Government and since David Porter will not be attending the House that day any rebellion is potentially already into double figures. David Harris gets me to come to the telephone to talk to trawler fleet owner Elizabeth Stevenson from Newlyn who is worried, not for the first time, that the fishermen are being drawn into a party political battle but if by now she can't see that what is really at stake is the very survival of the British fishing industry then she clearly hasn't understood, even yet, the real significance of the CFP.

A meeting of the Group of 8 on Monday 18 December discusses tactics in advance of tomorrow's Fisheries debate and decides in favour of abstaining on the Government motion. I personally declare that I shall vote against the Labour amendment, which will be put first, for the simple reason that it envisages the continuation of the CFP to which I am implacably opposed. With 17 signatures on our own amendment the Government are in real danger of being defeated. Come the day and I am at Billingsgate Fish Market before 7 a.m. being interviewed for the BBC 1 O'clock News and thankful for the opportunity to explain publicly what all the fuss is about. Before the debate gets under way the Agriculture department Whip, Roger Knapman, and the Scottish Secretary's PPS, Bernard Jenkin, give me an assurance that if I intervene on the Minister whilst he is at the Despatch Box I will not be disappointed by his response. Two interventions fail to elicit the undertakings that I have been led to believe would be forthcoming and whilst tempted to intervene again on the Minister's deeply flawed and highly unsatisfactory speech I realise that by doing so I shall prejudice the chances of being called to speak later in the debate. When the vote is called the Government motion is lost by 2 votes; Bill Cash and Michael Carttiss have voted against with Hugh Dykes (Harrow East), Peter Thurnham (Bolton North East) and David Wilshire joining the Group of 8 abstention.

On Wednesday 20 December the general impression amongst all that I meet – colleagues, press, even the House doorkeepers – is that we did right yesterday to the extent that Iain Duncan Smith goes out of his way to tell me that he's mad with himself for voting with the Government. ITV's political editor, Michael Brunson, tells me that Hezza and Douglas Hogg have been ever so busy briefing against us and that when Hogg told him that people like me shouldn't be expressing our opinions about fisheries matters he, Brunson, had felt constrained to point out to him that the Group of 8 had been following fisheries matters throughout the whole of the year. Nothing daunted Hezza goes on TV telling the world that it is the Eurosceptics who will cause the Conservatives to lose the next General Election as if the appalling crassness of the administration of which he is now Deputy Leader had absolutely nothing at all to do with it! Notwithstanding the fact that the Government lost last night's vote it will make absolutely no difference to what Government will actually do for the very simple reason that, in the final analysis, Government must, regardless of what the House of Commons thinks, honour the obligation imposed upon them by the Treaties. The Government have suffered the ignominy of a very public defeat, the House has delivered a negative verdict upon the central plank of Government policy, the Fishing industry and the general public have rejoiced at the democratic expression of common sense, but it all adds up to precisely nothing because the inescapable reality is that with Fisheries, as with so many other subject areas, Parliament is no longer sovereign. It is all a complete charade – the pretence that Parliamentary scrutiny of EU business counts for anything is little more than an extremely sick joke and it is on this sad note that the House rises for the Christmas recess. The end of another exciting but depressing and generally demoralising year.

CHAPTER THIRTEEN

1996

...a massive risk to human health as a result of eating beef

AT THE FIRST meeting of the Group of 8 in January I put it to my colleagues that we should take stock before launching ourselves into the New Year but the consensus is that we should press on regardless, a view shared by elder statesman John Biffen when I seek his opinion later in the day. Next week we will finalise our plans for the launch of our pamphlet about EU-inspired legislation entitled 'Dire Directives' as well as agreeing to visit fishing ports in Scotland, issuing a Press Release about the iniquitous Working Time Directive, responding to a reply we have received from the PM about a Referendum and, with the help of SBF, trying to flush out the views of our other colleagues on the subject of the CFP.

Speaking in the adjoining constituency of Wyre Forest at the weekend every single question from the audience is about Europe. The local Member, Anthony Coombs, is very impressed with my performance which he describes as 'bloody marvellous'. Quite apart from being in tune with the members of the Wyre Forest Conservative Association subsequent events lead me to believe that what I had to say on that occasion might have helped to persuade Anthony that there's more to Euroscepticism than he previously thought. Such 'non-conformism' as might have followed on from this 'conversion' is not allowed to develop however because by and by Anthony is invited to take the Trappist vows of silence that go with being a member of the Whips' Office. Whether his promotion is in any way accelerated by the support he gives me in an Adjournment debate that I initiate on 'the consequences of abolishing the pound sterling' I shall never know.

On 10 January David Atkinson (Bournemouth East) initiates a debate to discuss Russia's application to join the Council of Europe to which Foreign Office Minister Nick Bonsor (Upminster), a descendant of Horatio Nelson, replies, saying that HMG will be supporting Russia's candidature. Some days later Nick is not best pleased when I ask him if he really believes all that tosh that he gave by way of response to David Atkinson's Adjournment debate to which he says we have to support Russia's candidature in order to keep Yeltsin in power and to prevent Zhirinovsky or others from seizing the Presidency. I tell him that as far as I am concerned letting Russia join the Council of Europe sends out entirely the wrong signal. It will simply confirm that in the eyes of the rest of the world Russia can do what it likes with Chechnya, or anywhere else for that matter, with impunity and without risk of penalty or sanction. The Council of Europe was established under the tutelage of Winston Churchill in the aftermath of the Second World War to prevent a repetition of the appalling abuse of human rights that had occurred under the Third Reich. It is typical of the woolly thinking of the Foreign Office that notwithstanding that membership of the Council of Europe is conditional upon acceptance of and compliance with the European Convention on Human Rights it is prepared to promote Russia's candidature on the spurious basis that once in membership greater influence can then be exerted to make her comply. It is, of course, all of a piece with the absurd notion that only by dint of belonging can the UK hope to get the EU on our own terms. The CFP is a case in point. Following on from a meeting sponsored by Lord Pearson's Maastricht Study Group at which John Ashworth, Tom Hay, Keith Schofield and Chris Venmore put the case for Save Britain's Fish I manage to get Fisheries Minister Tony Baldry to concede that even the power of veto is useless in the context of our current problems. The fact of the matter is that only an unanimous vote in the Council of Ministers can amend the terms of the CFP and only an unanimous vote can prevent the time limited derogations from it, which the UK currently enjoys, running out at the end of 2002. The time when the UK might have used its veto to prevent the CFP being established in the first place is long since past and for any changes we are now entirely dependant upon obtaining the co-operation of our European 'partners' who have neither the incentive nor the intention of diluting the benefits they have gained by dint of the various treaties.

Still on the vexed question of Europe I put it to Home Secretary Michael Howard who, incidentally, expresses his pleasure at the prospect of addressing the LCCA Annual Dinner in July, that the PM has to come down firmly on one side or other of the European argument, otherwise potential mutineers on the fo'cs'le, deserters on the quarterdeck and a most unhappy ship in between is all that we've got to look forward to. Better, I say, to lose the likes of Hugh Dykes* and others of that ilk than to lose the General Election. This is the same proposition that I put to Lord McColl, Major's PPS in the House of Lords, who invites me to drop him a line as a consequence of our chance meeting in the Committee Room corridor earlier in the day.

The Group of 8 Press Conference on 21 January to launch 'Dire Directives' is well attended in spite of today's media preoccupation with the revelation that Harriet Harman (Lab. Peckham) is sending her child to a selective Grant Maintained school. The BBC Midland News tries to portray our event as a renewal of 'rebellion' on the Tory benches but I appreciate that

---

*Having lost his Harrow East seat in 1997 Hugh Dykes left the Conservative Party to join the Liberal Democrats.

it's expecting too much to think that the headlines will be about the substance of our pamphlet which is a résumé of how EU legislation is foisted onto the British Statute Book.

There is good news from Ludlow. According to Chairman Michael Wood there was a sea of hands at last night's meeting of the Finance & General Purposes Committee from people willing to second the proposition that a resolution be put to the AGM on 15 April adopting me as PPC for the next General Election. John Morgan is minuted as the actual seconder but long-term refuseniks Amy Corfield, Charles Dickie, Simon Kenyon-Slaney, Jackie Williams and Joe Meredith abstain on the vote which leaves me wondering whether the rumours that Joe has reported as being rife in Bishop's Castle about my not seeking re-election are not ones that he himself has invented. Be that as it may I am going to have to ignore my godfather's advice to serve in only two Parliaments so as to give the electors the opportunity to return their own verdict on what I have been making a nuisance of myself about these past nine years.

The 24 January is another red-letter day in the sense that the usually aloof John Redwood appears to want to have some dialogue with me. This is the first time that I have ever experienced this treatment from JR and as he shepherds me into a quiet corner of the lobby I can't help thinking that if he's ever going to make it in the leadership stakes then this is something that he's got to do a lot more of with many more of our colleagues. In the light of what John Townend told me before Christmas it may be that JR is our only hope as far as the leadership is concerned. When Major threw down the gauntlet last summer JR apparently told Michael Portillo that if he were to resign from Cabinet to challenge Major he, Redwood, would do likewise and back him. In spite of my meeting with him months before and the not inconsiderable bandwagon backing him at the time Michael Portillo's failure to rise to the occasion was both disappointing and surprising but on the other hand if he lacks the courage to seize the opportunities as they present themselves perhaps he isn't the right man for the job anyway.

Another Cabinet Minister that, in my opinion, is far from being the right man for the job is John Gummer. On 29 January I am well and truly after his blood when, at very short notice, he cancels my meeting with him originally scheduled for this evening. Coming on top of his persistent failure to reply to letters regarding the Local Government Commission Review this is the last straw and I both tell and write to my Whip, Roger Knapman, saying that I want a meeting with the Chief Whip so as to express my total dissatisfaction with the Secretary of State for the Environment's attitude. Discussing the matter briefly with my Shropshire colleague, John Biffen says that he is willing to come with me but I decline his offer because I don't want it to look as though I'm orchestrating a round robin. Saying that Gummer is of no use to us John gives me discretion to play his hand as appropriate but it is Saturday before I hear from the Chief Whip with a message in the mail timed at 1430 on Thursday. Sitting next to John at Shropshire Lord Lieutenant, Viscount Boyne's memorial service, John suggests that Gummer's intolerable attitude might not be entirely unconnected with the fact that the three Shropshire Conservative MPs are all Eurorealists. On Monday 5 February I make an appointment to see the Chief Whip at 1840 the next day. This in turn is postponed to the following day when new Chief Whip Alastair Goodlad (Eddisbury) appears to take my complaint about John Gummer's arrogant attitude at face value and asks me to leave it to him to deal with. Quite by chance my 14-minute meeting with the Chief Whip is preceded by an encounter with Gummer's PPS Douglas French (Gloucester) who asks me if I have yet had my meeting with his boss! A very lively conversation ensues in which Douglas tries to exonerate Gummer but I leave him in no doubt that, in my book, there is no excuse for not answering Members' letters and none at all for refusing to meet his colleagues to discuss the very serious implications of the Local Government Review upon Shropshire. In the meantime John Biffen has written to the PM on the same subject.

With my Association AGM looming I am delighted when, after some persuasion, Lord Hamilton of Dalzell agrees to be nominated as president of the LCCA in succession to the estimable David Hill. This appointment will ensure peace on the home front for the ensuing three years because the potential troublemakers will defer to his Lordship in a way that they are unlikely to defer to anyone else appointed to this position. When they realise that Lord Hamilton is firmly on my side of the European argument they will know that for the time being the game is up, not least because Michael Wood has another year to run as Chairman and there have never been any doubts as to where his loyalty lies.

Meeting on 6 February the Group of 8 decide to repeat last year's pattern of events at Party Conference – always supposing there is one and that we are not in the midst of a General Election campaign. We also decide to launch our own Green Paper on the forthcoming IGC. We will do this at a Press Conference in seven days time. On 7 February John Redwood's press conference to launch his draft proposals for the IGC is rather low key and causes me to ask Richard Shepherd and John Wilkinson about the advisability of going ahead with our own launch next Tuesday. They are both very bullish and say that our event will be very much more colourful and we are confident that Mike Penning will get more media attention for us than Ashley Gray achieved for JR.

According to today's *Daily Telegraph* NFU President David Naish engaged in Eurosceptic bashing at the farmers' AGM yesterday. Very shortly after he took office I made an appointment to meet him in his office at Agriculture

House to ascertain his opinion about the single currency. At the time I was appalled to hear him say that he didn't have one and that it was a decision for the politicians to make rather than himself or others in similar positions. At the time I wholeheartedly disagreed with him and took the view that he really should have an opinion on this important subject because of the effect it would have upon his members. The irony is that in the intervening period, as I have come to realise that David Naish's first pronouncement was correct – it is indeed a political decision – he, on the other hand, has abandoned his original position and has become an advocate of the single currency which is being sold to the farmers as the panacea for all ills without any attempt being made to point out that the crucial rate at which we might join the Euro is not something we can choose or decide for ourselves. The manner in which the rate at which a country may join the single currency is prescribed in Article 109L(5) of the Treaty on European Union and is most certainly not within the gift of the applicant country.*

As previously planned the Group of 8 press conference to launch our Green (discussion) Paper on the IGC goes ahead on 13 February but the resulting press coverage is not as extensive as we might have hoped having regard to the good attendance of journalists and TV cameras. Later in the day John Biffen, Derek Conway and I accompany Shropshire Conservative County Councillors to a meeting with John Gummer and Douglas French to remonstrate with Gummer about the Local Government Commission proposals for Shropshire. The meeting is inconclusive and only later does it transpire that implementation of the proposals will not in any case be before 1998. My original letters on this subject have still not been answered and I am subsequently obliged to present Douglas French with copies to substantiate my complaint.

A lively meeting of Redwood's Conservative 2000 group offers advice to JR as to what he should do should he be invited back into Cabinet. Personally I take the view that it will be difficult for him to refuse but in view of the two crises which are about to unfold it is unlikely that the circumstances will arise.

The first crisis begins innocuously on Thursday 15 February with the publication of the Scott Report into the sale of armaments to Iraq. A masterly statement in the House by Board of Trade President Ian Lang leaves the Opposition floundering and addressing the AGM of the Church Stretton branch of the LCCA the following evening I am rash enough to make the mistake of taking a position on this topic. I tell the assembled company how well the Government did yesterday and that 'we must all get behind the PM

---

*"…the Council of Ministers shall, acting with the unanimity of the Member States without a derogation (i.e. the member countries of the single currency) and the Member State concerned (in this case the UK), on a proposal from the European Commission and after consulting the European Central Bank, adopt the rate at which the Euro shall be substituted for the currency of the Member State concerned, and take the other measures necessary for the introduction of the Euro as the single currency in the Member State concerned.'

to see this thing through.' Less than twelve hours later those words are coming back to haunt me when I wake to hear Home Secretary Michael Howard getting the worst of the argument in an interview about the Scott Report on the BBC 'Today' programme. By the time the Group of 8 meet on Tuesday 20 February the picture is somewhat different to the one presented last Thursday. Our discussion is interesting but indeterminate. The lawyer in our midst, Nick Budgen, argues that busy people working in the law often make mistakes. Richard Shepherd and I, with our more practical backgrounds, take a more fundamentalist line which is supported by John Wilkinson. The upshot of this is that I tell my Whip that it will be much easier for me to vote for the Government next Monday if Attorney General Nicholas Lyell (Mid Bedfordshire) has in the meantime fallen on his sword. Like everybody else I speak to, Charles Wardle is deeply unhappy about Scott but intends to vote with the Government on Monday because although he believes that both Lyell and Chief Secretary to the Treasury William Waldegrave should go, he says that the danger of picking at this particular onion is that eventually it all leads to Major himself! At Thursday's meeting of the '22 Committee Quentin Davies expresses his fears about the Scott Report and whilst he gets no direct support this, I believe, is not a true reflection of how colleagues are thinking. All the other speakers on this subject help to persuade me that there is no need for me to put myself out on a limb next Monday but I haven't heard the end of the matter by a long chalk. Subsequently, finding me in the Library, Nick Budgen takes me to the Smoking Room to put the case for not kicking over the traces next Monday. I am not clear as to why he considers this matter so crucial to his own electoral prospects but he eventually confesses to having been put up to speaking to me by the Whips who are obviously fearing that I won't vote the ticket on Monday.

The following evening Nick and I attend a North East Wolverhampton Conservative Association function at the Whitmore Reans Conservative Club which is actually in Nick's constituency. We are there to support the North East PPC, David Harvey, but the occasion is somewhat marred by Nick's insistence on going on at great length about the Scott Report to the extent that I begin to wish that I had never agreed to go along in the first place. But that is not the end of the matter. On Sunday, ignoring all other media contacts, I speak to the *Sun* newspaper's Political Editor, Trevor Kavanagh, and later come to regret even that one contact with the press. At teatime Assistant Whip Liam Fox (Woodspring) telephones, not to find out about my voting intentions, but to ask what concessions I'm looking for! I tell him what I have previously told Roger Knapman which is that I should find it much easier to vote for the Government tomorrow if in the meantime the Attorney General has resigned. Later on in the evening Roger himself rings and I put his mind at rest by telling him that I shall be voting for the Government. Later still the phone rings again and it is my Chairman, Michael Wood, asking if I have seen the ITV News at 10 o'clock where Michael Brunson has reported that I shall be voting against the Government in tomorrow night's vote! I tell Michael that less than two hours ago I had told my Whip the very opposite but on Monday morning, in view of the false reports on ITN News, I am pleased to have the opportunity to put the record straight by telling my local media, Central TV and the *Shropshire Star*, that I shall indeed be voting with the Government which is just as well because the majority when the division is held is no more nor less than one! Roger Knapman thanks me for saving the Government, as do Paul Marland and Richard Alexander (Newark), and suggests that I register the point with the Deputy Chief Whip, Greg Knight (Derby North), whilst at the same time making it clear that they cannot count on my support on European matters.

The following day Michael Brunson apologises to me for his news report – he had talked to Trevor Kavanagh and between them they had made two and two equal five. Being the unfailingly courteous and punctilious gentleman that he is Michael says that he will have to do me a favour sometime! By the skin of its teeth the Government have escaped being defeated but there is no denying that the Scott Report has done nothing to allay the impression that there is something rotten about this administration and that when the time comes the Conservative Party is going to have to pay a heavy price.

Dispelling any lingering doubts that my stand on the European issue is not popular Adrian Lee tells me that he is now the Conservative PPC for the Tyne Bridge division which he ascribes to having told the selection committee that he 'agrees 100 per cent with Christopher Gill's views on Europe'. The following day, 28 February, I relay this news to the Minister for Europe, Nick Bonsor, adding that one of my constituents has recently made out a bank mandate in favour of the LCCA for £1000 per annum and also sent a cheque for £250 towards our Annual Dinner. I am under no illusion that feeding this sort of information into the system is going to make the slightest difference to the administration's determination to press on with European integration but at least they won't be able to say that they haven't been warned. Listening to the French Ambassador later in the day I hear him say, amongst other things, that Economic and Monetary Union (EMU) is necessary in order to enable France to regain monetary sovereignty! One simply couldn't make it up but in this *Alice in Wonderland* approach to European affairs the idiocy of some of the arguments deployed is apparently no obstacle to progress so long as it is all in the direction of harmonisation and integration.

Lunching with Enoch Powell on 29 February I ask him what he thinks we Eurorealists should do now to which he replies, 'Absolutely nothing.' He believes that public opinion will do the rest and instances Adrian Lee's selection as a PPC as evidence of the way in which the views of the electorate will eventually prevail. After lunch I have question No. 5 to the Prime Minister which, in John Major's absence, is answered by Deputy Prime Minister Michael Heseltine. I ask whether my right hon. Friend will '*assure the House that Her Majesty's Government would be prepared to walk away from the conference table at the forthcoming intergovernmental conference if they cannot get a deal that is acceptable to the majority of British voters?*' This is applauded by, amongst others, David Evans who tells me later that he has laid it on the line at the '22 Executive that if the Government doesn't change its attitude towards the European question they will have another rebel on their hands. He tells me that with only one exception the whole of the committee agreed with him including even the likes of Europhile Peter Hordern (Horsham).

On top of the Fresh Start Group, the European Research Group, the Group of 8 and the Conservative 2000 Group we now have the IGC Monitoring Group set up by Bill Cash to concentrate minds on the forthcoming IGC which will culminate in yet another European Treaty – the Amsterdam Treaty. The inescapable fact of the matter is that none of these groups within the Conservative Parliamentary Party, all of which have been created since John Major became Leader, would exist if we had a Government which was Conservative other than in name alone. In varying degrees they are all opposed to the Government's European policy and the fact that they are proliferating is a sad commentary upon the direction in which the Party is heading. The Party is, of course, aware of their existence as when Government Whip Patrick McLoughlin asks me if I will serve on a Standing Committee. When I explain that this would clash with an important meeting that I have to attend at least weekly he says, referring to the Group of 8, 'Do you mean the Cabinet?'! Interestingly at least one member of the real Cabinet is taking an interest in the Group of 8's pamphlet on EU legislation. When I apologise to the Chancellor of the Duchy of Lancaster, Roger Freeman (Kettering), the Cabinet Minister with responsibility for Deregulation, for my absence from his meeting with the Group of 8 on 20 February he says that he thinks 'Dire Directives' is very good, that he is holding meetings in Brussels on this very subject and for me to make arrangements for him to meet our group again in three weeks' time.

Not all of the groups are quite as robust or hardbitten as the Group of 8 and consequently, on 28 February, I feel constrained to tell the members present at a meeting of the Conservative 2000 Group that since we are playing a hard-ball game they must, when the next opportunity presents itself, be prepared to put their heads above the parapet instead of running for cover, irrespective of whether or not they risk losing their jobs as PPS to the Minister for Drains! That being said I get the impression that this is rather too hard-line for some of our colleagues, many of whom will seek to finesse the outcome of any future drama so as either to further their own careers or simply to salve their own consciences by being able to demonstrate that they were on the 'right side'. If I know anything about it their reluctance to stand up and be counted will continue to manifest itself in the future just as much as in the past and the Party will simply muddle on until the electorate wreaks its vengeance.

There is a rumpus on 5 March when it is announced that the European Court of Justice (ECJ) has found against the UK in the matter of compensation for Spanish fisherman prevented from fishing in UK waters by the Merchant Shipping Act. The Group of 8 immediately table an EDM and brief the press about this latest constitutional outrage. In 1988 the British Parliament passed into law the Merchant Shipping Act with the intention of curbing the exploitation of British fishing stocks by Spanish fishermen. As if the fact that the ECJ has previously struck down this British Act of Parliament is not bad enough it is now adding insult to injury to expect the British taxpayer to compensate Spanish trawler owners for their supposed consequential losses during the period in which the matter has been *sub judice*. The Europhile members can apparently overlook the fact that a law made in the British Parliament by the elected representatives of the British people is no longer supreme in that it can be overturned by an unelected Court comprising a majority of judges who are not even legally qualified, but to the rest of us this represents the very kernel of our case against the European Union – that it gives primacy to European law over and above National law and confers legitimacy upon EU laws over which the elected representatives have neither any say nor any control. This is the very antithesis of democracy and offends a principle for which democrats of all parties and none should be prepared to make a resolute stand. The unanswered question remains as to why the Conservative Party cannot or will not grasp this fundamental principle but, as we shall see, not even two disastrous General Election results will shake them out of their reverie.

My request for a PNQ on 6 March regarding the ECJ ruling on Fisheries is refused but Shadow Agriculture Minister Gavin Strang (Edinburgh East) is more successful. For forty minutes the Agriculture Minister, Douglas Hogg, is subject to some lively questioning from some of the 58 members of his own Party and 40 from the Opposition parties who make it their business to stay on in the Chamber after Foreign Office questions have ended. My consolation is that, whilst unsuccessful in obtaining permission for a PNQ on Fisheries, the Speaker has allocated me an Adjournment debate next week on the subject of 'HM Government's policy on the IGC'. This proves to be doubly fortuitous because later in the day I learn that the Government intend publishing their White Paper on the IGC on the very eve of my debate.

Proceedings on Monday 11 March are somewhat overshadowed by Jimmy Goldsmith's full page newspaper advertisements calling for a Referendum on

Europe – not on whether we should or should not accept the Treaty on European Union or the Single Currency but effectively on whether we should remain in the European Union or get out. With the publication of the Government's White Paper due tomorrow and the General Election barely twelve months away at the outside, Sir James' timing is impeccable but, for reasons which I am unable to discern, there is a very relaxed mood in the House today, particularly amongst Government Ministers. Perhaps they feel that the boil has at long last been lanced. Over dinner that evening Lord Harmar Nicholls, formerly the Member for Peterborough, says that he is the only Government Minister ever to have resigned over Europe but times have changed. Whereas Harmar's principled opposition to Europe led to Ted Heath kicking him upstairs with a Baronetcy our reward for taking an equally principled stand was to be kicked out of the Parliamentary Party by John Major!

On the day that the Government publishes its White Paper on the forthcoming IGC the European Court again finds against Britain, this time on the matter of the 48-hour maximum working week. The UK has argued, unsuccessfully as it now appears, that our opt-out from the social chapter means that we are not subject to EU maximum working hours provisions. As many of us had confidently predicted the ECJ would do, they have now ruled that the question of working hours is not one that is governed by the social chapter but by the health and safety provisions which the UK is already signed up to. Government reaction to this latest affront to national sovereignty is to take it on the chin because, as has already been seen with Fisheries, in its dealings with Europe it has no bottom line. There is apparently no insult to our nation's pride nor offence to its system of Parliamentary democracy that will cause the Major administration to deviate from its commitment to European integration. Travelling to Tamworth with Tim Rathbone (Lewes) and Jacqui Lait (Hastings & Rye) to campaign in the South East Staffordshire by-election caused by the death of David Lightbown I suggest to them that whilst canvassing they should keep their integrationist views to themselves so that we at least have a sporting chance of winning. Everybody that I meet on the doorstep who mentions the subject of Europe just wants out but this is a message that the Party top brass don't want to hear.

There's more trouble on the way but in a totally different and unexpected field. On 19 March Government Whip Derek Conway warns me that there will be a fairly devastating statement in the House this afternoon regarding Bovine Spongiform Encephalopathy (BSE). In the event it transpires that Derek's warning is premature by twenty-four hours but this will not prevent the Press leading with this topic tomorrow morning. At the Despatch Box on 20 March Health Secretary Stephen Dorrell reports to the House the findings of the Government surveillance unit in Edinburgh specialising in Creutzfeldt-

Jakob disease which claims to have identified a hitherto unrecognised variant of the disease. Had the Minister then gone on to say that he was confident that the measures already in place were adequate and proving satisfactory all would have been well but mention of additional measures to be instituted by both his department and MAFF exacerbate fears that there is a massive risk to human health as a consequence of eating beef. Such is the media hue and cry on BSE that I am barely able to concentrate on the debate on the IGC White Paper which takes place the following day. The Government motion is on the adjournment of the House so that, in spite of all the speculation to the contrary, there is no vote when the debate ends at 10 p.m. In contrast to the low level of interest in debates on European issues when I first entered the House, today the Speaker announces that more than 50 backbenchers have expressed a wish to speak but having had my own 1½ hour debate on this same subject last week I can hardly expect to be one of them.

The big issue in the aftermath of Stephen Dorrell's announcement is undoubtedly BSE. As a member of the Agriculture Select Committee at the time that it carried out its original investigation into BSE and as a practical butcher and farmer myself I have a reasonable understanding of the seriousness of the situation now unfolding but my first priority is to make contact with those most likely to be affected in my own constituency which is, after all, one of Britain's premier livestock producing areas. After meeting and talking to livestock auctioneers and producers on Friday and Saturday I telephone Agriculture Minister Douglas Hogg on Sunday (24 March) to advise him that the consensus in my area is in support of the slaughter of all cows born before the start of the Specified Bovine Offal ban in 1989. Douglas is courteous but doesn't invite any further information or advice which I can only ascribe to his scorn for people like me on account of our non-conformist views on European Union in general and CAP in particular. At 0650 on Monday morning I meet a BBC reporter and TV camera crew in Bridgnorth livestock market to be interviewed about the rapidly deteriorating BSE situation. Whilst the camera crew sort out the technical problems which are preventing the interview going ahead – 'water on the exciter' they say – I am not surprised to learn that the whole crew are vegetarian but that is far from today's worst news. In the afternoon Dorrell comes to the House again, this time to announce that the EU have banned the sale of British beef – not just within their own bailiwick but, to everybody's astonishment and incredulity, worldwide! This is quite outrageous. Apart from the constitutional impropriety of the EC going above the head of the elected Westminster Parliament they have quite arbitrarily and irrationally gone 'beyond the science', a point which I am at pains to make to Dorrell, Hogg, the Chief Whip and anybody else who will listen. I tell them that whilst the British Government's policy of acting strictly only in accordance with the best available scientific evidence has previously been correct, we are now in an entirely different situation in which they will have to take essentially political decisions in order to restore public confidence. In this context I will be surprised if a slaughter policy is not announced within the next forty-eight hours.

At the Group of 8 meeting on 26 March we agree to issue a Press Release supporting Goldsmith's idea of a Referendum, not on the narrow issue of the Single Currency, but on the broader question of the UK's continued EU membership. Earlier in the meeting Roger Freeman, true to his word, has taken time out to come and report progress on his deregulation efforts since being stimulated by our 'Dire Directives' publication.

After a meeting of Bill Cash's IGC Monitoring Group on 27 March at which they go back on decisions made only yesterday causing Robert Key (Salisbury) to say that 'if this is all John Major is up against then he's nothing to fear,' Teresa and I draft a Press release for the Group of 8 calling for a broad Referendum on remaining in the EU or seeking associate member status like Norway. We also draft EDM 677 on Beef which goes down after the 10 o'clock vote with no fewer than 116 signatories. My decision to abstain on this evening's vote on an amendment to the Finance Bill regarding VAT on Energy Saving Materials changes when my pair, Jeff Rooker, suddenly appears in the Chamber hot foot from the SE Staffordshire by-election campaign. The Duchess and I agree that this is not a big enough issue to rebel about and in the event the Government scrape by, once again, with a majority of one! But the rebels, or potential rebels, are not all on the Government benches as evidenced by the publication on 28 March of literature bearing the signatures of 50 Labour MPs in support of a campaign entitled 'A People's Europe'. According to their leaflets, 'this is an attempt to open a genuine debate in the Labour Party about the disastrous effects of a single currency under the monetarist terms of the Maastricht Treaty.' This comes seven weeks after the Governor of the Bank of England, Eddie George, has warned of the dangers inherent in the single currency and is further evidence of the strong feelings that this subject arouses – enough, one would imagine, to cause the Government to have second thoughts.

The debate on BSE is opened by Agriculture Minister Douglas Hogg, followed by Shadow Agriculture Minister Gavin Strang. After that it is the turn of the backbenchers and I am somewhat taken aback to be the first of them to be called. Despite not being able to say all that I had intended to say because of the Speaker's imposition of a 10 minute limit on backbench speeches my contribution is well received and there are several plaudits from colleagues as well as complimentary comments from doorkeepers who I wouldn't necessarily have thought would be much interested in this rather mundane subject. The following day Deputy Speaker Michael Morris says,

'What a powerful speech that was,' but the more satisfying aspect of the past few days is that the Minister has adopted some of the recommendations that I put to him earlier in the week when, with Chairman Paul Marland's permission, I attached myself to the deputation of backbench Agriculture Committee members which went to see Douglas Hogg in his office at MAFF. On that happy note I am glad to escape Westminster for the Easter recess but mindful of the fact that there won't be much happiness in the livestock and allied industries for some considerable time to come.

Whilst reports on the Agriculture front are extremely worrying there is better news on the Fisheries scene when John Ashworth telephones during the recess to say that John Redwood, in spite of his previous flat refusal, has now agreed to speak at the SBF rally in Westminster's Central Hall next Thursday. On the day in question JR makes himself readily available for media interviews against a backdrop of fishing vessels sailing up the Thames on the morning tide to support the rally. Ex-Chancellor Norman Lamont is another well known Conservative politician to put in an appearance and one is encouraged to believe that our efforts to raise the profile of the fishing issue must be succeeding if, as is now apparent, it is attracting the attention of some of our more prominent colleagues.

In spite of the best efforts of Tim Godfrey and partner, Alison Peppé, Bill Parr, David Lake, Peter Stock and Jackie Williams at the AGM of the LCCA, on 15 April, I am re-adopted as the PPC for the next election. John Morgan, in seconding the motion, tells the meeting how important it is to have a strong man representing us and new president Lord Hamilton's effusive praise for me and my efforts goes a long way towards deterring any other antis from getting uppity. David Foster tells the very well attended meeting that he has rejoined the Party – having resigned over Suez – so as to be able to vote for me and retiring President David Hill has inveigled Alan Screen into supporting the motion to keep face with the other area chairmen even though his preference would almost certainly be to do the opposite. At the Shirehall, later in the week, Conservative group leader Malcolm Pate tells Michael Wood that my speech to the AGM was brilliant and if only the PM would say the same sort of thing we wouldn't be in the trouble we are now.

Back in Westminster on 16 April for the beginning of the new sitting the Group of 8 meet to discuss future tactics. It is a stimulating meeting at which I argue that in the light of all the indications that the Government will make a manifesto commitment to hold a Referendum on the Single Currency we should now forget all about referenda and use our best endeavours to pressurise the Party into changing its whole approach towards Europe. Clearly this is not the PM's view and the following day, speaking in Prague, he takes the opportunity of attacking what he describes as Right-wing proposals for tax cuts, reduced public expenditure and greater Euroscepticism. It isn't considered good form to voice criticism on domestic issues whilst speaking in foreign countries but that apart there is now a dawning realisation that with Major at the helm we are, as a Party, going precisely nowhere. In agreeing to become a Party Treasurer David Evans tells the Conservative 2000 group that he has imposed certain conditions but he leaves us to draw our own conclusion as to what these might be.

Whatever Major might think or say the European issue will simply not go away. On 23 April 64 Conservatives, 8 Ulstermen, 4 Labour and 1 Liberal/Democrat pitch in to support Iain Duncan Smith's 10 Minute Rule Bill *'to amend the European Communities Act 1972 so as to provide by Order in Council for the disapplication within the United Kingdom of judgements, rules and doctrines propounded by the European Court'*. The combined Opposition of 59 Labour, 12 Liberal/Democrats, 6 Conservatives (David Ashby, Peter Bottomley, Hugh Dykes, Robert Hughes, David Knox and Hector Munro), 3 Plaid Cymru, 2 SDLP and 1 SNP ensures that Iain's Bill will make no further progress but yet another marker has been put down indicating that the Major line is far from being the Conservatives' settled view. This surfaces again the following day when Chief Whip Alistair Goodlad attends a meeting of the IGC Monitoring Group and is left in absolutely no doubt about the strength of feeling on the European issue. Mildly surprised to have been invited, at the weekend I travel to Cardiff to address a meeting of the Welsh area Young Conservative Patrons where I find everybody, apart from a few of the office holders, very much on my side of the argument. I come away delighted with the response, especially that from the young people themselves. Contrary to the disinformation put about by the Europhiles the younger generation are, generally speaking, more on our side than theirs. In my experience opposition to our views comes principally from big business and establishment figures such as, perhaps, former Secretary to the Queen Lord Charteris of Amisfield, to whom I am introduced at the beginning of May – he walks away from me without so much as a word and I can only conclude that, never having met him before, he is aware of my views and finds them distasteful or repugnant.

On Saturday 4 May listeners to the 'Today' programme hear Home Secretary Michael Howard refuse to answer John Humphreys' questions when he repeatedly asks him whether there are 'no circumstances in which he could contemplate leaving the European Union'. When I subsequently tell John Redwood that this is not what the British public want to hear he says that Cabinet Ministers cannot afford to be portrayed as extremists and that for Michael Howard to have given a better answer would have been to play straight into his opponents' hands. It is to be hoped that when the time comes the voters will appreciate these nuances but somehow I very much doubt it.

In advance of tomorrow's Press Conference to launch *In Their Own Words*, a publication compiled by my Research Assistant, Adrian Lee, I spend time on

Tuesday 7 May topping and tailing covering letters to accompany the complimentary copy which I am sending to all Members of Parliament. The booklet has been produced to draw attention to the direction in which the EU is really heading, as exemplified by the utterances of leading politicians in Europe generally, as opposed to the obfuscations and deceptions routinely propagated by domestic politicians who seek to disguise the full extent of the integrationist agenda in the certain knowledge that if the British people were to be told the truth about these matters they would find the whole concept unacceptable. Running to 116 pages, *In Their Own Words* contains scores of fully referenced quotations which I am hoping colleagues and others interested in the European debate will find useful in terms of advancing our cause. Unfortunately the Group of 8 press conference to launch my book is overtaken by events because earlier in the day John Redwood has launched his own publication, *Action not Words* and the press are understandably preoccupied with JR's comments about a Referendum and Teresa Gorman's intention to resurrect her own ideas on this subject as a 10 Minute Rule Bill. In this endeavour Teresa will be thwarted by Bill Cash who will sit up all night to make sure that he's first in line to get the necessary slot in the Parliamentary timetable and Teresa, arriving at the Private Bill office at 6 o'clock tomorrow morning, will find that she's been pipped at the post.

Foreign Secretary Malcolm Rifkind attends the backbench European Affairs Committee meeting on 8 May where he finds all the usual suspects gathered to ask him some leading questions. I draw Malcolm's attention to the remarks of the Unilever company's Chief Executive on 'Farming Today' when he said, in relation to the ongoing BSE crisis, that 'it's time we all stopped talking like lawyers and took some practical decisions.' As a QC himself it is perhaps not altogether surprising that the Foreign Secretary is reluctant to follow this advice and, putting it more bluntly, I feel constrained to tell him that what we actually need is 'not legal opinions, but votes'.

On 9 May Sir John Egan, Chairman of the British Airports Authority, welcomes MPs and Peers to a CBI Lunch at Centre Point where discussion centres on the single currency. Sitting next to Sir John* I despair of getting anything through to him although previous contacts with individual CBI Council members have revealed considerable sympathy for our point of view. CBI Director General Adair Turner is also seated at the top table but is, as if I didn't already know it, a lost cause as far as the Eurosceptics are concerned.

Already I am receiving replies from colleagues to the letter sent out with *In Their Own Words*. The best so far are from Ted Heath and John Major but compared with the total lack of response to the letters I wrote to colleagues in

---

*On assuming the Presidency of the CBI in 2002 Sir John, in an interview published in the *Daily Telegraph*, indicated that on the subject of the Single Currency his mind was much more sceptical than it had appeared to be in 1996.

November 1991 and May 1992 warning about the contents of the Maastricht Treaty this is progress indeed. There is movement too on the voluntary side of the Party. At the AGM of the West Midland Area Conservative Associations on 11 May, where incidentally I am made most welcome with all and sundry saying that they are right behind me and that I mustn't give in, my Chairman, Michael Wood, is voted on to the National Executive. Two years ago such a proposition would have been absolutely inconceivable but his nomination is indicative of a welcome and significant shift in opinion within the voluntary side of the Party. Nonetheless remarkable is the warm welcome I receive from Area Agent Rachel Dyche – what a contrast with two years ago!

On the 1 O'clock News that day it is announced that the PM has told the Scottish Conservative conference that there will be no referendum other than on the Single Currency as and when the situation arises. For sheer pigheadedness on anything to do with Europe the PM seldom scores less than top marks. The fact that his Parliamentary majority is wafer thin, that a substantial number of his Parliamentary colleagues see a referendum as the only way out of the current impasse, that an increasing proportion of the voluntary Party also want a referendum and that Sir James Goldsmith has now entered the lists campaigning solely for a referendum, isn't going to be allowed to deflect Major from his determination to keep the European project moving forward. Doubtless the Europhiles within Cabinet, principal amongst whom would be Heseltine, Clarke and Gummer, are keeping up the pressure upon him not to bow to public opinion and increasingly one is hearing senior figures in the Parliamentary Party disparage anything that might be termed 'populist', as though the garnering of votes was the least of our concerns. The whole situation is quite unreal particularly when there are so many influential people in the world of commerce who, like the Governor of the Bank of England, are counselling caution. On 14 May the Chairman of Morgan Grenfell tells the backbench Finance committee that, in his opinion, we should definitely not join the Single Currency. The fact that he is also on the board of the Deutsche Bank and is its only non-German director, lends force and credibility to his argument but sadly, as illustrated by the Government's blank refusal to produce a cost/benefit analysis, the question of joining the Single Currency is being driven by a momentum which has nothing to do with economics and everything to do with politics.

The beef crisis continues and on 15 May I am being interviewed by SkyNews saying how pleased I am that the PM is going to take a strong line with the EU if they don't lift the export ban when the studio door flies open and presenter Adam Boulton sweeps in to say that Foreign Secretary Malcolm Rifkind has just announced that the UK will not be taking any retaliatory measures! After the interview I bump into Sheila Gunn – ex-*Times* newspaper lobby correspondent now working as a senior Press Officer at CCO – who says that that isn't what Malcolm said at all. The plot thickens! Eight weeks after Dorrell's fateful announcement there is organised chaos. Government have taken sweeping decisions without apparently any real grasp of how they are going to be implemented. Bullied by the supermarket operators and the European Commission into taking ill considered measures they have created immense practical problems for which there is no obvious solution. In a debate on the CAP on 16 May I suggest that in order to get things moving MAFF should delegate some of its responsibilities to the industry's own body, the Meat and Livestock Commission (MLC), which is fully representative of all sections of the industry and probably better qualified than MAFF itself to deal with the intensely practical problems which have arisen. Three weeks later Colin McLean, Director General of the MLC, reveals that his organisation has barely been consulted about the BSE crisis let alone been invited to help. He gives MAFF and the Agriculture Minister very low marks for communication and confirms that the pressure for a ban on the sale of meat from cattle of over 30 months of age came originally from NFU President Sir David Naish, and the bosses of the major supermarket chains. Matters are scarcely better by 5 June when I tell the Chief Whip that I hope the Government knows what it is doing, rushing round Europe offering to kill more and more cattle, when a) NFU President David Naish has already said that he will not support an accelerated cull and b) it is highly unlikely that Parliament itself would support such measures. There is, however, just a small glimmer of light at the end of a very long and dark tunnel when today the EC confirms that it will lift the export ban on beef derivatives.

Guest speaker at the LCCA Annual Cocktail Party on 7 June is Home Office Minister David Maclean who emphasises the point that he 'likes and respects' their Member of Parliament and that the Home Secretary himself is coming to the Ludlow constituency only because he too 'likes and respects the local Member'. On the vexed question of Europe David tells the assembled company that the fact of the matter is that I am 'twelve months ahead of the Conservative Party' and, in the sense that many more people are now coming round to my point of view, his analysis is probably correct. I certainly hope so but regrettably twelve months is more than the Party have got before the last possible date for a General Election.

Notwithstanding the fact that the PM has ruled out any possibility of a general referendum on Europe, Bill Cash's 10 Minute Rule Bill on this subject attracts the support of 78 Conservatives when put to the vote on 11 June. Taking into account Iain Duncan Smith's earlier Bill, 91 different Conservative Members have now expressed themselves as sympathetic to the cause although there are doubtless several others who would have voted with us had they not been on the 'payroll'. Bill's initiative has well and truly put the cat amongst the pigeons because the following day we learn that the powers that be have homed in on the fact that his European Foundation is part financed by Sir James Goldsmith. The Chief Whip has issued an ultimatum – either renounce the Goldsmith money or resign from the European Foundation. Bill has the last laugh because within twenty-four hours of renouncing the Goldsmith money he has secured the equivalent funding from Margaret Thatcher. By Friday 14 June a free-for-all is developing with my constituent, National Union Chairman Robin Hodgson, joining in to condemn Lady Thatcher's action as if it is any business of his or the Conservative Party's as to whom individuals do or do not choose to donate their own money. Not to be outdone Jeffrey Archer goes on air on Saturday calling for Party unity, a cry of stinking fish that is repeated on the airwaves on Sunday by Deputy Prime Minister Michael Heseltine. On Monday the PM's PPS, John Ward, listens to what I have to say but doesn't hold out any promise of action when I point out that all the public pleas for party unity are entirely counter productive because they simply re-enforce the impression in the voters' minds that we are irredeemably split. On the other hand I do recognise that the 'management' need to create an alibi in advance of the inevitable electoral disaster that is now very much in prospect.

Dining in the Members' Dining Room on 17 June with David Martin, Angela Rumbold and Elizabeth Peacock (Batley & Spen) the ladies make no secret of their Euroscepticism – we're all Eurosceptics now, an impression that is heightened when Foreign Secretary Malcolm Rifkind, addressing a '92 Group dinner the following evening, says things that would have been unthinkable two years ago.

At 10 o'clock on Friday morning Teresa picks me up in her car en route to Heathrow for our flight to Scotland. At Aberdeen airport we are met by Tom Hay who whisks us off to tour the shipyard at Macduff prior to an early supper and a meeting with local farmers later in the evening. Saturday 22nd is taken up with more visits and interviews prior to the Public Meeting that we are scheduled to address in the Fishermen's Mission at Peterhead. At this meeting I am able to unveil the Opinion of Sir Patrick Neill QC obtained by SBF which concludes that the Government are not correct in asserting that coastal fisheries inside the 6 and 12 mile limits are protected. The Opinion confirms SBF's contention that with effect from 1 January 2003 the principle of 'equal access to the common resource' will apply which in turn means that fishing vessels registered in any other EU country will be legally entitled to fish right up to our very beaches. By the time we get back to London on Sunday the telephone lines have been busy and I receive a call from Christopher Booker who champions the fishermen's cause in the *Daily Mail* and the *Sunday Telegraph*, congratulating me on a good show at Peterhead. Once again it is demonstrably the case that public opinion is on our side of the argument rather than the Government's but not knowing what the next move should be I wonder whether now isn't the time to seek another interview with the PM. The upshot of this is a meeting on 3 July with Major's two PPSs, John Ward and Lord McColl, Shaun Williams from the No. 10 Policy Unit, Lord Pearson who has agreed to keep me company, and myself. I know that Shaun Williams has previously met Richard Body and SBF's John Ashworth and during the course of our meeting it transpires that he has also met with David Harris and David Porter. In spite of those meetings he clearly still hasn't understood the situation correctly and I find it necessary to bat him down more than once. Ian McColl appears very sympathetic to our cause but one swallow doesn't make a summer and if the truth be told we're probably not going to get any change in policy this side of a General Election.

Tuesday 25 June is an Opposition day and the Liberal Democrats table a motion of censure on the Agriculture Minister regarding the Government's handling of the BSE crisis. Telling junior Agriculture Minister Angela Browning (Tiverton) how lucky she is that we haven't cut up rough about the appalling way her department has handled the whole affair I hold my nose and vote the ticket. The following day Budgie expresses the opinion that we – the sceptics that is – saved the day for the Government. He makes a particular point of saying that there are many disgruntled colleagues with rural constituencies who would have followed my lead if I had chosen to make it hot for the Government but, whilst I can't agree with the PM who tells the Press that he thinks that Douglas Hogg has done a good job and that he has no thoughts of sacking him, I am not in the business of being a serial rebel and in any case there have been better opportunities to defeat the Government than this if that is what we really want to do. As always the calculation is a fine one. Defeat the Government in the Division lobby and precipitate a general Election which the Conservatives would almost certainly lose or stay our hand so that we remain in business at least until the PM chooses to go to the country. The reality of the situation as far as we are concerned is that the opportunities to spread the gospel are infinitely better for us as a 'rebel' group in what is now almost a hung Parliament than as a footnote to history in a Parliament with a substantial Labour majority.

It is in this spirit that on 27 June the Group of 8 travel to Chester where we are scheduled to address a public meeting in the City Hall. In advance of the meeting I do a long interview with BBC2 TV but as far as I know it is never used, probably because I wouldn't give the Beeb the sound bites they were looking for to suit their programme on xenophobia with which they were trying to associate us. The meeting goes well with each of us speaking for an average of six minutes before taking questions from the floor. Our departure is attended by the usual standing ovation and one cannot help wondering how many other Conservative MPs in these hard times are getting this size of audience or this sort of reception. If the opinion polls are anything to go by, not very many!

Chancellor Ken Clarke addresses the backbench European Affairs Committee on 3 July and manages to antagonise three-quarters of those present by saying that the Single Currency 'may have some merits' but 'will not necessarily lead to Political Union'! What more can one expect from someone who once famously declared that he hadn't read the Maastricht Treaty? Political Union will follow Economic and Monetary Union as surely as night follows day and anyone who says otherwise is either a fool or a knave. On the bus back from lunching at India House it is my pleasure to sit next to somebody who is quite definitely neither. During the course of our conversation former Speaker Bernard Weatherill, now Lord Weatherill, tells me that he remembers the days when it was very difficult to find Conservative MPs who wanted to be Ministers and that one of the great changes of the past thirty years and not, we agree, for the better, is that now it is practically impossible to find anyone who doesn't want to be a Minister! The consequence is that there are now all too few backbenchers willing to hold Government to account in the way that they should do for fear that they may thereby prejudice their advancement prospects, the end result of which is an executive which has become altogether too powerful for anybody's good including its own. As our conversation turns to other aspects of what we consider to be unfortunate developments I talk about 'the law of unintended consequences' whereupon Bernard produces pen and paper to note the expression down. It appears at column 1605 in the House of Lords' Official report the very next day when in an excellent and eminently sensible speech on the Constitution my travelling companion places on record much of the burden of our rather philosophical but nonetheless enjoyable discussion.

On what in the USA is known as Independence Day the Environment Secretary brings to the House the 'draft Shropshire (District of the Wrekin) (Structural Change) Order 1996'. This is the culmination of the long-running battle that John Biffen and I have had with Gummer concerning the Local Government Commission's review of local authority boundaries and we are not best pleased at the way in which the Executive has ridden roughshod over the elected representatives, even to the extent of instructing the Commission to hold a second inquiry in Shropshire after the first had recommended maintenance of the status quo. Having placed my dissatisfaction on the record I, together with former Wrekin MP Warren Hawksley, vote against the Order, as indeed John Biffen would have done but for a family bereavement. Whilst that particular battle is now ended the one concerning BSE continues to rage and on 9 July Douglas Hogg addresses the backbench Agriculture Committee on the subject of an 'accelerated cull' scheme. The reaction to his presentation is muted and the sight of Douglas sitting entirely alone in the 'No' Lobby later in the day seems to sum up the prevailing mood most eloquently.

As we approach the Summer Recess the Group of 8 is at somewhat of a loss to know what the next move should be. Our biggest problem is that there is no means of knowing whether there will be a General Election in the autumn in which eventuality there is nothing to be done other than go home and tend our own constituencies. On the other hand if the Election is not held until the spring the Government could limp on for almost another year with all the attendant risks of hitting more trouble or suffering further humiliation as when on 10 July 124 Conservatives vote in one Lobby, 116 in another and the rest of us wash our hands of the whole proceedings and go home. The motion on the Order Paper concerns Members' pay. Having sub-contracted the consideration of this matter to the Senior Salaries Review Board the Government now doesn't like what they have recommended which is that the Parliamentary salary be increased from £34,085 per annum to £42,300. Presumably recognising that to approve such a huge increase would be an electoral liability the Government propose a much more modest increase of 3 per cent which, predictably, the House rejects. One wonders who else other than John Major could have engineered the situation in which the Conservative vote is split three ways in almost equal proportions with $\frac{1}{3}$ voting with the Government because they're on the payroll, $\frac{1}{3}$ voting to support the recommendation of the SSRB which Government itself commissioned and $\frac{1}{3}$ abstaining in disgust at the impossible situation created entirely by our own side. Sadly this is yet another case of weak leadership and abdicated responsibility. On an entirely unrelated subject an all-Party group of MPs and Peers have been trying to persuade Government to sanction the building of a replacement Royal Yacht. This, we are confident, can be achieved mainly at the expense of the private sector although discussions that we have had with the Defence Secretary have established that he would personally be happy to man the proposed vessel out of the MoD budget. Following last night's Adjournment debate about the Royal Yacht initiated by Cyril Townsend (Bexleyheath) the All Party Royal Yacht Group, chaired by Lord Ashbourne, holds a Press Conference which is only moderately successful because we still lack any indication from Downing Street as to which way they want to go.* When on Saturday (13 July) it is announced that Lloyds Bank is prepared to put up £80m towards the building costs one can only conclude that here is another missed opportunity for Major and the Conservatives but, given the paralysis of decision making at the top, perhaps we shouldn't be too surprised.

Another sad commentary on our time is provided by Willie Ross who tells

---

*By the time a decision is finally taken the Election will be practically upon us and agreement to sanction HMY *Britannia*'s replacement just looks like so much window-dressing.

me that Government never consult the Ulster Unionist MPs and that many of the difficulties they encounter stem from the fact that Ministers take too much of their advice from civil servants. Given our recent experience in Shropshire I know exactly how he feels. An overweening executive can, more and more it appears, ignore the elected representatives with almost total impunity. With this knowledge in mind I am happy to congratulate Tony Wright (Lab. Cannock & Burntwood) on his contribution to a debate on Parliamentary Procedure on 11 July when, at the risk of being ruled out of order, I myself speak about the diminution of Parliamentary sovereignty. Notwithstanding our political differences the common ground between us is our shared concern about the excessive concentration of power in the hands of the executive and what this means for democracy. In saying that 'if we are honest, most of us are in the business of climbing greasy poles, falling off greasy poles or putting more grease on the pole to make sure people do not come up behind us,' Tony Wright analyses the situation not at all unfairly and in the final resort what we are up against is, as Nigel Spearing (Lab. Newham South) correctly points out, human nature!

At the Group of 8 meeting on 16 July a new avenue is explored. The proposition is that we should effectively take over the dormant Conservatives Against a Federal Europe (CAFE).

The 8 members of our group will all become its new Vice Presidents and Richard Body and Teddy Taylor, as our most senior members, will go to see Margaret Thatcher to invite her to become President. Mike Penning says that he has arranged to be the committee, pro tem, whilst we look around for a Chairman and other officers. It is proposed to hold a public meeting in Chelmsford at the end of September and looking ahead to the Party Conference we have booked an auditorium capable of holding somewhere between 650 and 1000 people.

On 15 July I sound out various colleagues to ascertain whether or not they would support an EDM about Douglas Hogg's mooted 'accelerated cattle cull'. To my surprise the Chairman of the backbench Agriculture Committee, Paul Marland, and the Chairman of the Agriculture Select Committee, Jerry Wiggin, are not keen but by the time I table it tomorrow evening I have six 'good' names to act as sponsors. On 17 July there is a press release from the Country Landowners' Association saying that it will be advising MPs to vote against the 'accelerated cattle cull' scheme and colleagues are telling me that they are drawing the attention of their local press to their support for my EDM whilst others are busy adding their names to the list of existing signatories. By Thursday our efforts appear to be paying off when it is announced on 'Farming Today' that the Government do not intend debating this matter this side of the recess. This proves to be duff information and practically the last thing that the House does before adjourning for the Summer Recess is to debate the

'Accelerated Slaughter Programme'. Winding up the debate the Parliamentary Secretary Angela Browning assures the House that the Orders implementing the accelerated cull, whilst drafted and available, would not be signed before Parliament returns in mid-October but that good news is tempered by the statement made earlier in the afternoon by her boss regarding a theoretical possibility that BSE might manifest itself in sheep.

Not all the news is bad. On 22 July it is rumoured that Paymaster General David Heathcoat-Amory has resigned from Government because he no longer supports the Government's European policy. This is soon confirmed when, quite by chance, I bump into him on the lower ground floor where his secretary, along with many other Members' secretaries, has her desk. When I say to David that if the news is true I salute him he says that it is indeed true and proceeds to show me a copy of his excellent letter of resignation together with the PM's pathetic reply.

Before Parliament adjourns for the summer there is a flurry of activity on the Fisheries front. Fisheries Minister Tony Baldry gets angry with me at a lively meeting of European Standing Committee A when I try, once again, to get him to accept that there cannot be and ultimately will not be any exception to the fundamental CFP principle of 'equal access to the common resource'. Subsequently, when the EC documents discussed in the Standing Committee are brought to the House, Nigel Spearing moves an amendment effectively to scrap the CFP and to replace it with a new policy based upon the mutual agreement of countries with recognised fisheries interest* working together in co-operation to achieve sustainable fish stocks and viable fishing communities. Believing co-operation to be infinitely preferable to coercion David Porter, Teddy Taylor and Warren Hawksley join me in the 'Aye' Lobby but there are more than enough of our Conservative colleagues in the 'No' Lobby to ensure that the Spearing amendment is lost. On 23 July Teresa and I have an appointment to see Secretary of State for Scotland Michael Forsyth (Stirling) to talk about the lessons to be learned from our recent visit to Peterhead. Michael is sympathetic and clearly concerned about the things we are able to tell him. 'God, what a mess,' he says. Whether at this stage his mind was still on Fisheries or whether his comment expressed a wider frustration is hardly the point – either way it seems to sum up our present situation quite succinctly.

At its first meeting after the Summer Recess the Group of 8 are keen to hear my views on the latest situation regarding beef and fish. Earlier in the day NFU President David Naish has told the backbench Agriculture committee that he has only gone along with the accelerated slaughter proposals since it became clear that this is what the Government has committed itself to. He

---

*Even though Austria and Luxembourg have no coastline, as members of the EU collective they are entitled to vote on Fisheries matters. It is a textbook example of how the collectivism which underscores all EU policies works in practice.

also confirms what Colin Maclean has previously told me when he admits that the 'Over Thirty Month' cull was instituted 'at the instigation of myself and the major retailers'. As far as Fisheries are concerned Richard Shepherd and I are able to report on a most successful visit to the Shetlands where we had been hosted by SBF member Magnie Stewart. One of my abiding memories of our visit is the sight of prime white fish in Scalloway fish market, fresh from the sea but covered in red dye. This, we were told, was because at the auction sale earlier that morning the fish in question hadn't reached the minimum sale price decreed by the EC and therefore had to be destroyed. The scandal of perfectly saleable, nutritious fresh fish being destroyed on shore, coupled with the even bigger tragedy of what goes on at sea where the quota system results in half of the fish that are caught being thrown back dead into the sea, makes it difficult to understand how any politicians, least of all Conservative ones, can go on supporting the CFP. Nevertheless, in spite of our best efforts, go along with it they do. On 24 July, in accordance with my regular practice of minuting formal meetings with Ministers by writing to them to confirm the salient points of our discussions, I had written to Michael Forsyth and it is to this letter that I refer when we speak again on 30 October. By now his attitude is quite different to the one he had adopted at our meeting in July. He flatly refuses to concede any ground at all and finishes up by saying that he is against getting out of Europe as if that answers my questions which are all Fisheries related. Perhaps I shouldn't be surprised that even erstwhile Thatcherites like Forsyth are now speaking in these terms when, according to James Cran, who as PPS to the Northern Ireland Secretary Patrick Mayhew (Tunbridge Wells) is seeing something of the inner workings of Government, the whole shoot is now being run by Clarke and Heseltine. On the other hand, as judged by the furore that is now building up on the question of firearms in the aftermath of the Dunblane gunning down of innocent children, there are serious doubts about whether even they are actually in control of the political agenda any more.

On 19 July Home Secretary Michael Howard had been the Guest of Honour at the LCCA Annual Dinner. On that occasion he was undoubtedly impressed by both the huge attendance – he'd never been to such a big constituency event, he said – and by the obvious support that I enjoyed amongst my constituents. In his speech Michael referred to me as his friend and talks about my 'fierce integrity' and 'the need for men of fierce integrity in Parliament'. In spite of the indifferent food the dinner is judged to have been the best yet which is more than can be said about my next meeting with the Home Secretary.

On 30 October I join a deputation of colleagues who go to see Michael Howard about his proposed firearms legislation. My 'fierce integrity' obliges me to tell him that as a backbencher I am becoming increasingly resentful

Home Secretary Michael Howard with l-r LCCA Vice Chairman Pam Twitchell, Sonny Twitchell, self, wife Patricia, Chairman Michael Wood and Rosemary Wood.

about being cut out of the deal either by review bodies set up by Government such as Scott, Nolan and the Senior Salaries Review Board or, in this case, the Snowdrop campaign, none of which have any democratic legitimacy whatsoever. In this particular instance even the views of the Home Affairs Select Committee and the Cullen Report appear to have become casualties of emotive tabloid press reporting and the Dunblane victims who have had the whole of the Summer Recess to wind up their campaign. Michael Howard's decision to give in to the anti-gun lobby is, as far as this administration is concerned, almost the final nail in the coffin. By the time we meet again in the Home Secretary's room with Conservative members of the Home Affairs Select Committee on 5 November it is obvious that the Firearms Amendment Bill is heading for trouble. The following day Jerry Wiggin chairs a meeting of shooting supporters at which John Carlisle (Luton North) and Tony Marlow threaten to vote against the Bill when it comes to the House for Second Reading next Tuesday. The consensus is that we should all abstain at Second Reading and vote against the subsequent Money resolution if, in the meantime, the Government have not come up with a lot more money to provide adequate compensation for the consequential losses that the legislation will undoubtedly cause.

Next day, 7 November, I leave my constituency Chairman, Michael Wood, drinking tea in the Pugin Room whilst I attend the weekly meeting of the '22 Committee where I have something to say. I remind the Committee that I have already, on a previous occasion, pointed out the hazard of Government sub-contracting difficult decisions since when we have had the SSRB and Cullen Reports, both of which the Government have ignored, so the first question to be answered is why Government commissioned them in the first place. I go on to tell the Committee what I have already told the Home Secretary which is that I am becoming increasingly resentful that editors of tabloid newspapers, spokespersons for the Snowdrop Campaign etc., who have absolutely no democratic legitimacy whatsoever, clearly have more influence with Government than its own backbenchers whose sole function, it appears, is to go through the correct voting lobby whenever told to do so. John Carlisle, Archie Hamilton and Ivan Lawrence all speak in support of what I have said and make the point that compensation will have to be much greater than presently envisaged, that this legislation is upsetting Conservative voters – this in response to Edwina Currie (Derbyshire South) who is worried about party unity and the effect upon marginal seats – and that it is contrary to Conservative principles. Following the meeting I have a long chat with Iain Duncan Smith who is seething about the Government and, as he says, every member of it. Not for the first time he says, 'I hate it.'

On the eve of the Second Reading I take John Biffen's amendment, which only he and I have signed, to the Table Office for it to be printed on tomorrow's Order Paper. Deliberately we are not advertising the fact that we are proposing that the Bill be not read a second time but by dinner time John Carlisle has discovered the existence of our amendment and he and others have appended their names. It appears on the Order Paper with 8 signatories and, without the slightest attempt to canvass support for it, attracts 31 Conservative votes when it is put to a division. Of the 384 Members who vote against the Biffen amendment only 209 are Conservatives which means that with 86 Conservative absences or abstentions the potential rebellion is very much greater than at first appears. The fact that the Speaker has selected John Biffen's amendment at all is in itself remarkable given that it effectively negates the Bill itself, an outcome that would more conventionally be achieved by voting against the Second Reading. By the time the Firearms Bill gets to Committee Stage the number of Conservatives openly opposed to this very illiberal measure will have doubled* but the damage that it will have done to Party morale and electoral prospects in the meantime is incalculable.

---

*In a division on an amendment to oblige Government to provide compensation to all those whose businesses would be adversely affected by the ban on handguns 62 Conservatives kick over the traces in the belief that putting people out of business as a consequence of arbitrary legislation is unacceptable and not what a so-called Conservative Government should be doing.

It will have destroyed any last remaining hope that this administration defends conservative principles and upholds traditional conservative values.

The next test for the Government will be how they deal with the European Court judgement on the Working Time Directive which is expected shortly. Meeting on 5 November the Group of 8 decide to hold a Press Conference on this topic next week. For the second week running Teresa has expressed her frustration that we are not doing more than we are and said that she would like to see us taking more direct action. Whilst there is no opposition to the sentiment it is not readily apparent what form that action should take and we decide to await the outcome of next week's press conference. In the event it is not one of our best and, perhaps because it is overshadowed by the Firearms Bill, attracts relatively little press coverage. We are urging Government to immediately introduce a period of non co-operation with the EU until the matter of the 48 hour week is satisfactorily resolved. At dinner that evening (12 November) I hear Nigel Evans (Ribble Valley), Rod Richards and Gary Streeter (Plymouth Sutton) all express varying degrees of Euroscepticism which are now widespread in the light of the ECJ ruling. Even David Harris, formerly PPS to the Foreign Secretary, is heard to express his frustration at the way the EU works. At a meeting of the IGC Monitoring Group on 13 November Norman Lamont says that the question of the 48 hour working week must be resolved now, not at the IGC. This is not dissimilar to the Group of 8 line of non co-operation pending settlement but, true to form, instead of kicking the ball into the back of the net, John Major kicks for touch saying that the matter will have to be thrashed out at the IGC. That evening a division on the Government's handling of the BSE crisis results in another cliff-hanger when the combined opposition musters 302 votes to the Government's 303.

On 18 November, referring to an article that appeared in yesterday's *Sunday Telegraph*, Teresa is anxious to explain that what she had said to journalist Matthew D'Ancona over lunch last week was on lobby terms and that he should not therefore have mentioned our names in his article. To put her mind at rest I tell her that it won't have done any harm because it will at least remind the public and the Whips' Office that we haven't gone away – nor have we, although next day Richard Body expresses the opinion at the regular Tuesday meeting of the Group of 8 that we may already have served our purpose! The meeting is reluctant to go the whole hog by calling for Britain to leave the EU but when, later in the day, I hear Michael Howard deliver a very strong Eurosceptic address at an ERG reception in which he says that the UK will simply not accept various aspects of EU policy and that we will be seeking the repatriation of powers already surrendered I can see Richard's point but then again I shall only believe it when I see it!

The following day there is a first class row at European Standing

On Westminster Bridge.

Committee B where the topic under discussion is the Euro, Convergence and Stability. John Whittingdale bravely votes with Labour and the Government is defeated. The consequence of this is that the business is destined to be debated on the floor of the House which is what the European Legislation Select Committee had recommended in the first place. On the 21st, at Question Time, the PM has a rough ride over the Government's refusal to agree to this in advance of the Chancellor going off to the meeting of Finance Ministers (Ecofin) next month. The Conservative benches are further outraged when we hear the PM say that the Stability Pact will not affect the UK! To deny that one of the EU collective's policies will have any effect upon one of its members is an insult to our intelligence. Following PMQs, Business Questions is equally lively as the Speaker, who only yesterday expressed her fears about the 'integrity' of Parliament, allows full rein on the same topic. At 1605 I see Marcus Fox, Chairman of the '22 Committee, and request an opportunity to speak at tonight's meeting and am heartened when he calls me first. I remind the Committee of the concern that I have previously expressed about the way in which the Government is conducting its business and go on to rail about the apparent contempt it holds for backbench opinion and the disgraceful way in which they are ramming three controversial EU finance regulations through Parliament without a proper debate. My theme is taken up by John Redwood, John Wilkinson and Tony Marlow and there are no dissenters. Later I learn that, for the first time in living memory, the executive of the '22 have reached unanimity and Marcus Fox is going to see the PM. That evening the lobby correspondents are anxious to know what it was that I said to the '22 and in the almost certain knowledge that they will already have been given the answer to that question by other colleagues I stick to the line that it was 'a private meeting'. I cannot help noticing how deferential everybody is being towards me and when the day ends with my being offered a glass of whisky in the Whips' Office I can scarcely believe how things have changed since, almost two years to the day, the decision was taken not to invite me in but to unceremoniously kick me out!

The sequel to today's events is that on 25 November, at 3 o'clock in the afternoon, Marcus Fox and '22 Committee Vice Chairman Geoffrey Johnson-Smith (Wealdon) see the PM, the upshot of which is that a debate on Economic and Monetary Union is now very much in prospect. In the meantime William Powell (Corby) rounds on me for having said at last week's meeting that 'there is no fund of goodwill for the Government on the backbenches'. His reason for objecting to my spelling out what most of our colleagues are thinking is that 'these things have a habit of getting into the Press'. In response to that I tell William that it's a pity the Party isn't a little less Stalinist so that more of our concerns could be aired at the '22 which is any case the right place to wash the Party's dirty linen rather than College Green.*

Prior to letting off steam at the '22 I had told the Chief Whip, Alistair Goodlad, my former territorial Whip, Roger Knapman, and my new Whip, Jacqui Lait, how angry I am and that they shouldn't gamble on the proximity of a General Election keeping myself and others in check. At the same time George Gardiner, Chairman of the '92 Group, has written to the Chief Whip saying that unless the debates are held on the floor of the House he will not in future vote with the Government on any other EU business. At dinner that night I am dumbfounded when Peggy Fenner, who has previously regarded Eurosceptics with unspeakable contempt, says that she will set out her opposition to the Single Currency in her Election Address and goes on to say how she has always been opposed to EMU and Political Union! It seems that even the out and out Europhile Michael Heseltine realises that the game is up. Earlier in the week David Evans has told me that Hezza has offered him big inducements to become his PPS, presumably having calculated that this will go some way towards softening his image as an arch integrationist. A week later David has just said, 'If there's a banana skin around, this Government will find it,' when the news breaks that tomorrow's Budget papers have been leaked to the *Daily Mirror* which means that there are no surprises when the Chancellor rises to make his Budget speech from the Despatch Box on 26 November.

Whilst 26 November is not a particularly brilliant day for the Chancellor, Fisheries Minister Tony Baldry appears to be on a 'high', talking about getting the problem of the 6 and 12 mile limits sorted out before the Election and the importance of doing everything possible to help colleagues with fishing constituencies. This is precisely what the Group of 8 have been trying to tell him ever since he was appointed in July 1995. He must know that in the remaining time available he can't possibly deliver on these undertakings but his waffle is good enough to satisfy Anthony Steen, the only other colleague to attend the meeting. Little wonder that Chris Venmore, Secretary of the South West Shell Fish Association, is putting up against him in South Hams. On the more topical EU related matter my Whip, Jacqui Lait, wants to know how much time I think should be allocated for the pending debate on EMU and also how I will vote on the motion to say that the EU Stability Pact Regulations have received proper scrutiny. I undertake to let her know in due course but stress that I would prefer not to be put in the position of having to vote against the Government. At a meeting of the 2000 Group, in response to

---

*Repeatedly the Europhiles would accuse the Eurosceptics of giving TV interviews on College Green, an open space on the opposite side of the road to Sovereign's entrance, claiming that this prejudiced Party unity. They conveniently overlooked the fact that they themselves never missed a media opportunity to put their own side of the argument but seldom, if ever, were they prepared to argue their case in the forum provided by the '22 Committee.

my question, John Redwood says that we must insist upon copper-bottomed guarantees that the Stability Pact regulations will not apply to the UK so long as we remain outside the Single Currency.

As things go from bad to worse one cannot help speculating how much more satisfactory it would have been if we had gone to the country in October, not least when the headlines on 29 January 'Ministers in Protest Over Mawhinney' scream trouble and strife at the highest level. According to the *Daily Telegraph* 'John Major is facing a growing Cabinet backlash against the 'heavy-handed' techniques being used by Dr Brian Mawhinney to force Ministers to go onto the offensive against Labour in the run-up to the General Election. Five Ministers have complained to Alistair Goodlad, the Chief Whip, that the Conservative Party Chairman is deliberately undermining them by briefing against them to the press.

After hearing Prime Minister's Questions and the Chancellor's Statement on Ecofin which follows, the members of the Group of 8 are so depressed and despondent when they meet on Tuesday 3rd December that the opportunity to defeat the Government on a VAT motion is not properly discussed and no action is taken. This is something that we soon come to regret. The mood of anger and resentment concerning the PM's answer to Tony Blair regarding the Single Currency* continues to build up throughout the rest of the week and on Thursday Teresa tells me that she has had a meeting with Alan Sked, the founder of the United Kingdom Independence Party. I tell Teresa that before I do anything rash I will tell her and very much hope that she will do the same for me. In the meantime I have told Roger Knapman that he needs to find a replacement for me on the Welsh Select Committee on which, to show willing, I have been prepared to serve for the past twelve months. The Parliamentary Party is in a fairly febrile mood as evidenced by the strength of feelings ventilated at Thursday's meeting of the '22 Committee following which it is reported that Tony Marlow is calling for Ken Clarke, the possible architect of so many of our misfortunes, to be sacked. A junior Minister from, on her own admission, a poor family which was helped by previous Conservative Governments to buy their own council house, cannot believe what is now happening. Both she and I had been clinging to the hope that at some stage before the General Election the PM would have abandoned his

---

*The exchange between the PM and the Leader of the Opposition was:

Mr Blair: 'Will the Prime Minister say clearly, without any qualification, that his statement of 3 April on behalf of the Government that at the next election he will not rule out the option of joining a single currency in the next Parliament, remains unequivocally the position of the Government'?

The Prime Minister: 'That remains unequivocally the position of the Government.'

Mr Blair: 'It is right to give the Prime Minister credit for such a clear reply. Let us see whether we can get another little clear reply. Can he tidy up one small loose end? Does he agree with the Deputy Prime Minister's statement on the radio at lunchtime, when he said of that position 'We are not going to change our position in the election campaign or in this Parliament?'

The Prime Minister: 'My right hon. Friend said that, that is our position.'

commitment to the Single Currency. When I tell the Minister that I could have wept when I heard what Major said on Tuesday, Angela Browning (Tiverton) responds by saying that this is indeed precisely what she herself did! On 4 December I am one of the 64 Conservatives who vote at the Report Stage of the Firearms Bill for an amendment, which the Government opposes, to pay compensation for consequential losses to gun clubs and businesses affected by the proposals to ban all handguns over .22 calibre. On all fronts anger is spilling over and as if from a different planet the stentorian voice of Nicholas Soames is heard to declaim, 'We must all get behind the Prime Minister,' oblivious of the fact that he has also given Blair the opportunity on a plate to upstage us on the Single Currency issue if he chooses to do so.

In advance of the impending General Election I am trying to help the Conservative PPC for the Wrekin constituency which, owing to boundary changes, will absorb some parts of the existing Ludlow division. On 3 December Peter Bruinvels and I are scheduled to meet Iain Sproat (Harwich), the Minister of State at the Department of National Heritage, in yet another attempt to get Lottery money for the Aerospace Museum at RAF Cosford. At the very last minute Iain cancels our meeting and Peter has a wasted journey and a lost opportunity to be photographed with a Government Minister. When no fewer than two Whips express their concern that Iain has let Peter and me down I get the impression that the last thing that anybody wants to do at the present time is to upset me. Subsequently, at the 10 o'clock vote, I overhear Secretary of State Virginia Bottomley (Surrey SW) discussing this morning's fiasco with Iain, the sequel to which is that the following day Virginia tells me that she is pulling out all the stops for Cosford and apologises once again for Sproat's failure to keep our appointment. How times have changed! When I originally approached Virginia on this subject she told me that I would 'have to speak to Jacob'. 'Who's Jacob?' I ask. 'Jacob Rothschild, he's the Chairman of the National Heritage Lottery Fund.' Quite apart from feeling disgruntled that the Secretary of State was giving me the brush-off, what annoyed me more was the fact that huge amounts of cash are being disbursed by unelected people who appear to have *carte blanche* to make awards to whomsoever they choose. Whilst lottery money cannot be equated with taxes it nevertheless rankles that the uses to which it is put is entirely in the hands of appointees who have no democratic legitimacy and, judged by the Secretary of State's response to me, little supervision.

Before adjourning for Christmas the House will have the opportunity, once again, to debate Fisheries. At a well attended SBF briefing on 5 December it is observed that Michael Stephen (Shoreham), the Fisheries Minister's PPS, is the first to arrive and the last to leave. Although it is clutching at straws one wonders whether this is a sign that the Government are at last seeing the light and that the policy really is about to change. A week later Roger Knapman goes literally on his knees to beg me to get the Group of 8 on board for the Fisheries vote on 16 December. He says that the Opposition parties, scenting a Government defeat, are primed for a vote of confidence on 17 December. Having consulted Richard Shepherd and Teddy Taylor earlier in the day we agree that we should make repatriation of Britain's Exclusive Fishing Zone the price for our support. On the day in question Roger telephones to say that the Government will definitely be defeated if we don't all vote the ticket but, determined to take the Government to the wire, I tell him that we will not be voting for the Fisheries motion. Very much at the eleventh hour we strike a bargain. At 2120, a bare forty minutes before the crucial vote, Teddy Taylor, Teresa Gorman and I agree to vote with the Government but only on the strict understanding that in winding up the debate, the Parliamentary Under-Secretary of State for Scotland, Raymond Robertson (Aberdeen South) responds satisfactorily to the intervention that I will make whilst he is at the Despatch Box. Mine is one of only two interventions that the Minister allows and I ask him if he will *give the House a categorical assurance that, unless a satisfactory agreement is reached on quota-hopping, Her Majesty's Government will veto the proposed treaty at the intergovernmental conference.* After quoting from the Foreign Secretary's broadcast interview with the BBC's 'On the Record' programme last evening Raymond Robertson secures our votes by saying that *'I can give my hon. Friend the Member for Ludlow the categorical assurance that he seeks.'* This assurance will, of course, be worthless if, as seems highly probable, Labour win the next election. Although down, Major is not yet out and the Opposition amendment criticising *'the failure of this Government in its seventeen years of office to tackle the problem facing the fishing industry'* etc. etc. is lost by 11 votes and the Government motion is carried by 12. Subsequently Roger tells me that had Teresa and I not given in the Ulster Unionists who abstained would otherwise have voted against the Government and the Government would have lost. Having seen Roger usher two of the Ulstermen out of the Chamber to talk to them, shortly after striking the bargain with us, his version of events seems entirely plausible. Once again, by the skin of their teeth, the Government have survived but by this time tomorrow a story will be breaking about how Government Whips have 'paired' individual Conservative Members with both Labour and Liberal Democrat Members. This is confirmed a couple of days later when Gareth Wardell (Lab. Gower) tells me that he was paired with Walter Sweeney but that the Whips had also paired Walter with Liberal Democrat leader, Paddy Ashdown! Since 'pairing' is an entirely unofficial arrangement which allows two opposing Members to be absent without affecting the outcome of a vote there can be no come-back if the Government are crafty enough to 'pair' one of their members with two Opposition Members. Doubtless there will be closer liaison between the Labour and Liberal Democrats Whips' offices in future to ensure that the Government isn't able to enhance its voting strength in this rather dubious way again but clearly, as far as the Government are concerned, desperate circumstances demand desperate measures.

On the day following the Fisheries debate the Group of 8 have a further meeting with Chancellor of the Duchy of Lancaster Roger Freeman, at which he says that he senses that the PM is teetering on the edge of a major decision on the European issue. There is, of course, the strong possibility that this is just another feint to try to calm things down before a General Election but on the other hand, if there is anything in it, at least it makes it look as though the pressure that we have brought to bear is paying off and that we have been right to stop short of defeating the Government in the division lobbies thus precipitating a premature Election. Conversely, given the fact that the Government have amongst other things missed the opportunity to veto the Stability Pact* at last weekend's Dublin summit one could easily be forgiven for thinking that the Cabinet's commitment to European integration is undiminished – 'what a tangled web we weave, when first we practise to deceive'!

---

*By dint of the Stability Pact a straitjacket will be imposed upon all those countries seeking to join the Single Currency which will oblige them to ensure that budget deficits do not exceed 3 per cent of GDP and total borrowings, 60 per cent of GDP. Fearful of the effect upon the strength of the Single Currency of excessive deficits in other EU countries this measure is being introduced at the insistence of Germany.

CHAPTER FOURTEEN

1997

*...the conclusion that I have behaved rather
more honourably than John Major ever deserved*

THE NEW YEAR begins, just like the old one had ended, with a public appeal for Party unity. On the day Parliament returns Deputy Prime Minister Michael Heseltine tells listeners to the BBC's 'Today' programme that the danger of disunity is stark. Ironically, on 28 December, former Party Vice-Chairman Jeffrey Archer had gone to press saying that party activists in the constituencies are sick and tired of seeing their work to secure victory ruined in minutes by MPs giving TV and radio interviews. On 20 January, a week after his 'Today' programme interview, Hezza gets a rough ride when he attends a meeting of the '92 Group. Having made the point that the Government no longer have an overall majority owing to the defection of three 'wets' (Alan Howarth, Emma Nicholson and Peter Thurnham) I tell him that prominent people in our Party, himself included, who make public appeals for unity simply confirm the public's worst suspicions. I also take the opportunity of saying that the Government's prospectus is bogus, firstly because saying that we will not go into a federal Europe doesn't square with having already signed three solemn and binding federalist treaties, and secondly because claiming that more discussions about the terms of the Single Currency are necessary, ignores the reality that what we have to do and when and how we do it is all spelt out in the Maastricht Treaty. For his part Bill Walker tells Hezza that it is apparent that something has changed in recent years and since it isn't himself it must be the Party. Hezza's response is that we must all stick to 'the agreed form of words' and that ' the policy won't change'. The endless search for a 'form of words' that deliberately avoids saying what we mean or meaning what we say, is now a major preoccupation of Government. Quite apart from being an electoral handicap the fudge is, in the longer term, unrealistic and unsustainable.

For the first seven days of the new sitting Teresa Gorman's 10 Minute Rule Bill *'to provide for the holding of a referendum on the United Kingdom's membership of the European Union'* is the centre of interest. At a meeting of Bill Cash's IGC group on 14 February John Redwood's appeal to Teresa to change the title of her Bill is turned down flat but not before Peter Tapsell has expressed disappointment that she did not consult the group before proceeding. The

Group of 8 are similarly unimpressed by Roger Knapman's threat that Teresa
will 'never come back to this place as a Conservative and that, if necessary, her
Association will be disbanded unless she withdraws her Bill'. The effect of the
Whips' Office blackmail is simply to strengthen the group's resolve to back
Teresa. The following day I make it my business to explain to the members of
the Conservative 2000 group that Teresa had deliberately not told anybody
about her timetable because when she did so last time she found herself
gazumped by Bill Cash of all people! Whilst recognising that JR himself might
have difficulty in supporting the Bill because it is so contrary to Government
policy I urge my colleagues, having regard to all the circumstances, to get
behind Teresa which most of them, with the notable exception of Bill Cash,
agree to do. JR says that he will give the matter careful thought over the
weekend before deciding what to do and, true to his word, he tells me on
Monday that he will support the Bill when Teresa brings it to the House on
Tuesday. After all the fuss (and threats) and in spite of Denis MacShane (Lab.
Rotherham) speaking against the Bill, there is no division because those
opposed decline to nominate Tellers. Irrespective of Party the last thing that
the Party hierarchies want is a vote at which all the political parties would be
seen to be opposed to giving the people a say in these important matters.
Correspondingly the last thing that the integrationists want is a referendum
which they might easily lose. Amongst others in the Aye lobby waiting to vote
when the division is called off are Norman Lamont, Peter Tapsell and John
Redwood. None of us are looking to make trouble for the Government – it's
perfectly capable of doing that for itself – but all of us have a vested interest in
trying to persuade the Cabinet to make the Party more electorally attractive
which, as things stand, it most certainly is not.

On 16 January the All Party Royal Yacht group holds a press conference to
publicise the progress that we are making in terms of a private sector solution
to the question of replacing HMY *Britannia*. Whilst it would be flattering to
think that this event succeeds in galvanising Government into action we are
all quite unprepared for the statement which Defence Secretary Michael
Portillo makes to the House on 22 January indicating that the Government
has at long last reached a decision which is to build a replacement, entirely at
taxpayers' expense. With barely three months to run before Major must go to
the country this decision is far too late to be regarded as other than pure
window dressing. It also raises the question as to why a Government which is
ostensibly committed to involving the private sector wherever possible has, in
this instance, not even bothered to contact those of us who have been working
to this end for some considerable time.

The death of Iain Mills on 16 January means that the Government no
longer has an overall majority and to make matters worse former PM Ted
Heath will use next Monday's 'Today' programme to attack the Government's

Commodore Anthony Morrow RN entertains the All Party Parliamentary Royal Yacht Group on board HMY Britannia.

Royal Yacht decision just as if he thought we hadn't got troubles enough already. I tell him that my constituency Chairman is not best pleased with his utterances and that there are times when we backbenchers must sing small!

Mounting speculation that the pending General Election will be held on 20 March is heightened when, on 22 January, '22 Chairman Marcus Fox refers to the inability of the Whips' Office to provide him with any information relating to next week's business. At Question Time on 23 January the PM tells the House that it is unlikely that the UK will join the Single Currency in 1999. That may suit Major's book but for those of us who do not want the Single Currency, now or ever, it poses a problem in terms of what we are going to say on the hustings. By the end of January the answer to the question is starting to emerge. On 28th I encounter David Martin on his way back from CCO in Smith Square, having taken the production of his election address out of their hands. John Biffen advises the IGC group that they will have to fight the election on the basis of their own personal manifestoes and next day Marcus Fox, responding to pressure from the '92 Group, tells the '22 Committee that there will be no censorship of colleagues' election addresses.

Sadly that is not the end of the matter. Within one hour of Marcus Fox making his statement at the '22 Committee my constituency Chairman is contacted by the President of the West Midlands area with a message from the Party Chairman urging me to back off. This prompts me to give top priority to writing the letter to all Cabinet Ministers that I have been contemplating for several weeks* and also a separate letter to Marcus Fox detailing the sequel to his pronouncement. Meanwhile Teresa tells me that the SkyNews Political Editor, Adam Boulton, has told her that John Major has told him that he wishes he had sought cross-party support for the Maastricht Treaty – a similar theme to that expressed in an article in last weekend's *Sunday Express* by his co-conspirator, Garel-Jones.

At the meetings of the IGC group and the Group of 8 on 4 February, colleagues are interested in hearing my account of the sequel to Marcus Fox's statement at last week's '22 Committee. That is more than can be said for the PM who clearly doesn't like the contents of my letter to him and studiously avoids meeting my eye when we encounter each other in the lobby next day. Not that I'm his only problem given that the Lords have today, whilst considering the provisions of the Firearms (Amendment) Bill, overturned Government decisions on the storage of guns and compensation for consequential loss. When the Lords' amendments are considered back in the Commons on 18 February no fewer than 95 Conservatives will defy the Party Whip to vote in favour of compensation for those whose livelihood has been adversely affected or completely destroyed by the imposition of arbitrary legislation. This is three times the number who opposed the Firearms Bill at Second reading and whilst, because of Opposition support, there is no danger of the Government losing the vote they have by this most illiberal legislation forfeited the goodwill of a substantial number of their own backbenchers, not to mention countless members of the public who will doubtless cast their votes accordingly.

A fortnight after Jack Aspinwall (Wansdyke) has expressed the opinion that 75 per cent of Conservative candidates will have a Single Currency disclaimer in their election addresses Foreign Secretary Malcolm Rifkind, tells the 'Today' programme that 'we are, on balance, hostile to a single currency'. Chancellor Ken Clarke then takes to the airwaves to tell the listeners that Rifkind's remark was 'a slip of the tongue under pressure from a very skilful interviewer' but that is not the end of the matter. On the BBC 'World at One' programme Rifkind is back again saying that he doesn't regret using the word 'hostile' in his earlier interview. Putting the record straight he says, 'No I don't regret it because, in the context in which I was using it, it was consistent with what the Government's policy is.' With the Foreign Secretary and the

*Appendix F.

Chancellor of the Exchequer singing from different song sheets it's anybody's guess as to where the centre of gravity is within Cabinet but of one thing we can be sure and that is that blaming backbenchers for party disunity is an irresponsible and cowardly cop-out – the problem is at the top and it's a poor leader who blames all his troubles on his foot-soldiers. Later in the day the Chancellor attends the '22 Committee where instead of addressing the assembled company as colleagues and equals he talks down to us and refuses to take questions. Unfortunately this is all too typical of the manner in which the Europhiles amongst us generally deport themselves – making assertions which they are unwilling to defend in open forum and taking care not to leave themselves open to challenge.

Catching up on my reading on the train home I am surprised to read in yesterday's *Shropshire Star* that Agriculture Minister of State Tony Baldry is to visit my constituency tomorrow. Convention decrees that Ministers visiting constituencies on official business advise the sitting Member accordingly. Whether out of ignorance, arrogance or sheer incompetence, notification of Baldry's impending visit consists of a single message left on my secretary's Ansaphone sometime after 5 p.m. on the evening prior to his arrival. When I take the matter up with him the following Monday the Minister undertakes to investigate. The next day there is an apologetic call from Baldry's office with a cock and bull story about his private office being prevented from advising Members about impending Ministerial visits until those affected have been written to by Civil Service officials. The letter to me relating to the visit which took place on 21 February arrives on 25 February and is dated 24 February! Although Baldry and I are in the same Party, judged by this experience, we might as well be on different planets, not least because of our diametrically opposed views on Europe. Whilst I was naïve enough when I first entered Parliament to believe that I was joining a team the reality is so totally different – little wonder that the permanent officials can, and do, run circles round the elected representatives, a task that is made much easier when so many Ministers are apparently driven by ambition rather than political conviction or genuine ability. According to my informant Bill Shelton, formerly the Member for Streatham, John Major, as one of his young councillors in the London Borough of Lambeth, had 'no conviction whatsoever' – little wonder that the Party is disintegrating around him! According to informed sources, even in Cabinet the PM does not encourage discussion or debate and is much more inclined to speak to his cronies in advance of Cabinet meetings to ensure that as far as possible business goes through on the nod. Not that one should be surprised at that – cronyism is endemic in politics as illustrated by the experience of my former colleagues Chris Butler and Tony Favell who were in the last three for the vacancy at Reigate caused by George Gardiner's deselection. Chris cannot understand how a complete unknown came to attract more votes than he and Tony, both experienced Parliamentarians, put together. The dice were clearly loaded against them when at the final selection meeting the public address system miraculously only functioned properly for Crispin Blunt and in contrast to their own CVs, which had been badly duplicated by the local Association, Crispin Blunt's CV was neat and tidy and altogether more presentable!

Back in the House of Commons Nick Budgen gets a very dusty answer at PMQs on 4 March when he raises the question of immigration. When at the following day's '22 Committee the question is posed as to whether or not the Government are prepared to make immigration an election issue the Chairman moves the business swiftly on without the least attempt or opportunity to discuss what is, after all, a very serious political issue. Marcus Fox's notion that the interests of the Conservative Party are best served by sweeping all controversial subjects under the carpet is profoundly mistaken but the assumption must be that this is what the top brass want. Mercifully the Stalinist mentality which pervades the '22 Committee is not at all evident at the smaller special interest group meetings which continue to provide fora for frank exchanges and meaningful discussion. With possibly only two, or maybe three, more meetings in prospect before Parliament is dissolved, I suggest that the Conservative 2000 group ought to discuss our post election strategy. David Evans agrees and says that that should be the only item on the agenda when we meet again next Wednesday. In the event discussion inevitably turns to the question of who will be the Leader in the next Parliament, the presumption being that the election result will make John Major's position untenable. As my modest contribution to the war effort I tell the group that I am willing to stand for election to the Executive of the '22 Committee and am pleased to receive pledges of support as well as John Redwood's acknowledgement of the importance of having a strong representation on that influential body.

On Sunday 9 March George Gardiner steals the headlines by announcing that he will contest the Reigate constituency as the candidate for Sir James Goldsmith's Referendum Party. As a Conservative Member of Parliament George has represented Reigate since 1974 and at the last election was returned with a majority of 17,664. The management still refuse to recognise the significance of the European dimension as far as Conservative and Conservative minded voters are concerned but in a series of open meetings in my own constituency it is obvious from the questions that I am asked that it is the one really big issue. When, as on 7 March, I am still on my feet at 2255 answering questions on this very subject it's no use pretending otherwise. Apart from my customary contribution to the Third Reading debate of the Finance Bill, flagging up the absurdity of capital taxes in a capitalist economy, the second week of March is like waiting for Godot. By Sunday 16th the press and media are full of speculation that the PM will announce the date of the election tomorrow. What is also reported is that the Chancellor is understood to have vetoed CCO election advertisements because of their Eurosceptic tinge. If Ted Heath is the Victor Meldrew of the Conservative Party then Ken Clarke must surely be the Bruce Grobbelaar!*

The press reports turn out to be entirely accurate and on Monday 17 March John Major goes to the Palace to seek the Queen's approval for the dissolution of Parliament. Parliament will be prorogued this coming Friday, 21 March, and the General Election will be held on Thursday 1 May. Few relish the prospect of an unusually long campaign and with strict rules regarding the amount of money that may be spent on election expenses it is a moot point as to when, during the course of the next six weeks, one should actually start the campaign proper. Fearing that I may have fallen into a trap by having previously agreed to speak at a hustings organised by the Three Tuns Inn & Brewery and its new owner, Sir Louis Blom Cooper QC, on 22 March I journey to Bishop's Castle to inform the meeting in person that I shall not, in the changed circumstances, be taking part as I have no intention of signalling the start of my own campaign until sometime in April.

Dining together that evening with Spencer Batiste (Elmet), William Powell and John Townend both Spencer and William express their doubts that we will be doing so again in two months time. With majorities of 3261 and 342 respectively they have little reason to be optimistic about retaining their seats and spirits are hardly raised by our Leader when he addresses the '22 on the 19th. On the eve of battle there is nothing inspirational about what Major has to say and his assertion that he is passionately opposed to socialism rings hollow when set against his track record of supine support for the European Union which is, with all its collectivist policies, socialism writ large. The following day as the PM leaves the tearoom he wishes everybody 'Good Luck' and patting me on the back of the head says that he hopes I'm going to 'behave myself'. It's a throw-away line without any apparent malice aforethought but in the fullness of time I may well come to the conclusion that I have behaved rather more honourably these past six years than John Major ever deserved.

---

*Liverpool F. C. goalkeeper accused of taking bribes to throw the matches.

Appendix A

Economic Affairs Section
Research Division
House of Commons Library
1 Derby Gate
London SW1A 2DG   1 November 1991

Dear Mr Gill

THE DUTCH PROPOSALS

You wanted to know just what the draft Treaty published on Monday would commit its signatories to with respect to a common currency.

Since I began to read the (draft) Treaty instead of reading press articles about it, what has struck me is not so much the let-out, or escape clause, but the immensity of what the UK would be bound by even with this clause inserted. Article 3 for example:-

2. Concurrently with the foregoing, and as provided for in this Treaty and in accordance with the timetable and the procedures set out therein, these activities shall include the irrevocable fixing of exchange rates between the currencies of the Member States leading to the introduction of a single currency, the ECU, the definition and conduct of a single monetary and exchange rate policy the primary objective of which shall be to maintain price stability and, without prejudice to this objective, to support the general economic policy in the Community, in a manner compatible with free and competitive market principles.

3. These activities of the Member States shall entail compliance with the following guiding principles: stable prices, sound public finances and monetary conditions and a sustainable balance of payments.

Similarly, by signing the UK government would accept the provisions of Article 104B – 'Member States shall avoid excessive government deficits', and as far as I can tell, be prepared to submit to Commission scrutiny (though not discipline) of public spending decisions made in the UK. The Commission intends that:-

7. Where the existence of an excessive deficit is established according to

217

paragraph 6, the Council shall make recommendations to the Member State concerned with a view to bringing that situation to an end within a given period. Subject to the provisions of paragraph 8, these recommendations shall not be made public.

8. Where it establishes that there has been no effective follow-up to its recommendations within the period laid down, the Council may, acting on a proposal from the Commission, make recommendations public.

The 'escape clause', as it has been described in the press, for the UK comes in Article 109G (2):-

2. The Council shall not oblige a Member State to participate in the third stage if a Member State has notified to the Council that the National Parliament of the Member State does not feel able to approve of the irrevocable fixing of its currency at the provisional date. Such a Member State shall be exempted from the decision as mentioned above, and will in this Treaty be called 'Member State with an exemption'. The Articles referred to in paragraph 4 do not apply to it.

The Articles of this Treaty which would no longer apply to a country that had sought the status of 'Member State with an exemption' are very few, barely half a dozen, and they deal with the narrow practicalities of the new Treaty. For example, the section of Article 104B which would not apply concerns the disciplinary powers that the Commission could use if a Member State refused to do anything about its excess budget deficit:-

- to issue a recommendation to the EIB to declare the Member State concerned ineligible for further EIB-borrowing;
- to require that the Member State concerned make a non-interest-bearing deposit of an appropriate size with the Community until the excessive deficit has, in the view of the Council, been corrected;
- to impose fines of an appropriate size;
- to suspend new commitments by the Structural Funds in the Member State until the excessive deficit has, in the view of the Council, been corrected.

An 'exempted Member' is also exempt from, Article 105, the provisions concerning the Central Bank and the note issue; Article 106 (7), the powers of the European System of the Central Banks; Article 107, the strict independence of the Central Bank (ECB) and, Article 108, the competence of the ECB; Article 109, the determination of the ECU exchange rate vis a vis the rest of the world; Article 109A (4), participation of Member States in choosing the Board Members of the Governing Council of the ECB (i.e., an exempted Member would have no say).

It is my impression, and I must stress the fact that I only received the 80 page draft yesterday, that despite the provisions of Article 109G, the UK will face a distinctly different set of constraints and obligations if it accepts the Treaty than if it does not. It might be argued that in agreeing to things such as prudent budget deficits etc, that this is so 'woolly' as not to be worth the description of a constraint, however, much the same could be said of previous economic agreements which have subsequently taken on a new meaning and importance. In addition, the Dutch proposals include a declaration that is separate from the Treaty. It notes:-

The Governments of the Member States,

express their strong preference for a swift transition to the third stage of EMU with the full participation of all Member States;

declare that their respective Member States shall contribute according to their ability to the realisation of the broadest base possible for the transition to stage three;

declare that as soon as for their respective Member States the conditions for the transition to stage three as referred to in Article 109F of this Treaty are fulfilled, it is their strongest intention to participate in stage three of EMU from the proposed date without exemption.

As has been pointed out, this is separate from the draft Treaty and does not have the same binding force as the latter. However, the declaration added to, for example, Article 3, places considerable persuasive pressure on governments not to 'opt-out' forever. The extent or degree of this force is perhaps best assessed by someone with skills in forensic diplomacy, rather than by a mere economist, which is of course exactly the point of the draft document in its present form: it can be all things to all parties.

To conclude, if the government signs this Treaty, and then if the House votes against the single currency monetary union concept, then the UK can opt-out of the immediate practical consequences of full union. But, in other respects the UK would have to act, in the short term, in a manner consistent with being in a union and, in the longer term, shape its actions consistent with ultimate membership.

Lastly, I enclose the Article from the Financial Times (30.10.91) that describes the content of the Treaty in more detail.

I hope that this is of some use.

Yours sincerely

Timothy Edmonds

Enc.

Christopher Gill Esq MP
House of Commons
London SW1A 0AA

Appendix B

A personal letter to each of my 335 Conservative colleagues

CHRISTOPHER GILL RD MP

HOUSE OF COMMONS
LONDON SW1A 0AA

May 1992

Now that copies of the Maastricht Treaty are available from
the Vote Office I thought that it might be helpful to draw
your attention to just a few of its more dramatic clauses.

In the preamble, for example, it is stated that the High
Contracting Parties :-

"Resolved to establish an Economic and Monetary Union
including a Single and Stable Currency" and

"Resolved to continue the process of creating an
Ever Closer Union"

Article 8 states that
"Citizenship of the Union is hereby established"

Article 99 that
"The Council shall .... adopt provisions for the
harmonisation of legislation concerning Turnover Taxes,
Excise Duties and other forms of Indirect Taxation"

Article J that
"A Common Foreign and Security Policy is hereby established".

There is much, much more in this Treaty which merits further
scrutiny and whilst it is true that the United Kingdom has
reserved its position on the Social Chapter and (for the time
being) on the Single Currency the fact remains that the overall
effect of the Maastricht Treaty is to institutionalise Socialism
throughout the Community.

If you thought that it would be helpful I should be only too
pleased to show you a marked copy of the Treaty which highlights
the meny serious and alarming developments which it contains.
I am keeping this copy at my desk in the East Cloisters so that
it is readily available should you wish to see it.

With kind regards,

Yours sincerely,

Appendix C

Treaty on European Union

His Majesty the King of the Belgians, Her Majesty the Queen of Denmark, the President of the Federal Republic of Germany, the President of the Hellenic Republic, His Majesty the King of Spain, the President of the French Republic, the President of Ireland, the President of the Italian Republic, His Royal Highness the Grand Duke of Luxembourg, Her Majesty the Queen of the Netherlands, the President of the Portuguese Republic, Her Majesty the Queen of the United Kingdom of Great Britain and Northern Ireland,

RESOLVED to mark a new stage in the process of European integration undertaken with the establishment of the European Communities,

RECALLING the historic importance of the ending of the division of the European continent and the need to create firm bases for the construction of the future Europe,

CONFIRMING their attachment to the principles of liberty, democracy and respect for human rights and fundamental freedoms and of the rule of law,

DESIRING to deepen the solidarity between their peoples while respecting their history, their culture and their traditions,

DESIRING to enhance further the democratic and efficient functioning of the institutions so as to enable them better to carry out, within a single institutional framework, the tasks entrusted to them,

RESOLVED to achieve the strengthening and the convergence of their economies and to establish an economic and monetary union including, in accordance with the provisions of this Treaty, a single and stable currency,

DETERMINED to promote economic and social progress for their peoples, within the context of the accomplishment of the internal market and of reinforced cohesion and environmental protection, and to implement policies ensuring that advances in economic integration are accompanied by parallel progress in other fields,

RESOLVED to establish a citizenship common to nationals of their countries,

RESOLVED to implement a common foreign and security policy including the eventual framing of a common defence policy, which might in time lead to a common defence, thereby reinforcing the European identity and its independence in order to promote peace, security and progress in Europe and in the world,

REAFFIRMING their objective to facilitate the free movement of persons, while ensuring the safety and security of their peoples, by including provisions on justice and home affairs in this Treaty,

RESOLVED to continue the process of creating an ever closer union among the peoples of Europe, in which decisions are taken as closely as possible to the citizen in accordance with the principle of subsidiarity,

In View of further steps to be taken in order to advance European integration,

HAVE DECIDED to establish a European Union and to this end have designated as their plenipotentiaries:

HIS MAJESTY THE KING OF THE BELGIANS:
Mark Eyskens,
Minister for Foreign Affairs;
Philippe Maystadt,
Minister for Finance;

HER MAJESTY THE QUEEN OF DENMARK:
Uffe Ellemann-Jensen,
Minister for Foreign Affairs;
Anders Fogh Rasmussen,
Minister for Economic Affairs;

THE PRESIDENT OF THE FEDERAL REPUBLIC OF GERMANY:
Hans-Dietrich Genscher,
Federal Minister for Foreign Affairs;
Theodor Waigel,
Federal Minister for Finance;

THE PRESIDENT OF THE HELLENIC REPUBLIC:
Antonios Samaras,
Minister for Foreign Affairs;
Efthymios Christodoulou,
Minister for Economic Affairs;

HIS MAJESTY THE KING OF SPAIN:
Francisco Fernandez Ordóñez,
Minister for Foreign Affairs;
Carlos Solchaga Catalán,
Minister for Economic Affairs and Finance;

THE PRESIDENT OF THE FRENCH REPUBLIC:
Roland Dumas,
Minister for Foreign Affairs;
Pierre Bérégovoy
Minister for Economic and Financial Affairs and the Budget;

THE PRESIDENT OF IRELAND:
Gerard Collins,
Minister for Foreign Affairs;
Bertie Ahern,
Minister for Finance;

THE PRESIDENT OF THE ITALIAN REPUBLIC:
Gianni De Michelis,
Minister for Foreign Affairs;
Guido Carli,
Minister for the Treasury;

HIS ROYAL HIGHNESS THE GRAND DUKE OF LUXEMBOURG:
Jacques F. Poos,
Deputy Prime Minister,
Minister for Foreign Affairs;
Jean-Claude Juncker,
Minister for Finance;

HER MAJESTY THE QUEEN OF THE NETHERLANDS:
Hans van den Broek,
Minister for Foreign Affairs;
Willem Kok,
Minister for Finance;

THE PRESIDENT OF THE PORTUGUESE REPUBLIC:
João de Deus Pinheiro,
Minister for Foreign Affairs;
Jorge Braga de Macedo,
Minister for Finance;

HER MAJESTY THE QUEEN OF THE UNITED KINGDOM OF GREAT BRITAIN
AND NORTHERN IRELAND:
The Rt. Hon. Douglas Hurd,
Secretary of State for Foreign and Commonwealth Affairs;
The Hon. Francis Maude,
Financial Secretary to the Treasury.

Appendix D

CHRISTOPHER GILL RD MP
HOUSE OF COMMONS
LONDON SW1A 0AA

Mrs J. Williams,
Chairman,
Ludlow Constituency Conservative Association,
54 Broad Street,
LUDLOW SY8 1NH.   19th March 1993

Further to our telephone conversation last evening I write to say that I find the situation in which you are clearly unable to support my position on the question of European Union quite intolerable.

From that conversation I learned that far from backing me in the stance that I have taken you question my judgement although on your own admission you know insufficient about the Treaty to know whether you are for or against it.

May I remind you that I purposefully made a copy of the Maastricht Treaty available to your household and never once have you said that you personally disagreed with my view. This in spite of the fact that there have been many occasions on which it would have been possible for you to do so – most recently on Monday 1st March when I visited you at your home and we discussed these matters at some length.

At our meeting on 1st March there was no hint of the reservations which you have now expressed in your Annual Report. I regret that you didn't see fit to discuss the contents of that report with me prior to publication and that furthermore the first I knew of it was when a copy reached me on Wednesday of this week, i.e. 2 days before the Constituency Annual General Meeting.

As to the contents of your Report as expressed in paragraph 3 you must know from your attendance at various Association meetings that the majority of our members support the line that I have taken and it is a matter of great regret to me personally that you feel unable to reflect that view.

In this context I remind you of the meeting held at my home shortly after you became Chairman when I stressed the vital necessity for the Member of Parliament and the senior Officers of the Association to be of one mind and totally loyal to each other. I very much regret that you have now chosen to declare your unwillingness to keep that bargain, not by intimating your differences to me but by making the damaging and hurtful statement that appears in your report to the full membership of the Association.

Reverting to our telephone conversation of last evening may I say that your statement that you were against a Referendum was also a revelation although you must have known exactly where I stood on that issue. May I remind you of the unequivocable statement in my election address which said 'let me assure you that I shall continue to resist all that which goes beyond creating a Common Market for goods, services, people and capital. Any changes to the original Treaty of Rome should, I believe, be made subject to a Referendum.'

In other words neither the Officers, nor the Members nor anyone else in the Ludlow Constituency was left in any doubt as to where I stood and it is of course a matter of fact that not only was the Conservative majority increased on 9th April from 11,699 to 14,152 but the number of Conservative votes that were cast also increased (from 27,499 to 28,719).

I am sorry that it is necessary for me to have to write to you in these terms but you should recognise that unless I receive an assurance that there will be no further breaches of trust between us then the year ahead under your continuing Chairmanship is likely to be less than satisfactory both from a personal point of view and also from the Association's point of view.

Yours sincerely,

Christopher Gill

P.S. I am enclosing herewith photocopies of correspondence from Mrs Mavis Burn who you seem to think has called for my deselection. Whilst Mrs Burn unreservedly supports my position on Maastricht she is, of course, not a member of our Party.

Appendix E

HOUSE OF COMMONS
LONDON SW1A OAA

Policy Paper From:

Sir Richard Body MP,	Tony Marlow MP,
Nick Budgen MP,	Richard Shepherd MP,
Christopher Gill MP,	Sir Teddy Taylor MP,
Teresa Gorman MP,	John Wilkinson MP.

As Statements from Government Ministers clearly indicate that the policy on Europe is being reviewed, the following proposals have been agreed by the eight excluded Conservatives as a formula which would take into account both public opinion and the seriousness of the situation which the Nation faces.

It is our hope that these proposals will be considered carefully by HM Government.

A Sense of Country
Since the expression of support for a free trade area in the Referendum of 1975 there has been no popular expression of agreement to the huge transfer of power from the people to Brussels that has since taken place. This is largely because the process has been gradual and surreptitious.

Consent is fundamental to such a profound change and acquiescence is insufficient to sustain the progressive transfer of the right to make our own laws to undemocratic and unaccountable foreign institutions. Indeed this process of political integration with Europe questions the very survival of the United Kingdom as a political entity and is fundamental to the Scottish National Party's argument.

We see in the attempted transfer of the British people's power to make law and to govern ourselves, the breakdown of the Rule of Law. We are increasingly anxious that these arrangements no longer enjoy even the acquiescence of the British people.

For any European policy to work it must enjoy the consent of the people. The Single European Act and the Maastricht Treaty are in opposition to the democratic imperative that has ensured our self-governance all the years of this century. The British Parliament and People are not Poodles. The question as to why Ministers value European political integration above our country's democratic imperative has to be addressed.

We hope that the issues we raise will find a resonance not only within our party but with the British People.

Basic Objective

EU acquisition of power and responsibility and its interference with issues which should be subject to National determination is a constant and accelerating problem. The aim of the 1996 negotiations should therefore be to seek substantial repatriation of decision making. If such an endeavour should prove to be impossible, our National aim should be to seek a separate relationship with the EU, possibly on the basis of free Trade and friendship only.

We should also make it clear that the UK will in no circumstances agree to further EU funding until progress is made.

Particular Aims

1. The Common Agricultural Policy is an absurd and costly protectionist racket which is constantly getting worse because of the inability of the EU to secure meaningful reforms. The basic objective must be the repatriation of responsibility for Agricultural policy subject to these policies being agreed within the EU to prevent unfair trading and subsidies.
2. The Common Fisheries Policy has developed in such a way that it will be impossible to ensure that the most basic rules are adhered to. The only feasible answer must be to repatriate responsibility for the management of fishing to Nation States.
3. The right of the European Court to intervene in National Policies should be revoked, and in particular the right to make decisions with retrospective effect should be removed.
4. The rights of member states to place a ban on the Export of Live animals should be restored, should they so wish.
5. The European Parliament is a costly nonsense which can never have any other than presentational powers within the existing EU structure. Its name should be changed to the European Assembly and the membership should be by nomination from elected national Parliaments.
6. Foreign Policy and Defence responsibilities should be removed from the Competence of EU Treaties.
7. The basic principle of Economic and Monetary Union should be scrapped with each nation having the entitlement to arrange its own economic policies and currency management.
8. The budget of the EU should be severely curtailed with the removal of all interventionist subsidies.

Appendix F

CHRISTOPHER GILL RD MP

HOUSE OF COMMONS

LONDON SW1A 0AA

30ᵗ January 1997

In the light of last night's welcome confirmation that
colleagues will, as ever, be free to write their own
election addresses I thought that I should write to
explain why it was always my intention to tell the
voters in the Ludlow constituency that I remain implacably
opposed to Economic and Monetary Union.

Government assurances that a Conservative government
would not take Britain into a federal Europe are bogus
given that the UK has already signed three solemn and
binding treaties which have created the blue print for
European integration.

Protestations that we must 'wait and see' before deciding
on a Single Currency are similarly bogus given that what has
to be done, how it has to be done and when it has to be done
are all spelt out clearly in the Maastricht Treaty.

On more prosaic matters such as Fisheries the Government's
policy is equally bogus given the fact that it steadfastly
refuses to accept that the basic tenet of the Common Fisheries
Policy is 'equal access to the common resource'.

As a Cabinet Minister you bear a heavy responsibility for
taking our Party into a General Election with policies on
Europe which at best will not bear scrutiny and at worst will
be seen as an attempt to hoodwink the electorate.

Whilst you may with every justification claim that its European
policies are Government policy you must surely recognise that
they no longer command majority support within the Party.

Yours sincerely,

Appendix G

Conservative 'rebel' votes cast in the 53 Divisions of the Committee stage of the European Communities (Amendment) Bill.

Cash	44	Sweeney	20
Taylor T.	44	Carlisle	19
Winterton N.	41	Hawksley	17
Gill	40	Legg	17
Jessel	40	Carttiss	16
Knapman	40	Porter	15
Winterton A.	40	Pawsey	14
Gorman	39	Boyson	11
Lawrence	37	Allason	10
Marlow	36	Duncan-Smith	8
Skeet	36	Townend	7
Walker	36	Hunter	6
Shepherd	35	Fry	5
Spicer	35	Greenway H.	4
Cran	33	Bendall	3
Lord	33	Moate	3
Budgen	32	Bonsor	2
Wilkinson	30	Jenkin	2
Body	27	Vaughan	2
Biffen	24	Whittingdale	2
Gardiner	24	Clark M.	1
Tapsell	24	Dunn	1
Butcher	20		

Appendix H

Conservative MPs who were openly critical of their Party's European policy.

1. THOSE WHO SIGNED BOTH 'FRESH START' EDMs

Rupert Allason	Bernard Jenkin
Sir Thomas Arnold	Toby Jessel
Vivian Bendall	Roger Knapman
Dr John Blackburn	Ivan Lawrence
Sir Richard Body	Barry Legg
Sir Nicholas Bonsor	Michael Lord
Sir Rhodes Boyson	Paul Marland
Nicholas Budgen	Tony Marlow
John Butcher	Sir Patrick McNair-Wilson
John Carlisle	Roger Moate
William Cash	James Pawsey
Dr Michael Clark	Barry Porter
James Cran	David Porter
Nirj Deva	Andrew Robathan
Den Dover	Marion Roe
Iain Duncan Smith	David Shaw
Bob Dunn	Richard Shepherd
Nigel Evans	Sir Trevor Skeet
Michael Fabricant	Michael Spicer
Peter Fry	John Sykes
Phil Gallie	Sir Teddy Taylor
Sir George Gardiner	John Townend
Christopher Gill	Sir Gerard Vaughan
Teresa Gorman	Bill Walker
Harry Greenway	John Whittingdale
John Greenway	John Wilkinson
Peter Griffiths	Ann Winterton
Warren Hawksley	Nicholas Winterton
Andrew Hunter	

2. THOSE WHO SIGNED ONLY THE FIRST EDM

Peter Ainsworth
Richard Alexander
Angela Browning
Geoffrey Clifton-Brown
David Congdon
Geoffrey Dickens
Alan Duncan
David Faber
Dr Liam Fox
Cheryl Gillan
Nick Hawkins
Charles Hendry

John Horam
Robert B. Jones
David Lidington
Raymond Robertson
Michael Shersby
Anthony Steen
Michael Stern
Roy Thomason
Nigel Waterson
John Watts
David Willetts
David Wilshire

3. THOSE WHO SIGNED ONLY THE SECOND EDM

Michael Carttiss
Sir Nicholas Fairbairn
Sir Michael Neubert

Sir Peter Tapsell
Walter Sweeney
Garry Waller

4. VOTED AGAINST THE PAVING MOTION 4/11/92

John Biffen
Sir Richard Body
Nicholas Budgen
John Butcher
John Carlisle
William Cash
Dr Michael Clark
James Cran
Iain Duncan Smith
Christopher Gill
Mrs Teresa Gorman
Toby Jessel
Roger Knapman

Barry Legg
Michael Lord
Tony Marlow
David Porter
Richard Shepherd
Sir Trevor Skeet
Michael Spicer
Sir Peter Tapsell
Sir Teddy Taylor
Bill Walker
John Wilkinson
Nicholas Winterton
Mrs Ann Winterton

5. ABSTAINED ON PAVING MOTION

Warren Hawksley
Bernard Jenkin
Sir Ivan Lawrence

Walter Sweeney
Sir Gerard Vaughan
John Whittingdale

Appendix I

Conservative 'Rebel' votes against the Treaty (Key Stages).

	2nd Reading 21/5/92	Paving Motion 4/11/92	Amendment 28 8/3/93	3rd Reading 20/5/93
Allason	✓			✓
Bendall				✓
Biffen	✓	✓	✓	✓
Body	✓	✓	✓	✓
Bonsor				✓
Boyson				✓
Budgen	✓	✓	✓	✓
Butcher	✓	✓		✓
Carlisle	✓	✓	✓	✓
Carttiss	✓			✓
Cash	✓	✓	✓	✓
Clark		✓		
Cran	✓	✓	✓	✓
Duncan Smith		✓		✓
Fry				✓
Gardiner			✓	✓
Gill	✓	✓	✓	✓
Gorman	✓	✓	✓	✓
Greenway H.	✓			✓
Hawksley			✓	✓
Hunter	✓		✓	
Jenkin				✓

	2nd Reading 21/5/92	Paving Motion 4/11/92	Amendment 28 8/3/93	3rd Reading 20/5/93
Jessel	✓	✓	✓	✓
Knapman		✓	✓	✓
Lawrence			✓	
Legg		✓		✓
Lord		✓	✓	✓
Marlow	✓	✓	✓	✓
Moate				✓
Pawsey				✓
Porter	✓	✓		✓
Shepherd	✓	✓	✓	✓
Skeet	✓	✓	✓	✓
Spicer	✓	✓	✓	✓
Sweeney			✓	✓
Tapsell		✓	✓	✓
Taylor	✓	✓	✓	✓
Townend				✓
Walker		✓	✓	✓
Whittingdale				✓
Wilkinson		✓	✓	✓
Winterton	✓	✓	✓	✓
Winterton	✓	✓	✓	✓
Robathan				✓
Rebel/Votes	22	26	26	41
Ayes/Noes	336/92	319/316	314/292	292/112

Index